· SERMONS ON ·

MEN OF THE
NEW TESTAMENT

Books of Sermons by Charles Spurgeon from Hendrickson Publishers

Sermons on the Lord's Supper

Sermons on the Passion of Christ

Sermons on Women of the Old Testament

Sermons on Men of the Old Testament

Sermons about Christmas

Sermons on the Prayers of Christ

Sermons on Cries from the Cross

Sermons on the Resurrection

Sermons on the Love of Christ

Sermons on the Holy Spirit

Sermons on Prayer

Sermons on Great Prayers of the Bible

Sermons on the Second Coming of Christ

Sermons on Heaven and Hell

Sermons on Women of the New Testament

Sermons on Men of the New Testament

· SERMONS ON ·
MEN OF THE
NEW TESTAMENT

HENDRICKSON PUBLISHERS

Sermons on Men of the New Testament

© 2016 Hendrickson Publishers Marketing, LLC
P. O. Box 3473
Peabody, Massachusetts 01961-3473

ISBN 978-1-61970-812-9

Originally published by Hendrickson Publishers in *Sermons on Men of the Bible*.

Printed in the United States of America

Cover photo of Charles Haddon (C. H.) Spurgeon by Herbert Rose Barraud is used by permission of the University of Minnesota Libraries, Special Collections and Rare Books.

Contents

In memory of Patricia Klein (1949–2014), our colleague
and friend, who spent her life caring for words
and who edited this series. She is truly missed.

Preface

Charles Haddon Spurgeon
1834–1892

Ask most people today who Charles Haddon Spurgeon was, and you might be surprised at the answers. Most know he was a preacher, others remember that he was Baptist, and others go so far as to remember that he lived in England during the nineteenth century. All of this is true, yet Charles Haddon Spurgeon was so much more.

Born into a family of Congregationalists in 1834, Spurgeon's father and grandfather were both Independent preachers. These designations seem benign today, but in the mid-nineteenth century, they describe a family committed to a Nonconformist path—meaning they did not conform to the established Church of England. Spurgeon grew up in a rural village, a village virtually cut off from the Industrial Revolution rolling over most of England.

Spurgeon became a Christian at a Primitive Methodist meeting in 1850 at age sixteen. He soon became a Baptist (to the sorrow of his mother) and almost immediately began to preach. Considered a preaching prodigy—"a boy wonder of the fens"—Spurgeon attracted huge audiences and garnered a reputation that reached throughout the countryside and into London. As a result of his great success, Spurgeon was invited to preach at the New Park Street Chapel in London in 1854, when he was just nineteen. When he first preached at the church, they were unable to fill even two hundred seats. Within the year, Spurgeon filled the twelve-hundred-seat church to overflowing. He soon began preaching in larger and larger venues, outgrowing each, until finally in 1861 the Metropolitan Tabernacle was completed, which seated six thousand persons. This would be Spurgeon's home base for the rest of his career, until his death in 1892 at age fifty-seven.

Spurgeon married Susannah Thompson in 1856 and soon they had twin sons, Charles and Thomas, who would later follow him in his work. Spurgeon opened Pastors' College, a training school for preachers, which trained over nine hundred preachers during his lifetime. He also opened orphanages for underprivileged boys and girls, providing education to each of the orphans. And with Susannah, he developed a program to publish and distribute Christian literature. He is said to have preached to over ten million people in his forty years of ministry. His sermons sold over twenty-five thousand copies each week and were translated into twenty languages. He was utterly committed to spreading the gospel through preaching and through the written word.

During Spurgeon's lifetime, the Industrial Revolution transformed England from a rural, agricultural society to an urban, industrial society, with all the attendant difficulties and horrors of a society in major transition. The people displaced by these sweeping changes—factory workers and shopkeepers—became Spurgeon's congregation. From a small village himself and transplanted to a large and inhospitable city, he was a common man and understood innately the spiritual needs of the common people. He was a communicator who made the gospel so relevant, who spoke so brilliantly to people's deepest needs, that listeners welcomed his message.

Keep in mind that Spurgeon preached in the days before microphones or speakers; in other words, he preached without benefit of amplifier systems. Once he preached to a crowd of over twenty-three thousand people without mechanical amplification of any sort. He himself was the electrifying presence on the platform: he did not stand and simply read a stilted sermon. Spurgeon used an outline, developing his themes extemporaneously, and speaking "in common language to common people." His sermons were filled with stories and poetry, drama and emotion. He was larger than life, always in motion, striding back and forth across the stage. He gestured broadly, acted out stories, used humor, and painted word pictures. For Spurgeon, preaching was about communicating the truth of God, and he would use any gift at his disposal to accomplish this.

Spurgeon's preaching was anchored in his spiritual life, a life rich in prayer and the study of Scripture. He was not tempted by fashion, be it theological, social, or political. Scripture was the cornerstone of Spurgeon's life and his preaching. He was an expositional preacher mostly, exploring a passage of Scripture for its meaning both within the text as well as in the lives of each member of his congregation. To Spurgeon, Scripture was alive and specifically relevant to people's lives, whatever their social status, economic situation, or time in which they lived.

One has a sense that Spurgeon embraced God's revelation completely: God's revelation through Jesus Christ, through Scripture, and through his own prayer and study. For him, revelation was not a finished act: God still reveals himself, if one made oneself available. Some recognize Spurgeon for the mystic he was, one who was willing and eager to explore the mysteries of God, able to live with those bits of truth that do not conform to a particular system of theology, perfectly comfortable with saying, "This I know, and this I don't know—yet will I trust."

Each of the sermons in this collection was preached at a different time in Spurgeon's career and each has distinct characteristics. These sermons are not a series, as they were not created or intended to be sequential, nor have they been homogenized or edited to sound as though they are all of a kind. Instead, they reflect the preacher himself, allowing the voice of this remarkable man to ring clearly as he guides the reader into a particular account, a particular event—to experience, with Spurgeon, God's particular revelation.

As you read, *listen*. These words were meant to be heard, not merely read. Listen carefully and you will hear the cadences of this remarkable preaching, the echoes of God's timeless truth traveling across the years. And above all, enjoy Spurgeon's enthusiasm, his fire, his devotion, his zeal to recognize and respond to God's timeless invitation to engage the Creator himself.

John the Baptist: Loosing the Shoe-Latchet

Delivered on Lord's Day morning, March 31, 1872, at the Metropolitan Tabernacle, Newington. No. 1044.

One mightier than I cometh, the latchet of whose shoes I am not worthy to unloose.—LUKE 3:16

It was not John's business to attract followers to himself but to point them to Jesus, and he very faithfully discharged his commission. His opinion of his Master, of whom he was the herald, was a very high one; he reverenced him as the anointed of the Lord, the King of Israel, and, consequently, he was not tempted into elevating himself into a rival. He rejoiced to declare, "he must increase but I must decrease." In the course of his self-depreciation, he uses the expression of our text, which is recorded by each one of the Evangelists, with some little variation. Matthew words it "whose shoes I am not worthy to bear"; he was not fit to fetch his Lord his shoes. Mark writes it "whose shoes I am not worthy to stoop down and unloose"; and John has it very much as in Luke. This putting on and taking off and putting away of sandals was an office usually left to menial servants; it was not a work of any repute or honor, yet the Baptist felt that it would be a great honor to be even a menial servant of the Lord Jesus. He felt that the Son of God was so infinitely superior to himself that he was honored if only permitted to be the meanest slave in his employ. He would not allow men to attempt comparisons between himself and Jesus; he felt that none could, for a moment, be allowed. Now this honest estimate of himself as less than nothing in comparison with his Master is greatly to be imitated by us. John is to be commended and admired for this, but better still he is to be carefully copied.

Remember that John was by no means an inferior man. Among all that had been born of women before his time there had not been a greater than he. He was the subject of many prophecies, and his office was a peculiarly noble one; he was the friend of the great Bridegroom and introduced him to his chosen bride. He was the morning star of the gospel day, but he counted himself no light in the presence of the Sun of Righteousness whom he heralded. The temperament of John was not that which bowed or cringed; he was no reed shaken by the wind, no man of courtly habits fitted for a king's palace. No. We see in him an Elijah, a man of iron, a son of thunder; he roared like a young lion on his prey, and feared the face of none. Some men are so naturally meek spirited, not to say weak-minded, that they naturally become subservient and set up others as their leaders. Such men are apt to err in depreciating themselves; but John was every inch a man, his great soul bowed only before that which was worthy of homage; he was in God's strength as an iron pillar and a brazen wall, a hero for the cause of the Lord, and yet he sat down in the presence of Jesus as a little child on a stool sits at his master's feet, and he cried, "whose shoe-latchet I am not worthy to stoop down and to unloose."

Recollect, moreover, that John was a man endowed with great abilities, and these are very apt to make a man proud. He was a prophet, yes, and more than a prophet. When he stood in the wilderness to preach, his burning eloquence soon attracted the people from Jerusalem and from all the cities round about, and the banks of Jordan saw a vast multitude of eager hearers crowding around the man clothed with a garment of camel's hair. Thousands gathered together to listen to the teaching of one who had not been brought up at the feet of the rabbis, neither had been taught eloquence after the fashion of the schools. John was a man of bold, plain, telling, commanding speech; he was no second-rate teacher, but a master in Israel, yet he assumed no airs of self-conceit, but accounted the lowest place in the Lord's service as too high for him. Note, too, that he was not only a great preacher, but he had been very successful not only in attracting the crowds but in baptizing them. The whole nation felt the effects of John's ministry and knew that he was a prophet: they were swayed to and fro by his zealous words, as the corn of autumn is moved in the breath of the wind. A man is very apt when he feels that he has power over masses of his fellow creatures to be lifted up and exalted above measure, but not so John. It was safe for the Lord to trust him with a great popularity and a great success, for though he had all those honors he laid them meekly down at Jesus' feet, and said, "I am not worthy to be even the lowest slave in Messiah's household."

Recollect, also, moreover, that John was a religious leader, and he had the opportunity, if he had pleased, of becoming the leader of a powerful sect. The people were evidently willing to follow him. There were some, no doubt, who would not have gone over to Christ himself if John had not bidden them go, and testified, "Behold the Lamb of God," and confessed over and over again, saying, "I am not the Christ." We read of some who years after the Baptist was dead still remained his disciples, so that he had the opportunity of leading away a multitude who would have become his followers, and so of setting up his own name among men; but he scorned it; his elevated view of his Master prevented his entertaining any desire for personal leadership and, putting himself down not in the place of a captain of the lord's hosts, but as one of the least soldiers in the army, he says, "His shoe-latchets I am not worthy to unloose." What was the reason, do you think, of John's always retaining his proper position? Was it not because he had a high idea of his Master and a deep reverence for him? Ah, brethren, because of our little estimate of Christ, it is often unsafe for the Lord to trust us in any but the very lowest positions. I believe many of us might have been ten times as useful, only it would not have been safe for God to have allowed us to be so; we should have been puffed up, and like Nebuchadnezzar we should have boasted, "Behold this great Babylon that I have built." Many a man has had to fight in the back ranks, and serve his Master but little, and enjoy but little success in that service, because he did not reverence Christ enough, did not love his Lord enough, and consequently self would soon have crept in to his own overturning, to the grief of the church, and to the dishonor of his Lord. Oh, for high thoughts of Christ, and low thoughts of ourselves! Oh, to see Jesus as filling all in all, and to be ourselves as less than nothing before him.

Having thus introduced the subject, our object this morning is to draw instruction from the expression which John here and elsewhere used with regard to himself and his Lord: "whose shoe-latchet I am not worthy to unloose."

I gather from this, first, that no form of holy service is to be lightly set by: second, that our unworthiness is apparent in the presence of any sort of holy work: but that, third, this unworthiness of ours, when most felt, should rather stimulate us to action than discourage us, for so it doubtless operated in the case of John the Baptist.

I. First, then, note *that no form of holy service is to be lightly set by.*

To unloose the latchets of Christ's shoes might seem very trivial; it might even seem as if it involved the loss of self-respect for a man of position and influence to stoop to offices which a servant might quite as well perform. Why should I bring myself down to that? I will learn of Christ; I will distribute bread among the multitude for Christ; I will have my boat by the seashore ready for Christ to preach in, or I will go and fetch the ass upon which he shall ride in triumph into Jerusalem; but what need can there be for the disciple to become a mere menial? Such a question as that is here forever silenced, and the spirit which dictates it is practically rebuked. Nothing is dishonorable by which Jesus may be honored. Nothing lowers a man if thereby he honors his Lord. It is not possible for any godly work to be beneath our dignity; rather ought we to know that the lowest grade of service bestows dignity upon the man who heartily performs it. Even the least and most obscure form of serving Christ is more high and lofty than we are worthy to undertake.

Now note that little works for Christ, little shoe bearings and latched loosings, often *have more of the child's spirit in them than greater works*. Outside in the streets, a man's companion will do him a kindness, and the action performed is friendly; but for filial acts you must look inside the house. There the child does not lend money to its father or negotiate business, yet in his little acts there is more sonship. Who is it that comes to meet father when the day is over? And what is the action which often indicates childhood's love? See the little child comes tottering forward with father's slippers, and runs off with his boots as he puts them off. The service is little, but it is loving and filial, and has more of filial affection in it than the servant's bringing in the meal, of preparing the bed, or any other more essential service. It gives the little one great pleasure, and expresses his love. No one who is not my child, or who does not love me in something like the same way, would ever dream of making such a service his specialty. The littleness of the act fits it to the child's capacity, and there is also something in it which makes it a suitable expression of a child's affection. So also in little acts for Jesus. Oftentimes men of the world will give their money to the cause of Christ, putting down large sums for charity or for missions, but they will not weep in secret over other men's sins, or speak a word of comfort to an afflicted saint. To visit a poor sick woman, teach a little child, reclaim a street urchin, breathe a prayer for enemies, or whisper a promise in the ear of a desponding saint, may show more of sonship than building a row of almshouses or endowing a church.

In little acts for Christ it is always to be remembered that the *little things are as necessary to be done as the greater acts*. If Christ's feet be not washed, if his sandals be not unloosed, he may suffer, and his feet may be lamed, so that a journey may be shortened, and many villages may miss the blessing of his presence. So with other minor things. There is as much need for the quiet intercessions of saints as for the public delivery of God's truth before the assembled thousands. It is as needful that babes be taught their little hymns as that monarchs be rebuked for sin. We remember the old story of the losing of the battle through the missing of a single nail in a horseshoe, and peradventure up to this moment the church may have lost her battle for Christ, because some minor work which ought to have been done for Jesus has been neglected. I should not wonder if it should turn out that many churches have been without prosperity because, while they have looked to the public ministry and the visible ordinances, they have been negligent of smaller usefulnesses. Many a cart comes to grief through inattention to the linchpin. A very small matter turns an arrow aside from the target. To teach a child to sing "Gentle Jesus," and to point its young heart to the Redeemer, may seem a trifle, but yet it may be a most essential part of the process of that gracious work of religious education by which that child shall afterward become a believer, a minister, and a winner of souls. Omit that first lesson, and it may be you have turned aside a life.

Take another instance. A preacher once found himself advertised to preach in an obscure village; the storm was terrible, and therefore, though he kept his appointment, he found only one person present in the place of meeting. He preached a sermon to that one hearer with as much earnestness as if the house had been crowded. Years after he found churches all over the district, and he discovered that his audience of one had been converted on that day and had become the evangelist of the whole region. Had he declined to preach to one, what blessings might have been withheld. Brethren, never neglect the loosing of the shoe-latchet for Christ, since you do not know what may hang upon it. Human destiny often turns upon a hinge so small as to be invisible. Never say within yourself, "This is trivial"—nothing is trivial for the Lord. Never say, "But this surely might be omitted without much loss." How do you know? If it be your duty, he who allotted you your task knew what he did. Do not in any measure neglect any portion of his orders, for in all his commands there is consummate wisdom, and on your part it will be wisdom to obey them, even to the jots and tittles.

Little things for Christ again are *often the best tests of the truth of our religion*. Obedience in little things has much to do with the character of a servant. You engage a servant in your own house, and you know very well whether she be a good or bad servant that the main duties of the day are pretty sure to be attended to; the meals will be cooked, the beds will be prepared, the house will be swept, the door will be answered; but the difference between a servant who makes the house happy and another who is its plague lies in a number of small matters, which, peradventure, you could not put down on paper, but which make up a very great deal of domestic comfort or discomfort, and so determine the value of a servant. So I believe it is in Christian life; I do not suppose that the most of us here would ever omit the weightier matters of the law; as Christian men we endeavor to maintain integrity and uprightness in our actions, and we try to order our households in the fear of God in great matters; but it is in the looking to the Lord upon minor details that the spirit of obedience is most displayed; it is seen in our keeping our eye up to the Lord, as the eyes of the handmaidens are to their mistresses for daily orders about this step and that transaction. The really obedient spirit wishes to know the Lord's will about everything, and if there be any point which to the world seem trifling, for that very reason the obedient spirit says, "I will attend to it to prove to my Lord that even in the minutiae I desire to submit my soul to his good pleasure." In small things lie the crucibles and the touchstones. Any hypocrite will come to the Sabbath worship, but it is not every hypocrite that will attend prayer meetings, or read the Bible in secret, or speak privately of the things of God to the saints. These are less things, so they judge, and therefore they neglect them, and so condemn themselves. Where there is deep religion prayer is loved: where religion is shallow only public acts of worship are cared for. You shall find the same true in other things. A man who is no Christian will very likely not tell you a downright lie by saying that black is white, but he will not hesitate to declare that whitish-brown is white— he will go that length. Now the Christian will not go halfway to falsehood, no, he scorns to go an inch on that road. He will no more cheat you out of two-pence farthing, than he would out of £2000. He will not rob you of an inch any more than of an ell [unit of length, about 45 inches]. It is in the little that the genuineness of the Christian is made to appear; the goldsmith's hallmark is a small affair, but you know true silver by it. There is a vast deal of difference between the man who gladly bears Christ's shoes, and another who will not stoop to anything which he thinks beneath him. Even a Pharisee will ask Christ to his house to sit at meat with him; he is willing to entertain a great religious leader at his table; but it is not everyone who will stoop down and unloose his shoes, for that very Pharisee who made the feast neither brought him water to wash his feet, nor gave him the kiss of welcome; he proved the insincerity of his hospitality by forgetting the little things. I will be bound to say Martha and Mary never forgot to unloose his shoe-latchets, and that Lazarus never failed to see that his feet were washed. Look then, I pray you, as Christians to the service of Christ in the obscure things, in the things that are not recognized by men, in the matters which have no honor attached to them, for by this shall your love be tried.

Mark, also, with regard to little works that very often *there is about them a degree of personal fellowship with Christ which is not seen in greater work.* For instance, in the one before us, to unloose the latchets of his shoes brings me into contact with himself, though it be only his feet I touch; and I think if I might have the preference between going forth to cast out devils and to preach the gospel and to heal the sick, or to stay with him and always loose the latchets of his shoes, I should prefer this last; because the first act Judas did—he went with the twelve and saw Satan like lightning fall from heaven, but he perished because he failed in the acts that came into contact with Christ—in keeping Christ's purse he was a thief, and in giving Christ the kiss he was a traitor. He who does not fail in things relating personally to Christ is the sound man; he has the evidence of righteousness of heart. There was never a grander action done beneath the stars than when the woman broke her alabaster box of precious ointment and poured it upon him; though the poor did not get anything out of it, though no sick man was the better for it, the act was done distinctly unto him, and therefore there was a peculiar sweetness in it. Oftentimes similar actions, because they do not encourage other people for they do not know of them, because they may not be of any very great value to our fellowmen, are lightly esteemed, yet seeing, they are done for Christ, they have about them a peculiar charm as terminating upon his blessed person. True, it is but the loosing of shoe-latchets, but then, they are his shoes, and that ennobles the deed.

Dear fellow Christians, you know what I mean, though I cannot put it into very good language this morning—I mean just this, that if there is some little thing I can do for Christ, though my minister will not know about it, though the deacons and elders will not know, and nobody will know, and if I leave it undone nobody will suffer any calamity because of it, but, if I do it, it will please my Lord, and I shall enjoy the sense of having done it to him, therefore will I attend to it, for it is no slight work if it be for him.

Mark, also, once more, concerning those gracious actions which are but little esteemed by the most of mankind, that we know *God accepts our worship in little things*. He allowed his people to bring their bullocks, others of them to bring their rams, and offer them to him; and these were persons of sufficient wealth to be able to afford a tribute from their herds and flocks, but he also permitted the poor to offer a pair of turtledoves, or two young pigeons, and I have never found in God's Word that he cared less for the turtledove offering than he did for the sacrifice of the bullock. I do know, too, that our ever blessed Lord himself, when he was here, loved the praise of little children. They brought neither gold nor silver like the wise men from the East, but they cried, "Hosanna," and the Lord was not angry with their hosannas, but accepted their boyish praise. And we remember that a widow woman cast into the treasury two mites, which only made a farthing, but, because it was all her living, he did not reject the gift, but rather recorded it to her honor. We are now quite familiar with the incident, but for all that, it is very wonderful. Two mites that make a farthing given to the infinite God! A farthing accepted by the King of kings! A farthing acknowledged by him who made the heavens and the earth, who said, "If I were hungry I would not tell thee, for the cattle on a thousand hills are mine." Two mites received with pleasure by the Lord of all! It was scarcely so much as a drop thrown into the sea, and yet he thought much of it. Measure not little actions by human scales and measures, but estimate them as God does, for the Lord has respect unto the hearts of his people; he regards not so much their deeds in themselves as the motives by which they are actuated. Therefore, value the loosing of the Savior's shoe-latchets, and despise not "the day of small things."

II. Now, brethren and sisters, I wish to conduct you, in the second place, to the consideration of *our own unworthiness*, which is sure to be felt by us whenever we come practically into contact with any real Christian service.

I believe that a man who does nothing at all thinks himself a fine fellow, as a general rule. You shall usually find that the sharpest critics are those who never write; and the best judges of battles those who keep at a prudent distance from the guns. Christians of the kid-gloved order, who never make an attempt to save souls, are marvelously quick to tell us when we are too rough or too light in our speech; and they readily detect us if our modes of action are irregular or too enthusiastic. They have a very keen scent for anything like fanaticism or disorder. For my part, I feel pretty safe when I have the censures of these gentlemen; we are not far wrong when they condemn us. Let a man begin earnestly to work for the Lord Jesus, and he will soon find out that he is unworthy of the meanest place in the employ of one so glorious. Let us turn over that fact a minute.

Dear brothers and sisters, when we recollect what we used to be, I am sure we must feel unworthy to do the very least thing for Christ. You know how Paul describes the wickedness of certain offenders, and he adds, "But such were some of you." What hardness of heart some of us exhibited toward God! What rebellion! What obstinacy! What quenching of his Spirit! What love of sin! Why, if I might stoop down to unloose the latchet of the shoe of that foot which was crucified for me, I must bedew the nail print with my tears, and say, "My Savior, can it be that I am ever allowed to touch your feet?" Surely, the prodigal, if he ever unloosed his father's shoes, could say to himself, "Why, these hands fed the swine, these hands were often polluted by the harlots; I lived in uncleanness and was first a reveler, and then a swineherd, and it is amazing love which permits me now to serve so good a father." Angels in heaven might envy the man who is permitted to do the least thing for Christ, and yet they never sinned. Oh, what a favor that we who are defiled with sin should be called to serve the sinless Savior.

But, then, another reflection comes at the back of it—we *recollect what we are as well as what we were*—I say, what we are, for though washed in Jesus' blood and endowed with a new heart and a right spirit, yet we start aside like a deceitful bow, for corruption dwells in us. It is sometimes hard work to maintain even a little faith, we are so double-minded, so unstable, so hot, so cold, so earnest, and then so negligent: we are so everything except what we ought to be, that we may well wonder that Christ allows us to do the least thing for him. If he were to shut us in prison and keep us there, so long as he did not actually execute us, he would be dealing with us according to mercy, and not giving us our full deserts; yet he calls us out of prison, and puts us in his service, and therefore we feel that we are unworthy to perform the least action in his house.

Besides, beloved, even *small services we feel require a better state of heart than we often have.* I am sure the service of preaching the gospel here often brings to my sight my unworthiness far more than I should otherwise see it. If it be a gracious thing to see one's sinfulness, I may thank God I preach the gospel, for it makes me see it. Sometimes we come to preach about Jesus Christ and glorify him, and yet our heart is not warm toward him, and we do not value him aright; while the text we are preaching from seats him on a high throne, our heart is not setting him there; and, oh, then we think we could tear our heart out of our very body, if we could get rid of the black drops of its depravity which prevent our feeling in unison with the glorious truth before us. Another time, perhaps, we have to invite sinners and seek to bring them to Christ, and that wants so much sympathy that if Christ were preaching our sermon he would bedew it with his tears; but, we deliver it with dry eyes, almost without emotion, and then we flog our hard heart that it will not stir and cannot be made to feel.

It is just the same in other duties. Have you not felt "I have to go and teach my class this afternoon, but I am not fit; I have been worried all the week with cares, and my mind is not up to the mark now; I hope I love my Lord, but I hardly know whether I do or not. I ought to be earnest about these boys and girls; but it is very likely I shall not be earnest; I shall sit down and go through my teaching as a parrot would go through it, without life, without love"? Yes, then you painfully feel that you are not worthy to unloose the latchets of your Lord's shoes. Possibly, you are going this afternoon to visit a dying man, and you will try and talk to him about the way to heaven. He is unconverted. Now you want a tongue of fire to speak with, and instead of that, you have a tongue of ice; you feel, "O God, how can it be that I shall sit by that bedside and think of that poor man, who will be in the flames of hell, perhaps, within a week, unless he receive Christ, and yet I shall coolly treat his tremendously perilous condition as though it were a matter of the very slightest consequence?" Yes, yes, yes, we have had hundred of times to feel that we are in and of ourselves not fit for anything. If the Lord wanted scullions in his kitchen, he could get better than we are; and if he needed someone to shovel out the refuse of his house, he could find better men than we are for that. To such a Master we are unworthy to be servants.

The same feeling arises in another way. Have we not to confess, brethren and sisters, in looking upon what we have done for Christ, that *we have far too much eye to self in our conduct.* We pick and choose our work, and the picking and choosing is guided by the instinct of self-respect. If we are asked to do that which is pleasant to ourselves, we do it. If we are requested to attend a meeting where we shall be received with acclamation, if we are asked to perform a service which will lift us up in the social scale or that will commend us to our fellow Christians, we jump at it like a fish at a fly; but suppose the work would bring us shame, suppose it would discover to the public rather our inefficiency than our ability, we excuse ourselves. The spirit which Moses felt a little of, when the Lord called him, is upon many of us. "If I were to speak for Christ," says one, "I should stutter and stammer." As if God did not make stuttering mouths as well as intent mouths; and as if, when he chose a Moses, he did not know what he was at. Moses must go and stammer for God and glorify God by stammering, but Moses does not like that; and many in similar cases have not had grace enough to go to the work at all. Why, if I cannot honor the Lord with ten talents, shall I refuse to serve him with one? If I cannot fly like a strong-winged angel through the midst of heaven and sound the shrill-mouthed trumpet so as to wake the dead, shall I refuse to be a little bee and gather honey at God's bidding? Because I cannot be a leviathan, shall I refuse to be an ant? What folly and what rebellion if we are so perverse.

And, if you have performed any holy work, have you not noticed that pride is ready to rise? God can hardly let us succeed in any work but what we become toplofty. "Oh, how well we have done it!" We do not want anybody to say, "Now that was very cleverly, and nicely, and carefully, and earnestly done," for we say all that to ourselves, and we add, "Yes, you were zealous about that work, and you have been doing what a great many would not have done, and you have not boasted of it either. You do not call in any neighbor to see it; you have been doing it simply out of love to God, and, therefore, you are an uncommonly humble fellow, and none can say you are vain." Alas!

What flattery, but truly "the heart is deceitful above all things, and desperately wicked." We are not worthy to unloose the latchets of Jesus' shoes, because, if we do, we begin to say to ourselves, "What great folks are we; we have been allowed to loose the latchets of the Lord's sandals." If we do not tell somebody else about it with many an exultation, we at least tell ourselves about it and feel that we are something after all, and ought to be held in no small repute.

My brethren, we ought to feel that we are not worthy to do the lowest thing we can do for Christ, because, *when we have gone to the lowest, Jesus always goes lower down than we have gone.* Is it a little thing to bear his shoes? What, then, was his condescension when he washed his disciples' feet? To put up with a cross-tempered brother, to be gentle with him, and feel, "I will give way to him in everything because I am a Christian," that is going very low; but then, our Lord has borne far more from us; he was patient with his people's infirmities and forgave even to seventy times seven. And, suppose we are willing to take the lowest place in the church, yet Jesus took a lower place than we can, for he took the place of the curse: he was made sin for us, even he that knew no sin, that we might be made the righteousness of God in him. I have sometimes felt willing to go to the gates of hell to save a soul; but the Redeemer went further, for he suffered the wrath of God for souls. If there should be any Christian here who is so humble that he has no lofty thoughts about himself, but prefers to be least among his brethren, and so proves his graciousness, yet, my dear brother, you are not so lowly as Christ made himself, for he "made himself of no reputation," and you have some reputation left; and he took upon himself the form of a servant, and he became obedient to death—you have not come to that yet—even the death of the cross—the felon's death upon the gibbet, you will never be brought to that. Oh, the stoop of the Redeemer's amazing love! Let us, henceforth, contend how low we can go side by side with him, but remember, when we have gone to the lowest, he descends lower still, so that we can truly feel that the very lowest place is too high for us, because he has gone lower still.

Beloved friends, to put these things in a practical shape, it may seem to be a very small duty for any of you to do, to speak to one person alone about his soul. If you were asked to preach to a hundred, you would try it. I ask you solemnly, in God's name, not to let the sun go down today till you have spoken to one man or woman alone about his or her soul. Will you not do that? Is it too little for you? Then I must be plain with you, and say you are not worthy to do it. Speak today to some little child about his soul. Do not say, "Oh, we cannot talk to children, we cannot stoop to them." Let no such feeling occupy any of our minds, for if this work be as the loosing of the Master's shoe-latchets, let us do it. Holy Brainerd, when he was dying and could no longer preach to the Indians, had a little Indian boy at his bedside, and taught him his letters; and he remarked to one who came in, "I asked God that I might not live any longer than I could be of use, and so, as I cannot preach anymore, I am teaching this poor little child to read the Bible." Let us never think that we are stooping when we teach children, but if it be stooping let us stoop.

There are some of you, perhaps, who have the opportunity to do good to fallen women. Do you shrink from such work? Many do. They feel as if they could do anything rather than speak to such. Is it the loosing of the latchet of your Master's shoe? It is, then, an honorable business; try it, brother. It is not beneath you if you do it for Jesus; it is even above the best of you, you are not worthy to do it. Possibly there is near your house a district of very poor people. You do not like going in among them. They are dirty and perhaps infected with disease. Well, it is a pity that poor people should so often be dirty, but pride is dirty too. Do you say, "I cannot go there"? Why not? Are you such a mighty fine gentleman that you are afraid of soiling your hands? You will not unloose your Master's shoe-latchet then. The Lord lived among the poor and was poorer even than they; for he had not where to lay his head. Oh, shame on you, you wicked and proud servant of a condescending, loving Lord! Go about your business and unloose the latchets of his shoes directly! Instead of imagining that you would be lowered by such work for Jesus, I tell you, it would honor you; indeed, you are not fit for it; the honor is too great for you and will fall to the lot of better men.

It comes to this, beloved, anything that can be done for Christ is too good for us to do. Somebody wanted to keep the door! Somebody wanted to rout out the back lanes! Somebody wanted to teach ragged roughs! Somebody wanted to ask people to come to the place of worship, and to lend them their seats, and stand in the aisle while they sit. Well, be it what it may; I had rather be a doorkeeper in the house of the Lord, or the doormat either, than I would be accounted among the noblest in the tents of wickedness. Anything for Jesus, the lower the better; anything for Jesus, the humbler the better; anything for Jesus. The more going down into the deeps, the more thrusting the arms up to the elbows in the mud to find out precious jewels, the more of that the better. This is the true spirit of the Christian religion. Not the soaring up there to sit among the choristers and sing in grand style, not the putting on of apparel and preaching in lawn sleeves; not the going through gaudy and imposing ceremonies—all that is of Babylon: but to strip yourself to the shirtsleeves to fight the battle for Christ, and to go out among men as a humble worker, resolved by any means to save some, this is what your Lord would have you to do, for this is the unloosing of the latchets of his shoes.

III. And, now, our last remark shall be that *all this ought to stimulate us and not discourage us.*

Though we are not worthy to do it, that is the reason why we should avail ourselves of the condescending grace which honors us with such employ. Do not say, "I am not worthy to unloose the latchets of his shoes, and, therefore, I shall give up preaching." Oh, no, but preach away with all the greater vigor. John did so, and to his preaching he added warning. Warn people as well as preach to them. Tell them of the judgment to come and separate between the precious and the vile. We should perform our work in all ways, not omitting the more painful part of it, but going through with whatever God has appointed to us. John was called to testify of Christ, he felt unworthy to do it, but he did not shirk the work. It was his lifelong business to cry, "Behold, behold, behold the Lamb of God!" and he did it earnestly; he never paused in that cry. He was busy in baptizing too. It was the initiatory rite of the new dispensation, and there he stood continually immersing those who believed. Never a more indefatigable worker than John the Baptist; he threw his whole soul into it, because he felt he was not worthy to do the work. Brethren and sisters, your sense of unworthiness will, if you be idle, sadly hamper you but if the love of God be in your soul you will feel, "Since I do so badly when I do my best, I will always do my utmost. Since it comes to so little when the most is done, I will at least do the most." Could I give all my substance to him, and give my life, and then give my body to be burned, it would be a small return for love so amazing, so divine, as that which I have tasted: therefore, if I cannot do all that, at any rate, I will give the Lord Jesus all I can, I will love him all I can, I will pray to him all I can, I will talk about him all I can, and I will spread his gospel all I can; and no little thing will I count beneath me if his cause require it.

Brethren, John lived hard, for his meat was locusts and wild honey; his dress was not the soft raiment of men who live in palaces, he wrapped about him the rough camel's skin; and as he lived hard he died hard too, his boldness brought him into a dungeon, his courageous fidelity earned him a martyr's death. Here was a man who lived in self-denial and died witnessing for truth and righteousness, and all this because he had a high esteem of his Master. May our esteem of Christ so grow and increase, that we may be willing to put up with anything in life for Christ, and even to lay down our lives for his name's sake!

Certain Moravian missionaries, in the old times of slavery, went to one of the West Indian islands to preach, and they found they could not be permitted to teach there unless they themselves became slaves; and they did so, they sold themselves into bondage, never to return, that they might save slaves' souls. We have heard of another pair of holy men who actually submitted to be confined in a lazar house, that they might save the souls of lepers, knowing as they did that they would never be permitted to come out again; they went there to take the leprosy and to die, if by so doing they might save souls. I have read of one, Thomé de Jesu, who went to Barbary among the Christian captives, and there lived and died in banishment and bondage, that he might cheer his brethren, and preach Jesus to them. Brethren, we have never reached to such devotion; we fall far short of what Jesus deserves. We give him little, we give him what we are ashamed not to give him. Often we give him our zeal for a day or two and then grow cool; we wake up suddenly and then sleep all the more soundly. We seem today as if we would set the world on fire, and tomorrow we scarce keep our own lamp trimmed. We vow at one time that we will push the church before us and drag the world after us, and by-and-by we ourselves are like Pharaoh's chariots with the wheels taken off, and drag along right heavily. Oh, for a spark of the love of Christ in the soul! Oh, for a living flame from off Calvary's altar, to set our whole nature blazing with divine enthusiasm for the Christ who gave himself for us that we might live! Henceforth, take upon yourselves in the solemn intent of your soul this deep resolve: "I will unloose the latchets of his shoes; I will seek out the little things, the mean things, the humble things, and I will do them as unto the Lord and not unto men, and may he accept me even as he has saved me through his precious blood." Amen.

Matthew: "A Man Named Matthew"

Intended for reading on Lord's Day, November 29, 1896; delivered on Lord's Day evening, April 12, 1885, at the Metropolitan Tabernacle, Newington. No. 2493.

> *As Jesus passed forth from thence, he saw a man, named Matthew, sitting at the receipt of custom: and he saith unto him, "Follow me." And he arose, and followed him.*—MATTHEW 9:9

This is a little bit of autobiography. Matthew wrote this verse about himself. I can fancy him, with his pen in his hand, writing all the rest of this gospel; but I can imagine that, when he came to this very personal passage, he laid the pen down a minute, and wiped his eyes. He was coming to a most memorable and pathetic incident in his own life, and he recorded it with tremulous emotion. "As Jesus passed forth from thence, he saw a man, named Matthew." The Evangelist could not have said much less about himself than this. "He saw a man, named Matthew, sitting at the receipt of custom: and he saith unto him, 'Follow me.' And he arose, and followed him." I do not think there is any part of Matthew's gospel that touched him more than this portion in which he was writing down the story of divine love to himself, and of how he himself was called to be a disciple of Christ.

I notice a very grave distinction between Matthew's way of recording his call and the very general style of converts relating their experience nowadays. The man seems to come boldly forth, with a springing step and a boastful air, and shouts out that he was the biggest blackguard who ever lived, and he tells with great gusto how he used to curse and to swear, and he talks as if there was something to be proud of in all that evil. Sit down, sir; sit down, and give us the story in this style, "As Jesus passed forth from thence, he saw a man, named Matthew"—that is about as much as we care to know. Tell us as briefly as you can how the Lord called you, and enabled you to follow him. There is a modesty about this narrative—not a mock modesty, by any means; there is no concealment of the facts of the case, there is no obscuration of the grace of Christ, but there is a concealment of Matthew himself. He mentions that he was a publican; in the list that he gives of the apostles he calls himself "Matthew the publican." The other Evangelists hardly ever call him a publican;

they do not even call him "Matthew," as a rule; they give his more respectable name "Levi," and they have more to say of him than he says of himself. It is always best for us, if there is anything to be said in our praise, not to say it ourselves, but to let somebody else say it. Brother, if your trumpeter is dead, put the trumpet away. When that trumpet needs to be blown, there will be a trumpeter found to use it; but you need never blow it yourself.

This verse reads to me so tenderly that I do not know how to communicate to you just how I feel about it. I have tried to imagine myself to be Matthew, and to have to write this story; and I am sure that, if I had not been inspired as Matthew was, I should never have done it so beautifully as he has done it, for it is so full of everything that is touching, tender, timid, true, and gracious: "As Jesus passed forth from thence, he saw a man, named Matthew, sitting at the receipt of custom: and he saith unto him, 'Follow me.' And he arose, and followed him."

Please notice—perhaps you did notice in our reading—whereabouts Matthew has put this story: it is placed immediately after a miracle. Some question has been raised, in a harmony of the Gospels, as to the exact position of this fact; whether it did occur just where Matthew tells it or whether he rather studied effect than chronology. Sometimes the Evangelists seem to overlook the chronological position of a statement, and put it out of its proper place that it may be more in its place for some other purpose. Well, I do not know about the chronology of this event; but it seems to me very beautiful on Matthew's part to record his call just here. "There," said he, "I will tell them one miracle about the Savior having made the palsied man take up his bed and walk, and then I will tell them of another miracle—a greater miracle still—how there was another man who was more than palsied, chained to his gains and to an injurious traffic, yet who, nevertheless, at the command of Christ, quit that occupation and all his gains, that he might follow his divine Master." Whenever you think about your own conversion, dear friend, regard it as a miracle, and always say within yourself, "It was a wonder of grace. If the conversion of anybody was ever a miracle of mercy, it was my conversion; it was extraordinary condescension on Christ's part to look on such a sinner as I was, and nothing but a miracle of grace could have saved me."

So Matthew tells his own story very tenderly, but he tells it very suggestively, putting it just after a most notable miracle; and I think that the Evangelist thought there was some similarity between the miracle and his own conversion, for there is nothing that palsies a man toward spiritual things like the lust of gold. Let a man be engaged in oppression and extortion, as the publicans were, and the conscience becomes seared as with a hot iron, and the extortioner is not likely to feel or desire that which is right. Yet here was a man, up to his neck in an evil occupation, but in a moment, at the divine call, he is made to part with all his hopes of gain that he may follow Christ. It was a miracle similar and equal to the raising of the palsied man who took up his bed and walked. You, too, dear friend, can trace a parallel, perhaps, between your conversion and some miracle of the Master. Was it, in your case, the casting out of devils? Was it the opening of the eyes of the blind? Was it the unstopping of deaf ears, and the loosing of a silent tongue? Was it the raising of the dead, or even more than that, was it the calling forth of corruption itself out of the grave, as when Jesus cried, "Lazarus, come forth," and Lazarus came forth? In any case, I invite you who know the Lord, in the silence of your souls just to sit down and think, not about Matthew, but about ourselves. I shall think about "a man named Spurgeon," and you can think about "a man named John Smith" or "Thomas Jones" or whatever your name may happen to be. If the Lord has looked upon you in love, you can just put your own name into the text, and say, "As Jesus passed forth from thence, he saw a man named James" or "John" or "Thomas," and you women may put in your names, too, you Marys and Janes, and so forth. Just sit and think how Jesus said to each one of you, "Follow me," and how in that happy moment you did arise and follow him, and from that hour you could truly sing, as you have often sung since—

> 'Tis done! the great transaction's done:
> I am my Lord's, and he is mine:
> He drew me, and I followed on,
> Charmed to confess the voice divine.
>
> High heaven, that heard the solemn vow,
> That vow renew shall daily hear:
> Till in life's latest hour I bow,
> And bless in death a bond so dear.

With some degree of rapidity, I will try to conduct your thoughts to various points of this interesting and instructive narrative.

I. The first is, that *this call of the man named Matthew seemed accidental and unlikely.*

"As Jesus passed forth from thence," just as he was going about some work or other, going away from Capernaum, perhaps, or merely going down one of its streets, it was as he "passed forth" that this event happened. As he passed, "he saw a man, named Matthew." That is the way we talk when we speak of things that, as we say, "happen" we scarcely know why. Now, dear friend, was that how you were converted? I do not know how long ago it was; but it did so happen, did it not? Yet it did not seem to you to be a very likely event ever to occur.

Looking back at the case of Matthew, it does seem now to have been a very unlikely thing that he should become a follower of Jesus. *Capernaum was Christ's own city, so he had often been there, yet Matthew remained unsaved.* Christ had not seen that "man, named Matthew," in the special way in which he saw him on this particular occasion; and you, dear friend, went to a place of worship a great many times before you were converted; perhaps you had been there regularly since you were a child. Yet it was not till that one particular day of grace that anything special happened to you, even as it was not till the time recorded in our text that something very special happened to the man named Matthew.

Further, at that time, *Jesus seemed as if he was about other business*; for, we read, "as Jesus passed forth from thence." And perhaps it seemed to you that the preacher was aiming at something else when his word was blessed to you. He was, maybe, comforting believers, yet God sent the message home to you, a poor unconverted sinner. Strange, was it not, both in Matthew's case, and your own?

At that time, also, *there are many other people in Capernaum, yet Christ did not call them.* He saw them, but not in the particular way in which he saw the man named Matthew. And, in like manner, on that day of mercy when you received the blessing of salvation, perhaps there was a crowded congregation, but, as far as you know, the blessing did not reach anybody but yourself. Why, then, did it come to you? You do not know, unless you have learned to look behind the curtains in the holy place, and to see by the light of the lamp within the veil. If you have looked there, you know that, when Jesus Christ is passing by, what men call his accidents are all intentional, the glances of his eye are all ordained from eternity; and when he looks upon anyone, he does it according to the everlasting purpose and the foreknowledge of God. The Lord had looked long before on that man named Matthew, so, in the fullness of time, Jesus Christ must needs pass that way, and he must look in love and mercy upon that man named Matthew. He saw him then because, long before, he foresaw him.

I cannot tell how you happen to be here, my dear friend—a stranger in London, perhaps, and a total stranger to this tabernacle; yet I believe you are brought here that my Lord and Master may see you—*you,* "a man, named

Matthew" or "John" or "James" or "Thomas" or whatever your name may be. And, oh! I pray that this may be the time when you shall see him, and hear him say, "Follow me," and you shall feel a blessed constraint to follow him without question or hesitancy, but at once leave whatever your sinful life may have been, and become a follower of Christ.

So, in the first place, this call of Matthew seemed accidental and unlikely, yet it was according to the purpose of God, and therefore it was duly given and answered.

II. In the second place, *this call of the man named Matthew was altogether unthought of and unsought.*

Matthew was not engaged in prayer when Christ called him. *He was in a degrading business:* "sitting at the receipt of custom." He was not listening to the Savior's preaching; he was taking from the people, against their will, the taxes for their Roman conqueror. As far as I can see, he had not even thought about Christ. I do not believe that he had been called before to be a disciple of Christ, and that he was on this occasion called to be an apostle; for I cannot imagine one who had been saved by Christ, returning to the publican business. It was an extortioner's occupation all through, and he who is called to be Christ's follower does not practice extortion from his fellowmen. If that is his employment before his conversion, he quits it when he comes to Christ.

Matthew was, further, *in an ensnaring business*. Nothing is more likely to hold a man fast than the love of gain. Sticky stuff is that gold and silver of which many are so fond; it has birdlimed many a soul for the best fowler, the devil, and many have been destroyed by it. The publicans usually made a personal profit by extorting more than was due; and, at this time, Matthew was not paying away money, but "sitting at the receipt of custom."

I do not know that, *even if Matthew has wished to follow Christ, he would have dared to do so.* He must have thought that he was too unworthy to follow Christ; and if he had dared to attempt it, I should suppose that *he would have been repulsed by the other apostles.* They would have snubbed him, and asked, "Who are you, to come among us?" They dared not do so after Christ himself had said to Matthew, "Follow me," but certainly there is no indication that this man named Matthew was seeking Christ, or even thinking about him; yet, while he sat taking his tolls and customs, Jesus came to him, and said, "Follow me."

O my dear hearer, if you have been converted, it may be that something like this was true in your case! At any rate, this I know is true; you were not the first to seek Christ, but Christ was the first to seek you. You were a wandering sheep and did not love the fold; but his sweet mercy went out after you.

His grace made you thoughtful and led you to pray; the Holy Spirit breathed in you your first breath of spiritual life, and so you came to Christ. It was so, I am sure; you did not first seek Christ, but he first sought you. Let us who are saved present the prayer to God now, that many here who have never sought the Lord may nevertheless find him; for it is written, "'I am found of them that sought me not': I said, 'Behold me, behold me, unto a nation that was not called by my name.'" See, then, the freeness of the grace of God, the sovereignty of his choice. Admire it in the man named Matthew; admire it still more in yourself, whatever your name may be.

III. Third, *this call of Matthew was given by the Lord Jesus with full knowledge of him.*

It is not said that Matthew first saw the Lord; but, "as Jesus passed forth from thence, he saw a man, named Matthew." I like to dwell upon those words, "He saw a man, named Matthew," because they seem to me to have a great deal of instruction in them.

Christ probably stopped opposite where Matthew was sitting, and looking at him, *he saw all the sin that had been in him, and all the evil that still remained in him.* "He *saw* a man, named Matthew." Christ has a searching look, a discerning look, a detecting look. He looked Matthew up and down, and he saw all that was in him. All that was secret to others was manifest before his piercing eyes. "He saw a man, named Matthew," and I believe that Jesus saw more in Matthew than was really in Matthew; I mean, that his love looked goodness into Matthew, and then saw it; his love looked grace into Matthew, and then saw it.

I do not know, but as far as I can see, Matthew had always been called "Levi" before. The Lord Jesus Christ did not see "a man named Levi." That was his old name; but, *he saw Matthew as he was to be:* "He saw a man, named Matthew." O beloved, when the Lord looked upon you even while you were a sinner, he saw a saint in you; though it was only his own eyes that could see so much as that. What he meant to make of you, he already saw in you, and he loved you as one who should yet be one of his redeemed servants.

I believe also that when the Lord Jesus Christ saw Matthew with the pen in his hand, he said to himself, "See what a nimble pen he has; *he is the man to write the first of the four Gospels.*" Jesus saw Matthew figuring away, as he put down the people's names, and how much they paid, and he said to himself, "That is the man to write one of the most regular and orderly of the Gospels; there is a clerkly habit about him, he is a good account keeper, that is the man for my service."

I do not know, dear friend, what the Lord may happen to see in you. I do not know all that he saw when he looked upon me. I fear that he saw nothing in me but sin and evil and vanity; but I believe that he did say to himself concerning me, "I see one to whom I can teach my truth, and who, when he gets a hold of it, will grip it fast, and never let it go, and one who will not be afraid to speak it wherever he is." So the Lord saw what use he could make of me, and I wonder what use he can make of you. Sit still, dear child of God, and wonder that the Lord should have made such use of you as he has made. And you who are just beginning to think of the Lord Jesus Christ, sit still, and each one of you say, "I wonder what use he can make of me."

There is an adaptation in men, even while they are unconverted, which God has put into them for their future service. Luke, you know, was qualified to write his gospel because he had been a physician; and Matthew was qualified to write the particular gospel which he has left us because he had been a publican. There may be a something about your habits of life, and about your constitution, and your condition, that will qualify you for some special niche in the church of God in years to come. Oh, happy day, when Jesus shall look upon you, and call you to follow him! Happy day, when he did look upon some of us, and saw in us what his love meant to put there, that he might make of us vessels of mercy meet for the Master's use!

IV. Pressing on a little further, I want you to notice, in the fourth place, that *Matthew's call was graciously condescending*: "As Jesus passed forth from thence, he saw a man, named Matthew, sitting at the receipt of custom: and he saith unto him, 'Follow me.'"

Christ had the choice of his followers, but *how came he to choose a publican?* The Roman yoke was so detestable to the freeborn son of Abraham that he could not bear the fact that the Roman, the idolater, should be lord in the Holy Land; so, if the Romans wanted Jews to collect the taxes, they could only get persons who had lost all care about public repute. They might be no worse than other people; perhaps they were not, but they were esteemed as being the very offscouring and pariahs of their race. But the Lord Jesus Christ sees this publican, and says to him, "Follow me." Not much of a credit will he be to his Master; so at least those around him will say. "See how this man, Jesus Christ, goes about, and picks up the scum of the people, the *residuum*. He is taking a publican as his follower—the man who has given himself up to be the servant of the oppressors and who has been himself an oppressor—he is going to have *him*. Now, if the Nazarene had passed by, and seen a learned rabbi or a Pharisee with his phylacteries, one who had made broad the borders of his garment, if Jesus had called *him*, it would have given a respectability to the community." Yes, but it so happens that the Lord Jesus Christ does not care about that sort of respectability at all. He is so respectable himself, in the highest sense of being respected, that he has honor enough and to spare for all his people, and he can condescend, without hazard, to call into his immediate company, to be one of his personal followers, "a man, named Matthew," even though he is a collector of the Roman taxes.

"Oh!" says one, "but I cannot think that he will ever call me." Yes, but I can think that he will! You remember John Newton, who had been a slave dealer, and more, who had been himself a slave, literally a slave, as well as a slave to the worst passions. Yet, let the church of St. Mary Woolnoth tell how from its pulpit there sounded through long years the glorious gospel of the blessed God from one who had been an African blasphemer, but who became a minister of Christ of the highest and noblest kind. Yes, the Lord Jesus Christ loves to look out for the *publicans*, the very lowest of the low, and to say to them, "Follow me. Come into my company. Walk behind me. Become my servant. Be entrusted with my gospel. I will make use of you." He still takes such as these to become the proclaimers of his Word; oh, that he may thus call some of you!

"Well," say you, "it was great condescension when the Lord called Matthew, the publican." Yes, but was it not equal condescension when he called you and me? O man or woman, whatever your name, sit and wonder and adore the condescending love that chose even you to be Christ's follower!

V. Again, dear friends—I hope I do not weary you while I try to bring this case of Matthew fully before you, wishing always that you may see yourself in it—observe next, that *this call of Matthew was sublimely simple*. Here it is in a nutshell: "He saith."

It was not John who said it or James or any of the apostles; but, *"He* saith." And it is not my preaching or your preaching or an archbishop's preaching, that can save souls; it is, *"He* saith," and it is when the Lord Jesus Christ, by the divine Spirit, says to a man, *"Follow me,"* that then the decisive work is done. Did he not say to the primeval darkness, "Light be!" and light was? And God, the omnipotent and eternal, has but to speak to man, and a like result will follow. "He saith unto him, 'Follow me'"; and then immediately, just as simply as possible, the record says, *"he arose, and followed him."* There is no palaver, no priestcraft, no sacramentalism. "He saith, 'Follow me.' And he arose, and followed him." That is the way of salvation; Christ bids you, while you are at your sin, leave it, and you leave it. He bids you trust him, and you trust him;

and trusting him, you are saved, for "he that believeth on the Son hath everlasting life."

Is that how you were saved, dear friend? I know it is; yet you used to fuss and fret and fume, and say to yourself, "I want to feel, I want to see, I want to experience." Now you have got clear of all those mistakes, I hope there is nothing more sublime than your conversion, but there is nothing more simple. And as for you, dear friends, who are looking for signs and wonders, or else you will not believe, I wish you would give up that foolish notion, for there is no sign and no wonder which is equal to this, that Christ should say to the dead heart, "Live," and it lives; that he should say to the unbelieving heart, "Believe," and it believes. In the name of Jesus Christ of Nazareth, I say to you, sinner, "Believe on the Lord Jesus Christ"; and if he is really speaking by me, you will believe in him, and you will arise and follow him.

So Matthew's call to follow Christ was sublimely simple.

VI. Notice, also, that it was immediately effectual. The Lord Jesus Christ said to him, "Follow me," and "he arose, and followed him." *Matthew followed at once.*

Some might have waited and put the coins away; but it does not appear that Matthew did so: "he arose, and followed him." He did not say to Christ, "I must enter the amounts to the end of this page; here is a lot of people with fish baskets, I must just see how much I can get out of them, and so finish up my reckoning." No, "he arose, and followed him." I believe that, when a man is converted, he is converted outright, and he will come right out from whatever wrong thing he has been doing. I have heard of a publican (I mean the other sort of publican, not a tax gatherer) who was very fond of drink, and he had by means of the drink sent many to perdition; but the day he was converted, he smashed his signboard, and had done with the evil traffic forever. When there is anything else that is wrong, whatever it is, I like to see men smash it up, and have done with it. Clear every trace of it out of your house; do not try to keep even a little piece of it or to do a wrong thing, and say, "I will give the profits to the Lord Jesus Christ." He will not take the money that is stained with the blood of souls. Quit the evil trade, and have done with it. Every kind of sin and every sort of evil, whatever it may be, will be left as soon as effectual grace comes to a man. I do not believe that anyone ever repents a little bit at a time; it is once for all that he does it, he turns straight around immediately, and obeys the Lord's call, "Follow me." Jesus said to Matthew. "'Follow me,' and he arose, and followed him."

"Oh!" says one, "was it so?" Yes, it was; I am not talking about things that are matters of question; I am speaking about facts. "As Jesus passed forth from thence, he saw a man, named Matthew, sitting at the receipt of custom, and he saith unto him, 'Follow me.' And he arose, and followed him." I know another man, not named "Matthew," but "Charles," and the Lord said to him, "Follow me"; and he also arose, and followed him. If I were to ask all the Christian men here now—John, James, Samuel, or whatever their names, who heard Jesus Christ say, "Follow me," and who followed him—to stand up, there would not be many of you left sitting, I hope. And you godly women, too, know that it was just the call of the Lord Jesus Christ to you that brought you to him there and then.

The call to Matthew was the call of effectual grace. "Where the word of a king is, there is power"; and Jesus Christ spoke to Matthew the word of *the* King. He said, "Follow me," and Matthew did follow him. I have heard that when the queen sends to anybody to come and see her, she does not "request the pleasure of his company," but she sends her command to him to come. That is the way kings and queens talk; and that is just the way with the Lord Jesus Christ, the King of kings, and Lord of lords. He says, "Follow me." And preaching to you in his name, we do not say, "Dear friend, do be converted, if you will"; but we say, "Thus saith the Lord: believe on the Lord Jesus Christ, and thou shalt be saved"; and with that command goes the power of the word of a king, and so sinners are saved. Jesus said to Matthew, "'Follow me,' and he arose, and followed him."

VII. Now, lastly, *Matthew's call was a door of hope for other sinners.*

I have been speaking mostly about personal conversion, and perhaps somebody says, "You know, sir, we are to think about other people as well as ourselves." Precisely so, and there is never a man who is saved who wants to go to heaven alone. So, when the Lord Jesus Christ saw "a man, named Matthew," and bade the publican follow him, *his salvation encouraged other publicans to come to Jesus.* Christ saw a great many other publicans and sinners whom he intended to draw to himself by means of that "man, named Matthew." He was to become a decoy duck for a great multitude of others like himself.

Next, *his open house gave opportunity to his friends to hear Jesus.* No sooner was Matthew called, and led to follow the Lord Jesus, than he said to himself, "Now, what can I do for my new Master? I have a good big room, where I have been accustomed to lock up the people's goods till they have paid their dues—

the *douane*, the customhouse, where I put away their goods in bond. Here, John, Thomas, Mary, come and clean out this room! Put a long table right down the middle. I am going to have in all my old friends; they have known what kind of man I have been, I am going to invite them all to supper; and it will not be a mean supper, either; it shall be the best supper they have ever had." Levi made a great feast in his own house, and he said to the Lord Jesus, "You have bidden me follow you, and I am trying to do so; and one way in which I am following you is that I am going to have a great feast in my house tonight, and to fetch in all my old companions. Will you, my Lord, be so good as to come and sit at the head of the table, and talk with them? They will be in a better humor for listening after I have fed them well. Will you come; and when they are all happy around my table, will you do for them what you have done for me? Maybe, Lord, if you will say that Matthew has become your follower, they will say, 'What! Matthew? Does he follow Christ? Well, then, who must this Christ be, that he will have such a follower as Matthew? Surely, he will have us, too, for we are like Matthew, and we will come to him as Matthew has come to him, if he will but speak the word of power to us as he did to Matthew.'" So the call of Matthew was Christ's way of bringing numbers of lost ones to a knowledge of the truth and to eternal salvation.

Now, has it been as with you, dear friend? Man, named John, Thomas, Samuel—woman, named Mary, Jane, or whatever it may be—have *you* brought any others to Jesus? Have you brought your children to Jesus? Have your prayers brought your husband to Jesus? Have your entreaties brought your brethren to Jesus? If not, you have failed as yet in accomplishing that which should be your life-work. Ask the Lord to help you now to begin with somebody or other of your own circle and your own standing, to whom you will be most likely to speak with the largest measure of influence and power of any man. The day you are converted, try to talk with those who were your schoolmates. Were you converted in a factory? Do not hesitate to speak to your fellow workmen. Are you a person of position? Do you occupy a high station in the fashionable world? Do not be ashamed of your Master, but introduce Christ into the drawing room, and let him have a footing among the highest of the land. Let each man, according to his calling, feel, "He who bade me follow him has bidden me do so that others may, through my instrumentality, be led to follow him too." God bless you in this holy service!

I feel as if I must close my discourse by just saying that, as the Lord saw "a man, named Matthew," and as he saw you, try now to return that look of love and see him; consider how great this man was; and, as Christ came to

Matthew's table, I now invite you who are believers in the Lord Jesus Christ to come to his table; and though you are not now numbered with publicans and sinners, but with his redeemed people, still it shall be your great joy to wonder as you sit here that your Master does still condescend to eat with publicans and sinners. God bless you, and save the whole of this great company, for his dear name's sake! Amen.

Simeon: "Nunc Dimittis"

Delivered on Lord's Day morning, January 15, 1871, at the Metropolitan Tabernacle, Newington. No. 1014.

Lord, now lettest thou thy servant depart in peace, according to thy word: for mine eyes have seen thy salvation.—LUKE 2:29–30

Blessed were you, O Simeon, for flesh and blood had not revealed this unto you; neither had it enabled you so cheerfully to bid the world farewell. The flesh clings to the earth; it is dust and owns affinity to the ground out of which it was taken; it loathes to part from mother earth. Even old age, with its infirmities, does not make men really willing to depart out of this world. By nature we hold to life with a terrible tenacity; and even when we sigh over the evils of life, and repine concerning its ills, and fancy that we wish ourselves away, it is probable that our readiness to depart lies only upon the surface, but down deep in our hearts we have no will to go.

Flesh and blood had not revealed unto Simeon that he saw God's salvation in that babe which he took out of the arms of Mary and embraced with eager joy. God's grace had taught him that this was the Savior, and God's grace at the same time loosened the cords which bound him to earth, and made him feel the attractions of the better land. Blessed is that man who has received by grace a meetness for heaven, and a willingness to depart to that better land: let him magnify the Lord who has worked so great a work in him. As Paul says, "Thanks be unto the Father, which hath made us meet to be partakers of the inheritance of the saints in light." Certainly none of us were meet by nature—not even Simeon; the fitness of the venerable man was all the handiwork of God, and so, also, was his anxiety to obtain the inheritance for which God had prepared him. I trust, brethren, while we consider this morning the preparedness of the saints for heaven, and turn over in our mind those reflections which will make us ready to depart, God's Holy Spirit, sent forth from the Father, may make us also willing to leave these mortal shores, and launch upon the eternal sea at the bidding of our Father, God.

We shall note, this morning, first, that *every believer may be assured of departing in peace*; but that, second, *some believers feel a special readiness to depart now*: "Now lettest thou thy servant depart in peace"; and, third, that *there are words of encouragement to produce in us the like readiness*: "according to thy word." There are words of Holy Writ which afford richest consolation in prospect of departure.

I. First, then, let us start with the great general principle, which is full of comfort; namely, this, that *every believer may be assured of ultimately departing in peace.*

This is no privilege peculiar to Simeon, it is common to all the saints, since the grounds upon which this privilege rests are not monopolized by Simeon, but belong to us all.

Observe, first, that *all the saints have seen God's salvation*, therefore, should they all depart in peace. It is true, we cannot take up the infant Christ into our arms, but he is "formed in us, the hope of glory." It is true, we cannot look upon him with these mortal eyes, but we have seen him with those eyes immortal which death cannot dim—the eyes of our own spirit which have been opened by God's Holy Spirit. A sight of Christ with the natural eye is not saving, for thousands saw him and then cried, "Crucify him, crucify him." After all, it was in Simeon's case the spiritual eye that saw, the eye of faith that truly beheld the Christ of God; for there were others in the temple who saw the babe; there was the priest who performed the act of circumcision, and the other officials who gathered round the group; but I do not know that any of them saw God's salvation. They saw the little innocent child that was brought there by its parents, but they saw nothing remarkable in him; perhaps, Simeon and Anna, alone of all those who were in the temple, saw with the inward eye the real Anointed of God revealed as a feeble infant. So, though you and I miss the outward sight of Christ, we need not regret it, it is but secondary as a privilege; if with the inner sight we have seen the incarnate God, and accepted him as our salvation, we are blessed with holy Simeon. Abraham saw Christ's day before it dawned, and even thus, after it has passed, we see it, and with faithful Abraham we are glad. We have looked unto him, and we are lightened. We have beheld the Lamb of God which taketh away the sins of the world. In the "despised and rejected of men" we have seen the anointed Savior; in the crucified and buried One, who afterward arose again, and ascended into glory, we have seen salvation, full, free, finished. Why, therefore, should we think ourselves less favored than Simeon? From like causes like results shall spring: we shall depart in peace, for we have seen God's salvation.

Moreover, believers already enjoy peace as much as ever Simeon did. No man can depart in peace who has not lived in peace; but he who has attained peace in life shall possess peace in death, and an eternity of peace after death.

"Being justified by faith we have peace with God through our Lord Jesus Christ." Jesus has bequeathed us peace, saying, "Peace I leave with you, my peace I give unto you." "For he is our peace," and "the fruit of the Spirit is peace." We are reconciled unto God by the death of his Son. Whatever peace flowed in the heart of Simeon, I am sure it was not of a diviner nature than that which dwells in the bosom of every true believer. If sin be pardoned, the quarrel is ended; if the atonement is made, then is peace established, a peace covenanted to endure forever. We are now led in the paths of peace; we walk the King's highway, of which it is written, "no lion shall be there"; we are led beside the still waters, and made to lie down in green pastures. We feel no slavish fear of God, though he be "a consuming fire" even to us; we tremble no longer to approach into his presence, who deigns to be our Father. The precious blood upon the mercy seat has made it a safe place for us to resort at all times; boldness has taken the place of trembling. The throne of God is our rejoicing, though once it was our terror.

> Once 'twas a seat of dreadful wrath,
> And shot devouring flame;
> Our God appeared "consuming fire,"
> And vengeance was his name.

Therefore, brethren, having peace with God, we may be sure that we shall "depart in peace." We need not fear that the God of all consolation, who has already enriched us in communion with himself, and peace in Christ Jesus, will desert us at the last. He will help us to sing a sweet swan song, and our tabernacle shall be gently taken down, to be rebuilt more enduringly in the fair country beyond Jordan.

Furthermore, we may rest assured of the same peace as that which Simeon possessed, since we are, if true believers, equally *God's servants*. The text says, "Lord, now lettest thou *thy servant* depart in peace." But, in this case, one servant cannot claim a privilege above the rest of the household. The same position toward God, the same reward from God. Simeon, a servant; you also, my brother, a servant; he who says to Simeon, "depart in peace," will say also the same to you. The Lord is always very considerate toward his old servants and takes care of them when their strength fails. The Amalekite of old had a servant who was an Egyptian, and when he fell sick he left him, and he would have perished if David had not had compassion on him; but our God is no Amalekite slave owner, neither doth he cast off his worn-out servants. "Even to your old age I am he; and even to hoar hairs will I carry you: I have made, and I will bear; even I will carry, and will deliver you." David felt this, for he prayed to God, and said, "Now, also, when I am old and gray-headed, O God, forsake me not." If you have been clothed in your Lord's livery of grace, and taught to obey his will, he will never leave you, nor forsake you; he will not sell you into the hands of your adversary, nor suffer your soul to perish. A true master counts it a part of his duty to protect his servants, and our great Lord and Prince will show himself strong on the behalf of the very least of all his followers, and will bring them every one into the rest which remains for his people. Do you really serve God? Remember, "his servants ye are to whom ye obey." Are you taught of the Spirit to obey the commandments of love? Do you strive to walk in holiness? If so, fear not death; it shall have no terrors to you. All the servants of God shall depart in peace.

There is also another reflection which strengthens our conviction that all believers shall depart in peace, namely, this: that up till now *all things in their experience have been according to God's word.* Simeon's basis of hope for a peaceful departure was "according to thy word"; and, surely, no Scripture is of private interpretation, or to be reserved for one believer to the exclusion of the rest? The promises of God, which are "Yea and amen in Christ Jesus," are sure to all the seed: not to some of the children is the promise made, but all the grace-born are heirs. There are not special promises hedged round and set apart for Simeon and a few saints of old time, but with all who are in Christ, their federal head, the covenant is made, and stands "ordered in all things and sure." If, then, Simeon, as a believer in the Lord, had a promise that he should depart in peace, I have also a like promise if I am in Christ. What God hath said in his Word, Simeon lays hold of, and none can say him no; but if, with the same grace-given faith, I also grasp it for myself, who shall challenge my right? God will not violate his promise to one of his people anymore than to another, and, consequently, when our turn shall come to gather up our feet in the bed and to resign our spirit, some precious passage in sacred Writ shall be as a rod and a staff to us that we may fear no evil.

These four considerations, gathered out of the text itself, may give four-fold certainty to the assurance that every believer, at the hour of his departure, shall possess peace.

For a moment, review attentively the words of the aged saint: they have much instruction in them. Every believer shall in death depart in the same sense as Simeon did. The word here used is suggestive and encouraging: it may be applied either to escape from confinement or to deliverance from toil. The Christian man in the present state is like a bird in a cage: his body imprisons his soul. His spirit, it is true, ranges heaven and earth, and laughs at the limits of matter, space, and time; but for all that, the flesh is a poor scabbard unworthy of the glittering soul, a mean cottage unfit for a princely spirit, a clog, a burden, and a fetter. When we would watch and pray, we find full often that the spirit is willing but the flesh is weak. "We that are in this body do groan." The fact is, we are caged birds; but the day comes when the great Master shall open the cage door, and release his prisoners. We need not dread the act of unfastening the door, for it will give to our soul the liberty for which it only pines, and then, with the wings of a dove, covered with silver, and its feathers with yellow gold, though aforetime it had lain among the pots, it will soar into its native air, singing all the way with a rapture beyond imagination. Simeon looked upon dying as a mode of being let loose—a deliverance out of durance vile, an escape from captivity, a release from bondage. The like redemption shall be dealt unto us. How often does my soul feel like an unhatched chick, shut up within a narrow shell, in darkness and discomfort! The life within labors hard to chip and break the shell, to know a little more of the great universe of truth, and see in clearer light the infinite of divine love. O happy day, when the shell shall be broken, and the soul, complete in the image of Christ, shall enter into the freedom for which she is preparing! We look for that, and we shall have it. God, who gave us to aspire to holiness and spirituality and to likeness to himself, never implanted those aspirations in us out of mockery. He meant to gratify these holy longings, or, else, he would not have excited them. Before long we, like Simeon, shall depart—that is, we shall be set free to go in peace.

I said that the word meant also a release from toil. It is as though Simeon had been standing at the table of his Master like a servant waiting on his Lord. You know the parable in which Christ says that the master does not first bid his servant sit down and eat bread, but commands him thus, "Gird thyself, and serve me." See then, Simeon stands yonder, girded and serving his Master; but by and by, when the Master sees fit, he turns around and says to Simeon, "Now you may depart, and take your own meat, your work is done." Or, we may use another simile, and picture Simeon sitting at the king's gate, like Mordecai, ready for any errand which may be appointed him, but at length his time of attendance expires, and the great monarch bids him depart in peace. Or, yet again, we may view him as a reaper toiling amid the harvest beneath a burning sun, parched with thirst and wearied with labor, and lo! the great Boaz comes into the field, and, having saluted his servant, says to him, "You have fulfilled like a hireling your day: take your wage, and depart in peace." The like shall happen to all true servants of Christ; they shall rest from their labors where no weariness shall vex them, "neither shall the sun light on them, nor any heat." They shall enter into the joy of their Lord, and enjoy the rest which remains for them. There is much of comfortable thought if we meditate upon this.

But note the words again. You perceive that the departure of the child of God is *appointed* of the Lord. "Now *lettest thou* thy servant depart." The servant must not depart from his labor without his master's permission, else would he be a runaway, dishonest to his position. The good servant dares not stir till his master says, "Depart in peace." Simeon was content to wait till he received permission to depart, and it becomes us all to acquiesce cheerfully in the Lord's appointment, whether he lengthens or shortens, our life. It is certain that without the Lord's will no power can remove us. No wind from the wilderness shall drive our souls into the land of darkness, no fiends with horrid clamor can drag us down to the abyss beneath, no destruction that wasteth at noonday, or pestilence waiting in darkness can cut short our mortal career. We shall not die till God shall say to us, "My child, depart from the field of service, and the straitness of this your tabernacle, and enter into rest." Till God commands us we cannot die, and when he bids us go it shall be sweet for us to leave this world.

Note, further, that the words before us clearly show that the believer's departure is attended with *a renewal of this divine benediction.* "Depart in peace," says God. It is a farewell, such as we give to a friend: it is a benediction, such as Aaron, the priest of God, might pronounce over a suppliant whose sacrifice was accepted. Eli said unto Hannah, "Go in peace: and the God of Israel grant thee thy petition that thou hast asked of him." Around the sinner's deathbed the tempest thickens, and he hears the rumblings of the eternal storm: his soul is driven away, either amid the thunderings of curses loud and deep, or else in the dread calm which evermore forebodes the hurricane. "Depart, ye cursed" is the horrible sound which is in his ears. But not so the righteous. He feels the Father's hand of benediction on his head, and underneath him are the everlasting arms. The best wine with him is kept to the last. At eventide it is light; and, as his sun is going down, it grows more glorious, and lights up all the surroundings with a celestial glow, whereat bystanders wonder, and exclaim, "Let me die the death of the righteous, and let my last end be like his." That pilgrim sets out upon a happy journey to whom Jehovah says, "Depart in peace." This is a sole finger laid upon the closing eyelid by a tender father, and it ensures a happy waking, where eyes are never wet with tears.

I cannot detain you longer over these words: suffice it to add, that whatever belonged to Simeon in this benediction must not be regarded as peculiar to him alone, but as, in their measure, the possession of all believers. "'This is the heritage of the servants of the Lord, and their righteousness is of me,' saith the Lord."

II. But now, second, we remind you, that *some believers are conscious of a special readiness to depart in peace.*

When do they feel this? Answer: first, *when their graces are vigorous.* All the graces are in all Christians, but they are not all there in the same proportion, nor are they at all times in the same degree of strength. In certain believers *faith* is strong and active. Now, when faith becomes "the evidence of things not seen," and "the substance of things hoped for," then the soul is sure to say, "Lord, now lettest thou thy servant depart in peace." Faith brings the clusters of Eshcol into the desert, and makes the tribes long for the land that flows with milk and honey. When the old Gauls had drunk of the wines of Italy, they said, "Let us cross the Alps, and take possession of the vineyards which yield such generous draughts." So when faith makes us realize the joys of heaven, then it is that our soul stands waiting on the wing, watching for the signal from the glory land.

The same is true of the grace of *hope,* for hope peers into the things invisible. She brings near to us the golden gates of the Eternal City. Like Moses, our hope climbs to the top of Pisgah, and beholds the Canaan of the true Israel. Moses had a delightful vision of the Promised Land when he gazed from Nebo's brow, and saw it all from Dan to Beersheba: so also hope drinks in the charming prospect of the goodly land and Lebanon, and then she exclaims exultingly, "Lord, now lettest thou thy servant depart in peace." Heaven realized and anticipated by hope renders the thought of departure most precious to the heart.

And the like, also, is the effect of the grace of love upon us. Love puts the heart, like a sacrifice, on the altar, and then she fetches heavenly fire and kindles it; and, as soon as ever, the heart begins to burn and glow like a sacrifice; what is the consequence? Why, it ascends like pillars of smoke up to the throne of God. It is the very instinct of love to draw us nearer to the person whom we love; and, when love toward God pervades the soul, then the spirit cries, "Make haste, my beloved, be thou like a roe or a young hart upon the mountains of separation." Perfect love, casting out all fear, cries, "up, and away."

> *Let me be with thee, where thou art,*
> *My Savior, my eternal rest!*
> *Then only will this longing heart*
> *Be fully and forever blest.*

I might thus mention all the graces, but suffer one of them to suffice, one which is often overlooked, but is priceless as the gold of Ophir—it is the grace of *humility*. Is it strange that the lower a man sinks in his own esteem the higher does he rise before his God? Is it not written, "Blessed are the poor in spirit, for theirs is the kingdom of heaven"? Simeon had no conceit of his own importance in the world, else he would have said, "Lord, let me stay, and be an apostle. Surely I shall be needed at this juncture to lend my aid in the auspicious era which has just commenced." But no, he felt himself so little, so inconsiderable, that now that he had attained his heart's wish and seen God's salvation, he was willing to depart in peace. Humility by making us lie low helps us to think highly of God and, consequently, to desire much to be with God. Oh, to have our graces always flourishing, for then shall we always be ready to depart and willing to be offered up. Lack of grace entangles us, but to abound in grace is to live in the suburbs of the New Jerusalem.

Another time, when believers are thus ready to go, is when their assurance is clear. It is not always so with even the most mature Christians, and some true saints have not yet attained to assurance; they are truly saved and possess a genuine faith, but as assurance is the cream of faith, the milk has not stood long enough to produce the cream; they have not yet come to the flower of assurance, for their faith is but a tender plant. Give a man assurance of heaven, and he will be eager to enjoy it. While he doubts his own security, he wants to linger here. He is like the psalmist when he asked that God would permit him to recover his strength before he went hence, and was no more. Some things were not yet in order with David, and he would stay a while till they were. But when the ship is all loaded, the crew on board, and the anchor heaved, the favoring breeze is desired that the bark may speed on its voyage. When a man is prepared for his journey, ready to depart, he does not care to linger long in these misty valleys, but pants for the sunny summits of the mount of God, whereon stands the palace of the great King. Let a man know that he is resting upon the precious blood of Christ, let him by diligent self-examination perceive in himself the marks of regeneration, and by the witness of his own spirit and by the infallible witness of the Holy Ghost bearing witness with his own spirit, let him be certified that he is born of God, and the natural consequence will be that he will say, "Now let me loose from all things here below and let me enter into the rest which is assuredly my own." O you that have lost your assurance by negligent living, by falling into sin, or by some other form of backsliding, I do not wonder that you hug the world, for you are afraid you have no other portion; but with those who read their titles clear to mansions in the skies it will be otherwise.

They will not ask to linger in this place of banishment, but will sing in their hearts, as we did just now:

Jerusalem my happy home,
Name ever dear to me;
When shall my labors have an end,
In joy and peace and thee?

Beloved, furthermore, saints feel most their readiness to go when *their communion with Christ is near and sweet*; when Christ hides himself we are afraid to talk of dying, or of heaven; but when he only shows himself through the lattices, and we can see those eyes which are "as the eyes of doves by the rivers of water, washed with milk and fitly set"; when our own soul melts even at that hazy sight of him, as through a glass darkly. Oh, then we fain would be at home, and our soul cries out for the day when her eyes shall see the King in his beauty, in the land that is very far off. Have you never felt the heavenly homesickness? Have you never pined for the home bringing? Surely, when your heart has been full of the Bridegroom's beauty, and your soul has been ravished with his dear and ever precious love, you have said: "When shall the day break, and the shadows flee away? Why are his chariots so long in coming?" You have swooned, as it were, with lovesickness for your precious Savior, thirsting to see him as he is, and to be like him. The world is black when Christ is fair; it is a poor heap of ashes when he is altogether lovely to us. When a precious Christ is manifested to our spirits, we feel that we could see Jesus and die. Put out these eyes, there is nothing more for them to see when they have seen *him*. "Black sun," said Rutherford, "black moon, black stars, but inconceivably bright and glorious Lord Jesus." How often did that devout man write words of this sort:

"Oh, if I had to swim through seven hells to reach him, if he would but say to me, like Peter, 'Come unto me,' I would go unto him not only on the sea, but on the boiling floods of hell, if I might but reach him, and come to him." I will pause here and give you his own words: "I profess to you I have no rest, I have no ease, till I be over head and ears in love's ocean. If Christ's love (that fountain of delight) were laid as open to me as I would wish, oh, how I would drink, and drink abundantly! I half call his absence cruel; and the mask and veil on Christ's face a cruel covering that hideth such a fair, fair face from a sick soul. I dare not upbraid him, but his absence is a mountain of iron upon my heavy heart. Oh, when shall we meet? Oh, how long is it to the dawning of the marriage day? O sweet Lord Jesus, take wide steps; O my Lord, come over the mountains at one stride! O my Beloved, be like a roe, or a young hart, on the mountains of separation. Oh, if he would fold the heavens together like an old cloak, and shovel time and days out of the way, and make ready in haste the Lamb's wife for her Husband! Since he looked upon me my heart is not mine; he hath run away to heaven with it."

When these strong throes, these ardent pangs of insatiable desire come upon a soul that is fully saturated with Christ's love, through having been made to lean its head upon his bosom, and to receive the kisses of his mouth, then is the time when the soul says, "Lord, now lettest thou thy servant depart in peace."

So again, beloved, saints have drawn their anchor up and spread their sails, when they have been *made to hold loose by all there is in this world*; and that is generally when they hold fastest by the world to come. To many this world is very sweet, very fair, but God puts bitters into the cup of his children; when their nest is soft, he fills it with thorns to make them long to fly. Alas, that it should be so, but some of God's servants seem as if they had made up their minds to find a rest beneath the moon. They are moonstruck who hope to do so.

All the houses in this plague-stricken land are worm-eaten and let in the rain and wind: my soul longs to find a rest among the ivory palaces of your land, O Emmanuel.

Brethren, it often happens that the loss of dear friends, or the treachery of those we trusted, or bodily sickness, or depression of spirit, may help to unloose the holdfasts which enchain us to this life; and then we are enabled to say with David in one of the most precious little psalms in the whole Book—131: "I have behaved and quieted myself, as a child that is weaned of his mother: my soul is even as a weaned child." I have often thought that if David had said, "my soul is even as a weaning child," it would have been far more like most of God's people. But to be weaned, quite weaned from the world, to turn away from her consolations altogether, this it is which makes us cry, "Lord, now lettest thou thy servant depart in peace." Even as the psalmist when he said, "And now, Lord, what wait I for? my hope is in thee."

Again, saints are willing to depart when their work is almost done. This will not be the case with many here present, perhaps, but it was so with Simeon. Good old man! He had been very constant in his devotions, but on this occasion he came into the temple, and there, it is said, he took the child in his arms, and blessed God. Once more he delivered his soul of its adoration—once more he blended his praise with the songs of angels. When he had done that, he openly confessed his faith: another important work of every believer, for he said, "mine eyes have seen thy salvation." He bore public testimony to the child Jesus and declared that he should be "a light to lighten the gentiles." Having done that, he bestowed his fatherly benediction upon the child's parents, Joseph and his mother; he blessed them, and said unto Mary, "Behold, this child is set for the fall and rising again of many in Israel." Now we read that David, after he had served his generation, fell on sleep; it is time for man to sleep when his life's work is finished. Simeon felt he had done all: he had blessed God; he had declared his faith; he had borne testimony to Christ; he had bestowed his benediction upon godly people; and so he said, "Now, Lord, lettest thou thy servant depart in peace." Ah, Christian people, you will never be willing to go if you are idle. You lazy lie-a-beds, who do little or nothing for Christ, you sluggish servants, whose garden is overgrown with weeds, no wonder that you do not want to see your master! Your sluggishness accuses you and makes you cowards. Only he who has put out his talents to good interest will be willing to render an account of his stewardship. But when a man feels, without claiming any merit, that he has fought a good fight, finished his course, and kept the faith, then will he rejoice in the crown which is laid up for him in heaven, and he will long to wear it. Throw your strength into the Lord's work, dear brethren, all your strength; spare none of your powers: let body, soul, and spirit be entirely consecrated to God and used at their utmost stretch. Get through your day's work, for the sooner you complete it, and have fulfilled like a hireling your day, the more near and sweet shall be the time when the shadows lengthen, and God shall say to you, as a faithful servant, "Depart in peace!"

One other matter, I think, helps to make saints willing to go, and that is *when they see or foresee the prosperity of the church of God.* Good old Simeon saw that Christ was to be a light to lighten the gentiles, and to be the glory of his people Israel; and, therefore, he said, "Lord, now lettest thy servant depart in peace." I have known many a godly deacon who has seen a church wither and decay, its ministry become unprofitable, and its membership become divided; the dear old man has poured out his soul in agony before God, and when at last the Lord has sent a man to seek the good of Israel, and the church has been built up, he has been overjoyed, and he has said, "now lettest thou thy servant depart in peace." It must have reconciled John Knox to die when he had seen the Reformation safely planted throughout all Scotland. It made dear old Latimer, as he stood tied to the stake, feel happy when he could say, "Courage, brother, we shall this day light such a candle in England as shall never be blown out." "Pray for the peace of Jerusalem." Yes, that we do, and we vehemently desire her prosperity, and if we can see Christ glorified, error defeated, truth established, sinners saved, and saints sanctified, our spirit feels she has all she wishes. Like dying David, when we have said, "Let the whole earth be filled with his glory," we can fall back upon the pillows and die, for our prayers like those of David the son of Jesse are ended. Let us pray for this peace and this prosperity, and when we see it come, it shall bring calm and rest to our spirits, so that we shall be willing to depart in peace.

III. I shall call your attention now, for a little while, to the third point, that *there are words to encourage us to the like readiness to depart.*

"*According to thy word.*" Now let us go to the Bible, and take from it seven choice words all calculated to cheer our hearts in the prospect of departure, and the first is Psalm 23:4: "Yea, though I walk through the valley of the shadow of death, I will fear no evil: for thou art with me; thy rod and thy staff they comfort me." "We walk"—the Christian does not quicken his pace when he dies; he walked before, and he is not afraid of death, so he calmly walks on. It is a walk through a "shadow." There is no substance in death, it is only a shade. Who needs fear a shadow? It is not a lonely walk—"thou art with me." Neither is it a walk that need cause us terror; "I will fear no evil": not only is there no evil, but no fear shall cloud my dying hours. It shall be a departure full of comfort: "thy rod and thy staff"—a duplicate means shall give us a fullness of consolation. "Thy rod and thy staff they comfort me."

Take another text, and so follow the direction, "according to thy word." Psalm 37:37: "Mark the perfect man, and behold the upright: for the end of that man is peace." If we are perfect, that is sincere; if we are upright, that is honest in heart; our end then shall assuredly be peace.

Take another word, Psalm 116:15: "Precious in the sight of the Lord is the death of his saints." It is no ordinary thing for a saint to die; it is a spectacle which the eyes of God are delighted with. As kings delight in their pearls and diamonds, and count them precious, so the deathbeds of the saints are God's precious things.

Take another, Isaiah 57:2: "He shall enter into peace: they shall rest in their beds, each one walking in his uprightness." Here is an entrance into peace for the saint, rest on his dying bed, rest for his body in the grave, rest for his spirit in the bosom of his Lord, and a walking in his uprightness in the immortality above. "According to thy word." O what force there is in these few syllables! When you can preach the Word of God you must prevail. Nothing has such marrow and fatness in it as a text of Scripture. It has a force of comfort all its own. Consider also 1 Corinthians 3:21–22: "For all things are yours; whether Paul, or Apollos, or Cephas, or the world, or life, or death, or things present, or things to come; all are yours." Now, if death is yours, there can be no sort of reason why you should be afraid of that which is made over to you as a part of your inheritance.

Take 1 Corinthians 15:54–57: "So when this corruptible shall have put on incorruption, and this mortal shall have put on immortality, then shall be brought to pass the saying that is written, Death is swallowed up in victory. O death, where is thy sting? O grave, where is thy victory? The sting of death is sin; and the strength of sin is the law. But thanks be to God, which giveth us the victory through our Lord Jesus Christ." With such a text we need not fear to depart.

And so that other word, the seventh we shall quote, and in that number seven dwells perfection of testimony. Revelation 14:13: "And I heard a voice from heaven saying unto me, 'Write, Blessed are the dead which die in the Lord from henceforth.' 'Yea,' saith the Spirit, 'that they may rest from their labors; and their works do follow them.'"

Now, I dare say, many of you have said, "I wish I had a word from God, just like Simeon had, to cheer me in my dying moments." You have it before you; here are seven that I have read to you, most sure words of testimony, unto which you do well to take heed, as unto a light shining in a dark place. These promises belong to all believers in our precious Lord and Savior, Jesus Christ. Fear not, then, be not afraid, but rather say, "Now lettest thou thy servant depart in peace."

I have done the sermon, but we must put a rider to it. Just a word or two to those of you who cannot die in peace because you are not believers in Christ: you have never seen God's salvation, neither are you God's servants. I must deal with you as I have dealt with the saints. I have given them texts of Scripture, for the text says, "according to thy word"; and I will give you also two passages of Scripture, which will show you those who may not hope to depart in peace.

The first one is negative: it shows who cannot enter heaven, and, consequently, who cannot depart in peace—1 Corinthians 6:9–10: "Know ye not that the unrighteous shall not inherit the kingdom of God?" the unjust, the oppressive, cheats, rogues, "the unrighteous shall not inherit the kingdom of God." I will read these words. I need not explain them, but let everyone here who comes under their lash submit to God's Word. "Be not deceived: neither fornicators"—plenty of them in London—"nor idolaters"—and you need not worship a God of wood and stone to be idolaters, worship anything but God, you are an idolater—"nor adulterers, nor effeminate, nor abusers of themselves with mankind, nor thieves, nor covetous, nor drunkards"—alas, some of these come to this house regularly—"nor revilers," that is, backbiters, cavilers, talebearers, swearers, and such like, "nor extortioners"—you fine 20 percent gentlemen! You who grind poor borrowers with usurious interest. None of you shall inherit the kingdom of God, not one of you. If you come within this list, except God renew your hearts and change you, the holy gates of heaven are shut in your face.

Now, take another text, of a positive character, from the book of Revelation 21:7–8: "He that overcometh shall inherit all things; and I will be his God, and he shall be my son. But the fearful"—that means the cowardly, those that are ashamed of Christ, those that dare not suffer for Christ's sake, those who believe everything, and nothing, and so deny the truth, because they cannot endure to be persecuted; "the fearful, and unbelieving"—that is, those who do not trust a Savior—"and the abominable"—and they are not scarce, some among the poor are abominable, and there are right honorables who ought to be called right abominables; yes, and greater than that, too, whose vices make them abominable to the nation; "and murderers"—"he that hateth his brother is a murderer"; and "whoremongers, and sorcerers"; those who have or pretend to have dealings with devils and spirits, your spirit rappers, the whole batch of them; "and idolaters, and all liars," and these swarm everywhere, they lie in print, and they lie with the voice; ". . . all liars, shall have their part in the lake which burneth with fire and brimstone: which is the second death."

Now these are no words of mine, but the words of God; and if they condemn you, you are condemned; but, if you be condemned, fly to Jesus. Repent and be converted, as says the gospel, and forgiveness shall be yours, through Jesus Christ. Amen.

John: "The Disciple Whom Jesus Loved"

⟿⟦⟵

Delivered on Lord's Day morning, May 23, 1880, at the Metropolitan Tabernacle, Newington. No. 1539.

The disciple whom Jesus loved following; which also leaned on his breast at supper.—JOHN 21:20

Our Lord loved all his disciples—"having loved his own which were in the world, he loved them unto the end." He said to all the apostles, "I call you not servants; for the servant knoweth not what his Lord doeth: but I have called you friends; for all things that I have heard of my Father I have made known unto you."

And yet within that circle of love there was an innermost place in which the beloved John was favored to dwell: upon the mountain of the Savior's love there was a knoll, a little higher than the rest of the mount, and there John was made to stand, nearest to his Lord. Let us not, because John was specially loved, think less, even in the slightest degree, of the love which Jesus Christ gave forth to the rest of his chosen. I take it, brethren, that those who display an extraordinary love to one are all the more capable of great affection to many; and therefore, because Jesus loved John most, I have an enhanced estimate of his love to the other disciples. It is not for a moment to be supposed that anyone suffered from his supreme friendship for John. John was raised, and they were not lowered, but raised with him. All believers are the dear objects of the Savior's choice, the purchase of his blood, his portion and inheritance, the jewels of his crown. If in John's case one is greater in love than another, yet all are eminently great, and therefore if it should so happen that you dare not hope to reach the height of John, and cannot look to be distinguished above others as "the disciple whom Jesus loved," yet be very thankful to be among the brotherhood who can each say, "He loved me, and gave himself for me." If you have not attained unto the first three, be happy to belong to the host of those who follow the Son of David. It is a matchless privilege, and an unspeakable honor, to enjoy the love of Jesus, even if you march among the rank and file of the armies of love. Our Lord's love to each of us has in it heights immeasurable and depths unfathomable; it passes knowledge.

Yet would I not utter this word of good cheer to make you remain at ease in a low state of grace; far rather would I excite you to rise to the highest point of love; for if already the Lord has loved you with an everlasting love, if already he has chosen you and called you, and kept you and instructed you, and forgiven you, and manifested himself to you, why should you not hope that another step or two may yet be taken, and that so you may climb to the very highest eminence? Why should you not before long be styled like Daniel, a "man greatly beloved," or like John, "that disciple whom Jesus loved"?

To be loved as John was, with a special love, is an innermost form of that same grace with which all believers have been favored. You must not imagine when I try to exhibit some of the lovable traits of John's character, that I would have you infer that the love of Christ went forth toward John in any other way than according to the law of grace; for whatever there was that was lovable in John, it was worked in him by the grace of God. Under the law of works John would have been as surely condemned as any of us, and there was nothing legally deserving in John. Grace made him to differ, just as truly as grace separates the vilest sinner from among the ungodly. Though it be granted that there were certain natural characteristics which made him amiable, yet God is the Creator of all that is estimable in man, and it was not till the natural had been by grace transformed and transfigured into the spiritual that these things became the subject of the complacency of Christ Jesus.

Brethren, we do not speak of John today as if he were loved because of his works or stood higher in the heart of Christ on the ground of personal merit, whereof he might glory. He, like all the rest of his brethren, was loved of Jesus because Jesus is all love and chose to set his heart upon him. Our Lord exercised a sovereignty of love and chose John for his own name's sake; and yet at the same time there was created in John much that was a fit object for the love of Christ. The love of Jesus was shed abroad in John's heart, and thus John himself was made fragrant with delightful odors. It was all of grace: the supposition of anything else is out of place. I look upon this special form of our Lord's love as one of those "best gifts" which we are bidden earnestly to covet—but a gift most emphatically, and not a wage or a purchasable commodity. Love is not bought. It never talks of price or claim. Its atmosphere is free favor. "If a man would give all the substance of his house for love, it would utterly be condemned." The supremest love is to be sought for, then, after the analogy of grace, as gracious men seek greater grace, and not as legalists chaffer and bargain for reward and desert. If ever we reach the upper chambers of love's palace, love herself must lead us up the stairs, yes, and be to our willing feet the staircase itself. Oh, for the help of the Holy Spirit while we speak upon such a theme.

I. And now, to come nearer to the text, first, dear friends, *let us consider the name itself*, "the disciple whom Jesus loved."

Our first observation upon it is—*it is a name which John gives to himself.* I think he repeats it five times. No other writer calls John "the disciple whom Jesus loved": John has thus surnamed himself, and all the early writers recognize him under that title. Do not suspect him, however, of egotism. It is one of the instances in which egotism is quite out of the question. Naturally, you and I would be rather slow to take such a title, even if we felt it belonged to us, because we should be jealous for our repute and be afraid of being thought presumptuous; but with a sweet naïveté which makes him quite forget himself, John took the name which he knew most accurately described him, whether others caviled at it or no. So far from there being any pride in it, it just shows the simplicity of his spirit, the openness, the transparency of his character, and his complete self-forgetfulness. Knowing it to be the truth, he does not hesitate to say it: he was sure that Jesus loved him better than others, and, though he wondered at it more than anyone else did, yet he so rejoiced in the fact that he could not help publishing it whatever the consequences to himself might be. Often there is a deal more pride in not witnessing to what God has done for us than in speaking of it. Everything depends upon the spirit which moves us. I have heard a brother with the deepest humility speak with full assurance of the divine love, and while some have thought that he was presumptuous, I have felt within myself that his positive testimony was perfectly consistent with the deepest humility, and that it was his simple modesty which made the man so utterly forget himself as to run the risk of being thought forward and egotistical. He was thinking of how he should glorify God, and the appearance of glorifying himself did not alarm him, for he had forgotten himself in his Master. I wish we could bear to be laughed at as proud for our Lord's sake. We shall never have John's name till like John we dare wear it without a blush.

It is a name in which John hides himself. He is very chary of mentioning John. He speaks of "another disciple," and "that other disciple," and then of "that disciple whom Jesus loved." These are the names by which he would travel through his own gospel "incognito." We find him out, however, for the disguise is too thin, but still he intends to conceal himself behind his Savior; he wears his Master's love as a veil, though it turns out to be a veil of light. He might have called himself if he had chosen "that disciple who beheld visions of God," but he prefers to speak of love rather than of prophecy. In the early church we find writings concerning him, in which he is named "that disciple who leaned on Jesus' bosom," and this he mentions in our text. He might have been called "that disciple who wrote one of the Gospels" or "that disciple who knew more of the very heart of Christ than any other"; but he gives the preference to love. He is not that disciple who did anything, but who received love from Jesus; and he is not that disciple who loved Jesus, but "whom Jesus loved." John is the man in the silver mask; but we know the man and his communications, and we hear him say, "We have known and believed the love that God hath to us. God is love, and he that dwelleth in love dwelleth in God, and God in him."

The name before us is *a name in which John felt himself most at home.* No other title would so well describe him. His own name, "John," means the "gift of God," and he was a precious gift from God the Father to his suffering Son, and a great comfort to the Savior during the years of his abode among men. Jesus doubtless counted him to be his Jonathan, his John, his God gift, and he treasured him as such; but John does not so much think of his being of any service to his Lord, as of that which his Lord had been to him. He calls himself "that disciple whom Jesus loved," because he recognized the delightful obligation which springs out of great love, and wished ever to be under its royal influence. He looked on Jesus' love as the source and root of everything about himself which was gracious and commendable. If he had any courage, if he had any faithfulness, if he had any depth of knowledge, it was because Jesus had loved these things into him. All the sweet flowers which bloomed in the garden of his heart were planted there by the hand of Christ's love, so when he called himself "that disciple whom Jesus loved," he felt that he had gone to the root and bottom of the matter, and explained the main reason of his being what he was.

This endearing name was very precious to him, because it evoked the sunniest memories of all his life. Those short years in which he had been with Jesus must have been looked upon by him in his old age with great transport, as the crown and glory of his earthly existence. I do not wonder that he saw Christ again in Patmos, after having seen him once in Palestine as he did see him; for such sights are very apt to repeat themselves. Such sights, I say; for John's view of his Lord was no ordinary one. There is at times an echo to sights as well as to sounds; and he who saw the Lord with John's eagle eye, with his deep-seated inner eye, was the likeliest man in all the world to see him over again in vision as he did see him amid the rocks of the Aegean Sea. All the memories of the best part of his life were awakened by the name which he wore, and by its power he often renewed that intimate communion with the living Christ which had lived on during the horrors of the crucifixion and lasted to the end of his days. That charming name set all the bells of his soul a-ringing: does it not sound right musically—"the disciple whom Jesus loved"?

That name was a powerful spring of action to him as long as he lived. How could he be false to him who had loved him so? How could he refuse to bear witness to the gospel of the Savior who had loved him so? What leagues of journeying could be too long for the feet of that disciple whom Jesus loved? What mobs of cruel men could cow the heart of the disciple whom Jesus loved? What form of banishment or death could dismay him whom Jesus loved? No, henceforth in the power of that name John becomes bold and faithful, and he serves his loving Friend with all his heart. I say, then, that this title must have been very dear to John, because he felt himself most at home in it; the secret springs of his nature were touched by it, he felt his whole self, heart, soul, mind, memory, all comprehended within the compass of the words "the disciple whom Jesus loved."

It was a name which was never disputed. You do not find anyone complaining of John for thus describing himself. General consent awarded him the title. His brethren did quarrel with him a little when his fond mother, Salome, wanted thrones for her two sons on the right and the left hand of the Messiah; but the love of Jesus to John never caused any ill will among the brethren, nor did John take any undue advantage of it. I believe that the apostles tacitly acknowledged that their Lord was perfectly right in his choice. There was something about John which made his brethren love him, and therefore they did not marvel that their Lord should make him his most intimate friend. The truly loved one of God generally receives the love of his brethren, yes, and even the love of the ungodly after a sort; for when a man's ways please the Lord, he makes even his enemies to be at peace with him. While David walked with God, all Israel loved him, and even Saul was forced to cry, "Thou art more righteous than I." John was so loving that he gained love everywhere. We may well be eager after this choice blessing, since it alone of all known treasures excites no envy among the brethren, but the rather makes all the godly rejoice. Inasmuch as saints wish to be greatly loved themselves, they are glad when they meet with those who have obtained that blessing. If we would ourselves smell of myrrh and aloes and cassia, we are glad to meet with those whose garments are already fragrant. You never find John lecturing his brethren or acting as a lord over God's heritage, but in all gentleness and lowliness he justified the affection which our Lord manifested toward him.

II. Thus much, then, with regard to the name. Second, *let us look at the character which lay below it.*

I can only give a miniature of John: it is quite impossible in the few moments of a sermon to draw a full-length portrait; and, indeed, I am not artist enough to accomplish it if I should attempt the task. In the character of John we see much that is admirable.

First, let us look at *his personality as an individual.* His was a large and warm heart. Perhaps his main force lies in the intensity of his nature. He is not vehement, but deep and strong. Whatever he did he did right heartily. He was simpleminded, a man in whom there was no guile: there was no division in his nature, he was one and indivisible in all that he felt or did. He did not entertain questions, he was not captious, he was not apt to spy out faults in others, and as to difficulties, mental or otherwise, he seems to have been happily without them. Having pondered and come to a conclusion, his whole nature moved in solid phalanx with forceful march; whichever way he went he went altogether, and right resolutely. Some men go two ways, or they tack about, or they go toward their object in an indirect manner; but John steams straight forward, with the fires blazing and the engine working at full speed. His whole soul was engaged in his Lord's cause, for he was a deep thinker, a silent student, and then a forceful actor. He was not impetuous with the haste of Peter, but yet he was determined and thoroughgoing, and all on fire with zeal.

He was exceedingly livid in his beliefs, and believed to the utmost what he had learned of his Lord. Read his epistle through, and see how many times he says, "we know," "we know," "we know." There are no "ifs" about him; he is a deep and strong believer. His heart gives an unfeigned assent and consent.

Withal there was an intense warmth about John. He loved his Lord; he loved his brethren; he loved with a large heart, for he had a grand nature. He loved constantly, and he loved in such a way as to be practically courageous for his Master, for he was a bold man, a true son of thunder. He was ready to go to the front if he was bound to do so, but it is in quite a quiet way, and not with a rush and a noise: his is not the dash of a cataract, but the still flow of a deep river.

Putting all together that we know about his personality, we look upon him as a man who was the reverse of your cold, calculating, slow-moving son of diffidence. You know the sort of persons I mean, very good people in their way, but by no means fascinating or much to be imitated. He was quite the reverse of those dried, juiceless brethren who have no human nature in them—men who are somewhere about perfect, for they have not life enough to sin, they do no wrong, or they do nothing at all. I know a few of those delightful people, sharp critics of others and faultless themselves, with this one exception, that they are heartless. John was a hearty man: a man of brain, but of soul too—a soul which went out to the tips of his fingers, a man who was permeated with intense but quiet life: a man to be loved. His life was not that of an ice plant, but of the red rose. He carried summer in his countenance, energy in his manner, steady force in all his movements. He was like that other John of whom he was once a disciple, "a burning and a shining light." There was warmth as well as light in him. He was intense, sincere, and unselfish by nature, and a fullness of grace came upon him and sanctified these virtues.

Let us now view him *in his relation to his Lord.* The name he takes to himself is *"the disciple* whom Jesus loved." Jesus loved him as a disciple. What sort of disciples do masters love? You that have ever been teachers of youth know that if teachers had their choice certain persons would be selected before others. If we teach we love teachable people: such was John. He was a man quick to learn. He was not like Thomas, slow, argumentative, cautious; but having once assured himself that he had a true teacher, he gave himself right up to him, and was willing to receive what he had to reveal.

He was a disciple of very keen eye, seeing into the soul of his instructor's teaching. His emblem in the early church was the eagle—the eagle which soars, but also the eagle which sees from afar. John saw the spiritual meaning of types and emblems; he did not stop at the outward symbols, as some of the disciples did, but his penetrating soul read into the depths of truth. You can see this both in his gospels and in his epistles. He is a spiritually minded man; he stays not in the letter, but he dives beneath the surface. He pierces through the shell and reaches the inner teaching. His first master was John the Baptist, and he was so good a disciple that he was the first to leave his teacher. You hint that this did not show that he was a good disciple. Indeed it did, for it was the Baptist's aim to send his followers to Jesus. The Baptist said, "Behold the Lamb of God, which taketh away the sin of the world," and John was so good a follower of the forerunner that he immediately followed the Lord himself, to whom the forerunner introduced him. This he did without a violent jerk: his progress was natural and even. Paul came to Jesus with a great start and twist, when he was put upon the lines on the road to Damascus: but John glided gently to the Baptist and then from the Baptist to Jesus. He was not obstinate, neither was he weak, but he was teachable, and so he made steady progress in his learning: such a disciple is one that a teacher is sure to love, and John was therefore "the disciple whom Jesus loved."

He was full of faith to accept what he was taught. He believed it, and he believed it really and thoroughly. He did not believe as some people do, with the fingertips of their understanding, but he gripped the truth with both hands, laid it up in his heart, and allowed it to flow from that center and saturate his whole being. He was a believer in his inmost soul; both when he saw the blood and water at the cross, and the folded grave clothes at the sepulcher, he saw and believed.

His faith worked in him a strong and enduring love, for faith works by love. He believed in his Master in a sweetly familiar way, "for there is no fear in love; but perfect love casteth out fear." Such a trustful, confiding disciple is sure to be loved of his teacher.

John had great receptiveness. He drank in what he was taught. He was like Gideon's fleece, ready to be saturated with the dew of heaven. His whole nature absorbed the truth as it is in Jesus. He was not a great talker: I should think he was almost a silent disciple. So little did he say that we have only one saying of his recorded in the Gospels. "Why," one might say, "I remember two or three." Do you remind me that he asked that he might sit on the right hand of Christ? I have not forgotten that request, but I answer that his mother, Salome, spoke on that occasion. Again, you tell me that at the supper he asked, "Lord, who is it?" Yes, but it was Peter who put that question into his mouth. The only utterance that I remember in the gospel which was altogether John's, is that at the sea of Tiberias, when he said to Peter, "It is the Lord." This was a very significant little speech—a recognition of his Lord such as the quick eye of love is sure to make. He who lived nearest to Jesus could best discern him as he stood upon the shore. "It is the Lord," is the gladsome cry of love, overjoyed at the sight of its Beloved. It might have served John as his motto—"It is the Lord." Oh, that we were able amid darkness and tossing to discern the Savior, and rejoice in his presence. "Blessed are the pure in heart, for they shall see God"; and such was the beloved disciple.

One great trait in John's character as a disciple was his intense love for his teacher; he not only received the truth, but he received the Master himself. I take it that the leaning of a man's faults often betrays his heart more than his virtues. It may seem a strange observation to make, but it is true. A true heart may as well be seen in its weakness as in its excellence. What were the weak points about John, as some would say? On one occasion he was intolerant. Certain persons were casting out devils, and he forbade them because they followed not with the disciples. Now, that intolerance, mistaken as it was, grew out of love to his Lord; he was afraid that these interlopers might set up as rivals to his Lord, and he wanted them to come under the rule of his beloved Jesus. At another time the Samaritans would not receive them, and he asked his Master that he might call down fire from heaven on them. One does not commend him, but still it was love to Jesus which made him indignant at their ungenerous conduct to their best friend. He felt so indignant that men should not entertain the Savior who had come into the world to bless them that he would even call fire from heaven: it showed his burning love for Jesus. Even when his mother asked that he and the brother might sit upon thrones at the right hand and the left hand of Christ, it was a deep and thoughtful faith in Jesus which suggested it. His idea of honor and glory was bound up with Jesus. If he gives way to ambition it is an ambition to reign with the despised Galilean. He does not want a throne unless it be at his Leader's side. Moreover, what faith there was in that request! I am not going to justify it, but I am going to say something to moderate your condemnation. Our Lord was going up to Jerusalem to be spat upon, and to be put to death, and yet John so thoroughly threw himself into his Lord's career that he would fain share in the fortune of his great Caesar, assured that it must end in his enthronement. He is content, he says, to be baptized with his baptism, and to drink of his cup; he only asks to share with Jesus in all things. As a good writer says, it reminds one of the courage of the Roman who when Rome was in the hands of the enemy purchased a house within the walls: John heroically asks for a throne at the side of one who was about to die on the cross, for he feels sure that he will triumph. When the cause and kingdom of Christ seemed ready to expire, yet so wholehearted was John in his faith in God and his love to his beloved Lord, that his highest ambition was still to be with Jesus and take shares with him in all that he would do and be. So, you see, all through he loved his Lord with all his heart, and therefore Jesus Christ loved him: or let me turn it the other way—the Lord loved John, and therefore he loved the Lord Jesus. It is his own explanation of it: "We love him because he first loved us."

I must ask you to look at John once more, as an instructed person. He was a beloved disciple, and remained a disciple, but he grew to know more and more, and in that capacity I would say of him, that doubtless our Lord Jesus loved him because of the tenderness which was produced by grace out of his natural warmth. How tender he was to Peter, after that apostle's grievous fall, for early in the morning John goes with him to the sepulcher. He is the man who restored the backslider. He was so tender that our Lord did not say to John, "Feed my lambs"; for he knew he would be sure to do it; and he did not even say to him, "Feed my sheep," as he did to Peter; he knew that he would do so from the instincts of his loving nature. He was a man who under the tutorship of Christ grew, moreover, to be very spiritual and very deep. The words he uses in his epistles are mostly monosyllables, but what mighty meanings they contain. If we may compare one inspired writer with another, I should say that no other Evangelist is at all comparable to him in depth. The other Evangelists give us Christ's miracles, and certain of his sermons, but his profound discourses, and his matchless prayer, are reserved for that disciple whom Jesus loved. Where the deep things of God are concerned, there is John, with sublime simplicity of utterance, declaring unto us the things which he has tasted and handled. Of all the disciples John was most Christlike. Like will to like. Jesus loved John for what he saw of himself in him, created by his grace. Thus I think you will see that, without supposing John to have possessed any merit, there were points in his personal character, in his character as a disciple, and in his character as an educated, spiritual man, which justified our Savior in making him the object of his most intimate affection.

III. Very briefly, in the third place, *let us review the life which grew out of this extraordinary love of Christ.*

What was the life of John? First, it was a life of *intimate communion*. John was wherever Christ was. Other disciples are put away, but Peter and James and John are present. When all the disciples sit at the table, even Peter is not nearest to the Lord Jesus, but John leans his head upon his bosom. Their intercourse was very near and dear. Jesus and John were David and Jonathan over again. If you are a man greatly beloved you will live in Jesus, your fellowship will be with him from day to day.

John's was a life of *special instruction*. He was taught things which no others knew, for they could not bear them. At the latter end of his life he was favored with visions such as even Paul himself, though not a whit behind the chief of the apostles, had never seen. Because of the greatness of his Lord's love to him he showed him future things, and lifted up the veil so that he might see the kingdom and the glory. They shall see most who love most; they shall be taught most who most completely give up their hearts to the doctrine.

John henceforth became a man in whose life there was *amazing depth*. If he did not say much as a rule while his Lord was with him, he was taking it all in for future use. He lived an inner life. He was a son of thunder, and could boldly thunder out the truth, because, as a thundercloud is charged with electricity, so had he gathered up the mysterious force of his Lord's life, love, and truth. When he did break out there was a voice like the voice of God in him;

a deep, mysterious, overwhelming power of God was about him. What a flash of lightning is the Apocalypse! What awful thunders sleep within the voils and the trumpets! His was a life of divine power because of the great fire which burned within; his was not the flash of crackling thorns beneath a pot, but the glow of coals in a furnace when the whole mass is molten into a white heat. John is the ruby among the twelve, he shines with a warm brilliance reflecting the love which Jesus lavished on him.

Hence his life was one of *special usefulness*. He was entrusted with choice commissions involving high honor. The Lord gave him to do a work of the most tender and delicate kind, which I am afraid he could not commit to some of us. As the Redeemer hung upon the tree dying he saw his mother standing in the throng, and he did not commit her to Peter, but to John. Peter would have been glad of the commission, I am sure, and so would Thomas, and so would James; but the Lord said to John, "Behold thy mother!" and to his mother, "Woman, behold thy son!" And from that hour that disciple took her to his own home. So modest, so retiring, I was going to say so gentlemanly, was John, that he was the man to take charge of a brokenhearted mother. Said I wrong that he was a true gentleman? Divide the word, and surely he was the gentlest of men. John has a delicate air and considerate manner, needful to the care of an honored woman. Peter is good, but he is rough; Thomas is kind, but cold; John is tender and affectionate. When you love Jesus much he will trust his mother to you; I mean his church and the poorest people in it, such as widows and orphans, and poor ministers. He will trust them to you because he loves you much. He will not put everybody into that office. Some of his people are very hard and stony of heart, and fitter to be tax collectors than distributors of alms. They would make capital officers in an army, but not nurses in a hospital. If you love Jesus much you shall have many delicate offices to perform which shall be to you proofs of your Lord's trust in you, and renewed tokens of his love.

John's life was, moreover, one of *extraordinary heavenliness*. They call him John the Divine, and he was so. His eagle wings bore him aloft into the heavenly places, and there he beheld the glory of the Lord. Whether in Jerusalem or in Antioch, in Ephesus or in Patmos, his conversation was in heaven. The Lord's Day found him in the spirit, waiting for him that cometh with clouds, so waiting that he who is the Alpha and Omega hastened to reveal himself to him. It was the love of his Lord which had thus prepared him for visions of the glory. Had not that love so enkindled his own love as to hold him faithfully at the cross all through the agony, he might never have been able to gaze upon the throne. He had lovingly followed him who had been pointed out to him as the "Lamb of God," and therefore he was made meet to see him as the Lamb in the midst of the throne, adored of angels and redeemed saints, whose harps and viols are engrossed with his praise. Oh, that we, too, could be freed from the grossness of earth, and borne aloft into the purer atmosphere of spiritual and heavenly things.

IV. We close by saying, very briefly, *let us learn lessons for ourselves* from that disciple whom Jesus loved. May the Holy Spirit speak them to our inmost hearts.

First, I speak to those of you who are still young. If you wish to be "the disciple whom Jesus loved," *begin soon.* I suppose that John was between twenty and twenty-five when he was converted; at any rate, he was quite a young man. All the representations of him which have been handed down to us, though I attach no great value to them, yet unite in the fact of his youth. Youthful piety has the most profitable opportunity of becoming eminent piety. If you begin soon to walk with Christ, you will improve your pace, and the habit will grow upon you. He who is only made a Christian in the last few years of his life will scarcely reach to the first and highest degree, for lack of time, and from the hampering influence of old habits; but you who begin soon are planted in good soil, with a sunny aspect, and should come to maturity.

Next, if we would be like John in being loved by Christ, let us *give our heart's best thoughts to spiritual things.* Brethren and sisters, do not stop in the outward ordinance, but plunge into its inner sense. Never allow your soul, on the Lord's Day for instance, to be thankful and happy merely because you have been to the place of worship. Ask yourself, "Did I worship? Did my soul commune with God?" In the use of the two ordinances of baptism and the Supper, content not yourself with the shell, but seek to get at the kernel of their inner meaning. Rest not unless the Spirit of God himself dwell within you. Recollect that the letter kills; it is the spirit that gives life. The Lord Jesus Christ takes no delight in those who are fond of broad phylacteries and multiplied sacraments and holy performances and superstitious observances. The Father seeks those to worship him who worship him in spirit and in truth. Be spiritual, and you are among those who are likely to be men greatly beloved.

Next to that, *cherish a holy warmth.* Do not repress your emotions and freeze your souls. You know the class of brethren who are gifted with refrigerating power. When you shake hands with them, you would think that you had hold of a fish: a chill goes to your very soul. Hear them sing. No, you cannot hear them! Sit in the next pew, and you will never hear the gentle hiss or mutter which they call singing. Out in their shops they could be heard a quarter of a mile off, but if they pray in the meeting, you must strain your ears. They do all Christian service as if they were working by the day for a bad master and at scanty wages: when they get into the world, they work by the piece as if for dear life. Such brethren cannot be affectionate. They never encourage a young man, for they are afraid that their weighty commendation might exalt him above measure. A little encouragement would help the struggling youth mightily, but they have none to offer. They calculate and reckon and move prudently; but anything like a brave trust in God they set down as rashness and folly. God grant us plenty of rashness, I say, for what men think imprudence is about the grandest thing under heaven. Enthusiasm is a feeling which these refrigerators do not indulge. Their chant is, "As it was in the beginning, is now, and ever shall be, world without end. Amen"; but anything like a dash for Christ and a rush for souls they do not understand. Mark this, if you trace such brethren home, you will find that they have little joy themselves and make very little joy for others. They are never quite certain that they are saved, and if they are not sure of it we may readily guess that other people are not. They spend in anxious thought the strength which ought to have gone in hearty love. They were born at the north pole and live amid perpetual frost: all the furs of Hudson's Bay could not warm them. About them you see none of the rich tropical flowers which bedeck the heart upon which the Sun of Righteousness shines with perpendicular beams. These chilly mortals have never traversed the sunny regions of heavenly love where the spices of holy delight load all the air, and apples of gold are everywhere within the reach of glowing hearts. The Lord bring us there!

Jesus Christ loves warm people; he never shines on an iceberg except to melt it. His own life is so full of love that its holy fire kindles the like flame in others, and thus he has fellowship with those whose hearts burn within them. The fitness for love is love. To enjoy the love of Jesus we must overflow with love. Pray for earnest, eager, intense affection. Lay your hearts among the coals of juniper till they melt and glow.

Dear brother, if you want to be the man that Jesus loves, cultivate strong affection and *let your nature be tender and kind.* The man who is habitually cross, and frequently angry, cannot walk with God. A man of a quick, hot temper who never tries to check it, or a man in whom there is a malicious remembrance of injuries, like a fire smoldering amid the embers, cannot be the companion and friend of Jesus, whose spirit is of an opposite character. A pitiful, compassionate, unselfish, generous heart is that which our Lord approves. Forgive your fellow as if you never had anything to forgive. When brethren injure you, hope that they have made a mistake, or else feel that if they knew you better they would treat you worse. Be of such a mind toward them that you will neither give nor take offense. Be willing to lay down, not only your comfort, but even your life for the brethren. Live in the joy of others, even as saints do in heaven. Love others so as to forget your own sorrows. So shall you become a man greatly beloved.

Last of all, may the Spirit of God help you to rise to heavenliness. Do not be miserable money-grubbers, or sordid earthworms; do not be pleasure hunters and novelty seekers, do not set your affection upon these children's toys, which will be so soon broken up. Be no more children, but men of God. Oh, to find your joy in Christ, your wealth in Christ, your honor in Christ, your everything in Christ—this is peace. To be in the world but not to be of it: to linger here as if you were an angel sent from heaven to dwell for a while among the sons of men, to tell them of heaven, and point them the way—this is to abide in Christ's love. To be always ready to fly, to stand on tiptoe, waiting for the heavenward call, to expect to hear the trumpet ring out its clarion note, the trumpet of the coming of your Lord—this is to have fellowship with Christ. Sit loose, I pray you, by this world; get a tighter grip of the world to come—so shall Jesus' love be shed abroad within you. Throw your anchor upward, into the placid sea of divine love, and not like the seamen, downward, into a troubled ocean. Anchor yourselves to the eternal throne, and never be divided even in thought from the love of God, which is in Christ Jesus our Lord. May it be my privilege and yours, brothers and sisters, to lean these heads of ours on Jesus' bosom, till the day break and the shadows flee away. Amen and amen.

Andrew: Everyday Usefulness

Delivered on Lord's Day morning, February 14, 1869, at the Metropolitan Tabernacle, Newington. No. 855.

And he [Andrew] brought him [Peter] to Jesus.—JOHN 1:42

We have a most intense desire for the revival of religion in our own midst, and throughout all the churches of our Lord Jesus. We see that error is making great advances, and we would fain lift up a banner for the cause of truth; we pity the mighty populations among whom we dwell, for they are still godless and Christless, and the things of their peace are hid from their eyes, therefore would we fain behold the Lord performing miracles of grace. Our hope is that the set time to favor Zion is come, and we intend to be importunate in prayer that God will reveal his arm and do great things in these latter days. Our eager desire, of which our special services will be the expression, is a right one. Challenge it who will, be it ours to cultivate it, and prove by our zeal for God that the desire is not insincere or superficial.

But, my brethren, it is very possible that in addition to cultivating a vehement desire for the revival of religion, we may have been daydreaming, and forecasting in our minds a conception of the form which the divine visitation shall take. Remembering what we have heard of former times of refreshing, you expect a repetition of the same outward signs, and look for the Lord to work as he did with Livingstone at the Kirk of Shotts or with Jonathan Edwards in New England or Whitefield in our own land. Perhaps you have planned in your mind that God will raise up an extraordinary preacher whose ministry will attract the multitude, and while he is preaching, God the Holy Spirit will attend the word, so that hundreds will be converted under every sermon; other evangelists will be raised up of a like spirit, and from end to end this island shall hear the truth and feel its power.

Now it may be that God will so visit us. It may be that such signs and wonders as have frequently attended revivals may be again witnessed—the Lord may rend the heavens and come out and make the mountains to flow down at his feet; but it is just possible that he may select quite another method. His Holy Spirit may reveal himself like a mighty river swollen with floods, and sweeping all before its majestic current; but if so he wills, he may rather unveil his power as the gentle dew which, without observation, refreshes all the earth. It may happen unto us as unto Elijah when the fire and the wind passed before him, but the Lord was not in either of those mighty agencies: he preferred to commune with his servant in a still, small voice. Perhaps that still, small voice is to be language of grace in this congregation. It will be useless then for us to be mapping out the way of the eternal God, idle for us to be rejecting all the good which he may be pleased to give us because it does not happen to come in the shape which we have settled in our own minds to be the proper one. Idle, did I say? Such prejudice would be wicked in the extreme.

It has very frequently happened that while men have been sketching out imaginary designs, they have missed actual opportunities. They would not build because they could not erect a palace; they therefore shiver in the winter's cold. They would not be clothed in homespun, for they looked for scarlet and fine linen before long; they were not content to do a little, and therefore did nothing. I want, therefore, to say this morning to every believer here, it is vain for us to be praying for an extensive revival of religion, and comforting each other in the hope of it, if meanwhile we suffer our zeal to effervesce, and sparkle, and then to be dissipated: our proper plan is, with the highest expectations, and with the largest longings, to imitate the woman of whom it is written, "She hath done what she could," by laboring diligently in such holy works as may be within our reach, according to Solomon's precept, "Whatsoever thy hand findeth to do, do it with thy might." While believers are zealously doing what God enables them to do, they are in the high road to abundant success; but if they stand all the day idle, gaping after wonders, their spiritual want shall come upon them as an armed man. I have selected the text before us in order that I may speak upon matters which are practical and efforts within the reach of all. We shall not speak of the universal triumph of the gospel, but of its victory in single hearts; nor shall we deal with the efforts of an entire church, but with the pious fervor of individual disciples. If the Christian church were in a proper and healthy state, the members would be so studious of the word of God, and would themselves have so much of the Spirit of Christ, that the only thing they would need in the great assemblies, over and above worship, would be a short encouraging and animating word of direction addressed to them, as to well-drilled and enthusiastic soldiers, who need but the word of command, and the deed of valor is straightaway performed. So would I speak, and so would I have you hear at this hour.

Coming then, to the subject, Andrew was converted by Christ to become his disciple. Immediately he sets to work to recruit the little army by discipling others. He finds his brother Peter, and he brings him to Jesus.

I. First, I shall call your attention, this morning, to *the missionary disciple.*

Andrew is the picture of what all disciples of Christ should be. To begin, then. This first successful Christian missionary *was himself a sincere follower of Jesus.* Is it needful to make that observation? No, will it ever be needless while so many make a profession of a faith which they do not possess? While so many will wantonly thrust themselves into the offices of Christ's church, having no concern for the glory of his kingdom, and no part or lot in it, it will be always needful to repeat that warning, "Unto the wicked God saith, 'What hast thou to do to declare my statutes?'" Men who have never seen the beauties of Emmanuel are not fit persons to describe them to others. An experimental acquaintance with vital godliness is the first necessity for a useful worker for Jesus. That preacher is accursed who knows not Christ for himself. God may, in infinite sovereignty, make him the means of blessing to others, but every moment that he tarries in the pulpit he is an impostor; every time he preaches he is a mocker of God, and woe unto him when his Master calls him to his dread account. You unconverted young people who enter upon the work of Sunday school instruction, and so undertake to teach to others what you do not know yourselves, do place yourselves in a position of unusual solemnity and of extraordinary peril. I say "of extraordinary peril," because you do by the fact of being a teacher profess to know, and will be judged by your profession, and I fear condemned out of your own mouths. You know the theory only of religion, and of what use is that while you are strangers to its power? How can you lead others along a way which you yourself refuse to tread?

Besides, I have noticed that persons who become active in church work before they have first believed in Christ are very apt to remain without faith, resting content with the general repute which they have gained. O dear friends, beware of this. In this day hypocrisy is so common, self-deceit is so easy, that I would not have you place yourselves where those vices become almost inevitable. If a man voluntarily puts himself where it is taken for granted that he is godly, his next step will be to mimic godliness, and by and by he will flatter himself into the belief that he really possesses that which he so successfully imitates. Beware, dear hearers, of a religion which is not true; it is worse than none. Beware of a form of godliness which is not supported by the fervor of your heart and soul. This age of shams presents but few assistances to self-examination, hence am I the more earnest that every one of us, before he shall seek to bring others to Christ, should deliberately ask himself, "Am I a follower of Christ myself? Am I washed in his blood? Am I renewed by his

Spirit?" If not, my first business is not in the pulpit, but on my knees in prayer: my first occupation should not be in the Sunday school class, but in my closet, confessing my sin and seeking pardon through the atoning sacrifice.

Andrew was earnest for the souls of others, though he was but a young convert. So far as he can gather, he appears to have beheld Jesus as the Lamb of God one day, and to have found out his brother Peter the next. Far be it from us to forbid you who but yesterday found joy and peace, to exert your newborn zeal and youthful ardor. No, my brethren and sisters, delay not, but make haste to spread abroad the good news which is now so fresh and so full of joy to you. It is right that the advanced and the experienced should be left to deal with the captious and the skeptical, but you, even you, young as you are, may find some with whom you can cope; some brother like Simon Peter, some sister dear to you who will listen to your unvarnished tale, and believe in your simple testimony. Though you be but young in grace, and but little instructed, begin the work of soul winning, and

> *Tell to sinners 'round*
> *What a dear Savior you have found.*

If the religion of Jesus Christ consisted in abstruse doctrines, hard to be understood, if the saving truths of Christianity were metaphysical points, difficult to handle, then a matured judgment would be needed in every worker for God, and it would be prudent to say to the young convert, "Hold back till you are instructed"; but, since that which saves souls is as simple as A, B, C, since it is nothing, but this, "He that believeth and is baptized, shall be saved," he that trusts the merit of Christ shall be saved. You who have trusted him know that he saves you, and you know that he will save others; and I charge you before God, tell it, tell it right and left, but especially tell it to your own kinsfolk and acquaintance, that they also may find eternal life.

Andrew was a disciple, a new disciple, and, I may add, *a commonplace disciple,* a man of average capacity. He was not at all the brilliant character that Simon Peter his brother turned out to be. Throughout the life of Jesus Christ, Andrew's name occurs, but no notable incident is connected therewith. Though in afterlife he no doubt became a most useful apostle, and according to tradition sealed his life's ministry by death upon a cross, yet at the first Andrew was, as to talent, an ordinary believer, one of that common standard and nothing remarkable. Yet Andrew became a useful minister, and thus it is clear that servants of Jesus Christ are not to excuse themselves from endeavoring to extend the boundaries of his kingdom by saying, "I have no remarkable talent or singular ability." I very much disagree with those who decry ministers of slender gifts, sneering at them, as though they ought not to occupy the pulpit at all. Are we, after all, brethren, as servants of God, to be measured by mere oratorical ability? Is this after the fashion of Paul, when he renounced the wisdom of words lest the faith of the disciples should stand in the wisdom of man, and not in the power of God? If you could blot out from the Christian church all the minor stars, and leave nothing but those of the first magnitude, the darkness of this poor world would be increased sevenfold. How often the eminent preachers, which are the church's delight, are brought into the church by those of less degree, even as Simon Peter was converted by Andrew! Who shall tell what might have become of Simon Peter if it had not been for Andrew? Who shall say that the church would ever have possessed a Peter if she had closed the mouth of Andrew? And who shall put their finger upon the brother or sister of inferior talent and say, "These must hold their peace"? No, brother, if you have but one talent, the more zealously use it. God will require it of you: let not your brethren hold you back from putting it out to interest. If you are but as a glowworm's, lamp, hide not your light, for there is an eye predestinated to see by your light, a heart ordained to find comfort by your faint gleam. Shine, and the Lord accept you.

I am putting it in this way that I may come to the conclusion that every single professor of the faith of Christ is bound to do something for the exten- sion of the Redeemer's kingdom. I would that all the members of this church, whatever their talents were, would be like Andrew in *promptness*. He is no sooner a convert than he is a missionary; no sooner taught than he begins to teach. I would have them like Andrew, *persevering,* as well as prompt. He first finds Peter—that is his first success, but how many afterward he found, who shall tell? Throughout a long life of usefulness it is probable that Andrew brought many stray sheep to the Redeemer's fold, yet certainly that first one would be among the dearest to his heart. "He first" found Peter: he was the spiritual father of many sons, but he rejoiced most that he was the father of his own brother Peter—his brother in the flesh, but his son in Christ Jesus.

Could it be possible for me to come to every one of you personally, and grasp you by the hand, I would with most affectionate earnestness—yes, even with tears—pray you, by him to whom you owe your souls, awake and render personal service to the Lover of your souls; make no excuse, for no excuse can be valid from those who are bought with so great a price. Your business, you will tell me, requires so much of your thoughts, I know it does; then use your business in such a way as to serve God in it. Still there must be some scraps of time which you could devote to holy service; there must be some opportuni- ties for directly aiming at conversions. I charge you, avail yourselves of such occasions, lest they be laid to your door. To some of you the excuse of "business" would not apply, for you have seasons of leisure. Oh, I beseech you, let not that leisure be driveled away in frivolities, in mere talk, in sleep and self-indulgence! Let not time slip away in vain persuasions that you can do nothing, or in mere preparations for grand experiments, but now, like Andrew, hasten at once to serve Jesus; if you can reach but one individual, let him not remain unsought.

Time is hastening, and men are perishing. The world is growing old in sin. Superstition and idolatry root themselves into the very soil of human nature. When, when will the church become intent upon putting down her Master's foes? Possessing such little strength, we cannot afford to waste a jot of it. With such awful demands upon us, we cannot afford to trifle. Oh, that I had the power to stir the heart and soul of all my fellow Christians by a description of this huge city wallowing in iniquity, by a picture of the graveyards and cemeteries fattening on innumerable corpses; by a portrayal of that lake of fire to which multitudes yearly descend.

Surely sin, the grave, and hell are themes which might create a tingling even in the dull cold ear of death. Oh, that I could set before you the Redeemer upon the cross dying to ransom souls! Oh, that I could depict the heaven which sinners lose, and their remorse when they shall find themselves self-excluded! I would, I could even set before you in vivid light the cases of your own sons and daughters, the spiritual condition of your own brothers and sisters, without Christ, and therefore without hope, unrenewed, and therefore "heirs of wrath, even as others," then might I expect to move each believer here to an immediate effort to pluck men as brands from the burning.

II. Having described the missionary disciple, we shall now speak briefly in the second place upon *his great object*.

The great object of Andrew seems to have been to bring Peter to Jesus. This, too, should be the aim of every renewed heart—to bring our friends to Jesus, not to convert them to a party. There are certain unbrotherly sectarians, called Brethren, who compass sea and trod land to make proselytes from other churches. These are not merchants seeking goodly pearls in a legitimate fashion, but pirates who live by plunder; they must not excite our wrath so much as our pity, though it is difficult not to mingle with it something of disgust. While this world remains so wicked as it is, we need not be spending our strength as Christian denominations in attacking one another: it will be better for us to go and fight with the Canaanites than with rival tribes which should be one united Israel.

I should reckon it to be a burning disgrace if it could be said, "The large church under that man's pastoral care is composed of members whom he has stolen away from other Christian churches." No, but I value beyond all price the godless, the careless, who are brought out from the world into communion with Christ. These are true prizes, not stealthily removed from friendly shores, but captured at the edge of the sword from an enemy's dominions. We welcome brethren from other churches if in the providence of God they are drifted to our shores, but we would never hang out the wrecker's beacon to dash other churches in pieces in order to enrich ourselves with the wreck. Far rather would we be looking after perishing souls than cajoling unstable ones from their present place of worship. To recruit one regiment from another is no real strengthening of the army; to bring in fresh men should be the aim of all.

Furthermore, the object of the soul winner is not to bring men to an outward religiousness merely. Little will you have done for a man if you merely make the Sabbath breaker into a Sabbath keeper, and leave him a self-righteous Pharisee. Little will you have done for him if you persuade him, having been prayerless, to be a mere user of a form of prayer, his heart not being in it. You do but change the form of sin in which the man lives; you prevent him being drowned in the salt water, but you throw him into the fresh; you take one poison from him, but you expose him to another. The fact is, if you would do real service to Christ, your prayer and your zeal must follow the person who has become the object of your attention, till you bring him absolutely to close with grace and lay hold on Jesus Christ, and accept eternal life as it is found in the atoning sacrifice. Anything short of this may have its usefulness for this world, but must be useless for the world to come. To bring men to Jesus—Oh, be this your aim and mine!—not to bring them to baptism, nor to the meetinghouse, nor to adopt our form of worship, but to bring them to his dear feet who alone can say, "Go in peace; your sins which are many are all forgiven you."

Brethren, as we believe Jesus to be the very center of the Christian religion, he who gets not to Christ gets not to true godliness at all. Some are quite satisfied if they get to the priest and obtain his absolution; if they get the sacraments, and eat bread in the church; if they get to prayers, and pass through a religious routine; but we know that all this is less than nothing and vanity, unless the heart draws near to Jesus. Unless the soul accepts Jesus as God's appointed sin offering and rests alone in him, it walks in a vain show and disquiets itself in vain. Come then, brethren, nerve yourselves to this point, that from this day forth let your one ambition be in dealing with your fellowmen, to bring them to Jesus Christ himself. Be it determined in your spirit that you will never cease to labor for them till you have reason to believe that they are trusting in Jesus, loving Jesus, serving Jesus, united to Jesus, in the hope that they shall be conformed to the image of Jesus and dwell with him, world without end.

But some will say, "We can very clearly understand how Andrew brought Peter to the Lord, because Jesus was here among men, and they could walk together till they found him." Yes, but Jesus is not dead, and it is a mistake to suppose that he is not readily to be reached. Prayer is a messenger that can find Jesus at any hour. Jesus is gone up on high as to his body, but his spiritual presence remains to us, and the Holy Ghost as the Head of this dispensation is always near at hand to every believer.

Intercede, then, for your friends. Plead with Christ on their account; mention their names in your constant prayers; set apart special times in which you plead with God for them. Let your dear sister's case ring in the ears of the Mediator; let your dear child's name be repeated again and again in your intercessions. As Abraham pleaded for Ishmael, so let your cry come up for those who are round about you, that the Lord would be pleased to visit them in his mercy. Intercession is a true bringing of souls to Christ, and this means will avail when you are shut out from employing any other. If your dear ones are in Australia, in some settler's hut where even a letter cannot reach them, prayer can find them out; no ocean can be too wide for prayer to span, no distance too great for prayer to travel. Far off as they are, you can take them up in the arms of believing prayer, and bear them to Jesus and say, "Master, have mercy upon them." Here is a valuable weapon for those who cannot preach or teach; they can wield the sword of all-prayer. When hearts are too hard for sermons, and good advice is rejected, it still remains to love to be allowed to plead with God for its wayward one. Tears and weepings are prevalent at the mercy seat, and if *we* prevail there, the Lord will be sure to manifest his prevailing grace in obdurate spirits.

To bring men to Jesus you can adopt the next means, with most of them, namely, that of instructing them, or putting them in the way of being informed concerning the gospel. It is a very wonderful thing that while to us the light of the gospel is so abundant, it should be so very partially distributed in this country. When I have expounded my own hope in Christ to two or three in a railway carriage, I have found myself telling my listeners perfect novelties. I have seen the look of astonishment upon the face of many an intelligent Englishman when I have explained the doctrine of the substitutionary sacrifice of Christ; persons who have even attended their parish church from their youth up, I have met with, who were totally ignorant of the simple truth of justification by faith; yes, and some who have been to Dissenting places of worship do not seem to have laid hold of the fundamental truth that no man is saved by his own doings, but that salvation is procured by faith in the blood and righteousness of Jesus Christ.

This nation is steeped up to the throat in self-righteous doctrine, and the Protestantism of Martin Luther is very generally unknown. The truth is held by as many as God's grace has called, but the great outlying world still talk of doing your best, and then hoping in God's mercy, and I know not what beside, of legal self-confidence, while the master doctrine that he who believes in Jesus is saved by Jesus' finished work, is sneered at as enthusiasm, or attacked as leading to licentiousness. Tell it, then, tell it on all sides, take care that none under your influence shall be left in ignorance of it; I can bear personal witness that the statement of the gospel has often proved in God's hand enough to lead a soul into immediate peace.

Not many months ago I met with a lady holding sentiments of almost undiluted popery, and in conversing with her I was delighted to see how interesting and attractive a thing the gospel was to her. She complained that she enjoyed no peace of mind as the result of her religion, and never seemed to have done enough. She had a high idea of priestly absolution, but it had evidently been quite unable to yield repose to her spirit. Death was feared, God was terrible, even Christ an object of awe rather than love. When I told her that whosoever believeth on Jesus is perfectly forgiven, and that I knew I was forgiven—that I was as sure of it as of my own existence; that I feared neither to live nor to die, for it would be the same to me, because God had given me eternal life in his Son, I saw that a new set of thoughts were astonishing her mind. She said, "If I could believe that, I should be the happiest person in the world." I did not deny the inference, but claimed to have proved its truth, and I have reason to believe that the little simple talk we had has not been forgotten. You cannot tell how many may be in bondage for want of the simplest possible instruction upon the plainest truths of the gospel of Jesus Christ.

Many, too, may be brought to Christ through your example. Believe me, there is no preaching in this world like the preaching of a holy life. It shames me sometimes, and weakens me in my testimony for my Master, when I stand here and recollect that some professors of religion are a disgrace not only to their religion, but even to common morality. It makes me feel as though I must speak with bated breath and trembling knees, when I remember the damnable hypocrisy of those who thrust themselves into the Church of God, and by their abominable sins bring disgrace upon the cause of God and eternal destruction upon themselves. In proportion as a church is holy, in that proportion will its testimony for Christ be powerful. Oh! Were the saints immaculate, our testimony would be like fire among the stubble, like the flaming firebrand in the midst of the sheaves of corn. Were the saints of God less like the world, more disinterested, more prayerful, more godlike, the tramp of the armies of Zion would shake the nations, and the day of the victory of Christ would surely dawn. Freely might the church barter her most golden-mouthed preacher if she received in exchange men of apostolic life. I would be content that the pulpit should be empty if all the members of the church would preach Jesus by their patience in suffering, by their endurance in temptation, by exhibiting in the household those graces which adorn the gospel of Jesus Christ. Oh, so live, I pray you, in God's fear and by the Spirit's power, that they who see you may ask, "Whence hath this man this holiness?" and may follow you till they are led by you to Jesus Christ to learn the secret by which men live unto God.

You can bring men to Jesus by your example, then. And once again, let me say, before I close this point, our object should be to bring men to Jesus, having tried intercession, and instruction, and example, by occasionally, as time and opportunity may serve us, giving a word of importunate entreaty. Half a dozen words from a tender mother to a boy who is just leaving home for an apprenticeship may drop like gentle dew from heaven upon you. A few sentences from a kind and prudent father given to the daughter, still unconverted, as she enters upon her married life, and to her husband, kindly and affectionately put, may make that household forever a house for God. A kind word dropped by a brother to a sister, a little letter written from a sister to her brother, though it should be only a line or two, may be God's arrow of grace. I have known even such little things as a tear or an anxious glance work wonders.

You perhaps may have heard the story of Mr. Whitefield, who made it his wont wherever he stayed to talk to the members of the household about their souls—with each one personally; but stopping at a certain house with a colonel, who was all that could be wished except a Christian, he was so pleased with the hospitality he received and so charmed with the general character of the good colonel and his wife and daughters, that he did not like to speak to them about decision as he would have done if they had been less amiable characters. He had stopped with them for a week, and during the last night, the Spirit of God visited him so that he could not sleep. "These people," said he, "have been very kind to me, and I have not been faithful to them; I must do it before I go; I must tell them that whatever good thing they have, if they do not believe in Jesus they are lost." He arose and prayed. After praying he still felt contention in his spirit. His old nature said, "I cannot do it," but the Holy Spirit seemed to say, "Leave them not without warning." At last he thought of a device, and prayed God to accept it; he wrote upon a diamond-shaped pane of glass in the window with his ring these words: "One thing thou lackest." He could not bring himself to speak to them, but went his way with many a prayer for their conversion. He had no sooner gone than the good woman of the house, who was a great admirer of him, said, "I will go up to his room: I like to look at the very place where the man of God has been." She went up and noticed on the windowpane those words, "One thing thou lackest." It struck her with conviction in a moment. "Ah!" said she, "I thought he did not care much about us, for I knew he always pleaded with those with whom he stopped, and when I found that he did not do so with us, I thought we had vexed him, but I see how it was; he was too tender in mind to speak to us." She called her daughters up. "Look there, girls," said she, "see what Mr. Whitefield has written on the window, 'One thing thou lackest.' Call up your father." And the father came up and read that too, "One thing thou lackest!" and around the bed whereon the man of God had slept they all knelt down and sought that God would give them the one thing they lacked, and before they left that chamber they had found that one thing, and the whole household rejoiced in Jesus.

It is not long ago since I met with a friend, one of whose church members preserves that very pane of glass in her family as an heirloom. Now, if you cannot admonish and warn in one way, do it in another; but take care to clear your soul of the blood of your relatives and friends, so that it may never crimson your skirts and accuse you before God's bar. So live and so speak and teach, by some means or other, that you shall have been faithful to God and faithful to the souls of men.

III. I must now take you to a third point. We have had the missionary disciple and his great object; we have now, third, *his wise methods.*

I have trenched upon this subject already, but I could not help it. Andrew being zealous was wise. Earnestness often gives prudence, and puts a man in the possession of tact, if not of talent. *Andrew used what ability he had.* If he had been as some young men are of my acquaintance, he would have said, "I should like to serve God. How I should like to preach! And I should require a large congregation." Well, there is a pulpit in every street in London; there is a most wide and effectual door for preaching in this great city of ours beneath God's blue sky. But this young zealot would rather prefer an easier berth than the open air; and, because he is not invited to the largest pulpits, does nothing. How much better it would be if, like Andrew, he began to use the ability he had among those who are accessible to him, and from that stepped to something else, and from that to something else, advancing year by year! Sirs, if Andrew had not been the means of converting his brother, the probabilities are that he never would have been an apostle. Christ had some reason in the choice of his apostles to their office, and perhaps the ground of his choice of Andrew as an apostle was this: "He is an earnest man," said he, "he brought me Simon Peter; he is always speaking privately to individuals; I will make an apostle of him." Now, you young men, if you become diligent in tract distribution, diligent in the Sunday school, you are likely men to be made into ministers; but if you stop and do nothing until you can do everything, you will remain useless—an impediment to the church instead of being a help to her. Dear sisters in Jesus Christ, you must none of you dream that you are in a position in which you can do nothing at all. That were such a mistake in providence as God cannot commit. You must have some talent entrusted to you, and something given you to do which no one else can do. Out of this whole structure of the human body, every little muscle, every single cell, has its own secretion and its own work; and though some physicians have said this and that organ might be spared, I believe that there is not a single thread in the whole embroidery of human nature that could well be spared—the whole of the fabric is required. So in the mystical body, the church, the least member is necessary, the most uncomely member of the Christian church is needful for its growth. Find out, then, what your sphere is and occupy it. Ask God to tell you what is your niche, and stand in it, occupying the place till Jesus Christ shall come and give you your reward. Use what ability you have, and use it at once.

Andrew proved his wisdom in that *he set great store by a single soul*. He bent all his efforts at first upon one man. Afterward, Andrew, through the Holy Spirit, was made useful to scores, but he began with one. What a task for the arithmetician, to value one soul! One soul sets all heaven's bells ringing by its repentance. One sinner that repents makes angels rejoice. What if you spend a whole life pleading and laboring for the conversion of that one child? If you win that pearl, it shall pay you your life worth. Be not therefore dull and discouraged because your class declines in numbers, or because the mass of those with whom you labor reject your testimony. If a man could earn but one in a day, he might be satisfied. "One what?" says one. I meant not one penny, but £1000. "Ah," say you, "that would be an immense reward." So if you earn but one soul you must reckon what that one is; it is one for numeration, but for value it exceeds all that earth could show. What would it profit a man if he gained the whole world and lost his soul? And what loss would it be to you, dear brother, if you did lose all the world and gained your soul, and God made you useful in the gaining of the souls of others? Be content and labor in your sphere, even if it be small, and you will be wise.

You may imitate Andrew in *not going far afield to do good*. Many Christians do all the good they can five miles off from their own house, when the time they take to go there and back might be well spent in the vineyard at home. I do not think it would be a wise regulation of the parochial authorities if they required the inhabitants of St. Mary, Newington, to remove the snow from the pavement of St. Pancras, and the inhabitants of St. Pancras to keep clean the pavement of St. Mary, Newington. It is best and most convenient that each householder should sweep before his own door; so it is our duty to do, as believers, all the good we can in the place where God has been pleased to locate us, and especially in our own households. If every man has a claim upon me, much more my own offspring. If every woman has some demand upon me as to her soul, so far as my ability goes, much more such as are of my own flesh and blood. Piety must begin at home as well as charity. Conversion should begin with those who are nearest to us in ties of relationship. Brethren and sisters, during this month I stir you up, not to be attempting missionary labors for India, not to be casting eyes of pity across to Africa, not to be occupied so much with tears for popish and heathen lands, as for your own children, your own flesh and blood, your own neighbors, your own acquaintance. Lift up your cry to heaven for them, and then afterward you shall preach among the nations. Andrew goes to Cappadocia in his afterlife, but he begins with his brother; and you shall labor where you please in years to come, but first of all your own household, first of all those who are under your own shadow must receive your guardian care. Be wise in this thing; use the ability you have, and use it among those who are near at hand.

Perhaps somebody will be saying, "How did Andrew persuade Simon Peter to come to Christ?" Two or three minutes may be spent in answering that inquiry. He did so, first, by narrating his own personal experience; he said, "We have found the Messiah." What you have experienced of Christ tell to others. He did so next by intelligently explaining to him what it was he had found. He did not say he had found someone who had impressed him, but he knew not who he was; he told him he had found Messiah, that is, Christ. Be clear in your knowledge of the gospel and your experience of it, and then tell the good news to those whose soul you seek. Andrew had power over Peter because of his own decided conviction. He did not say, "I hope I have found

Christ," but, "I have found him." He was sure of that. Get full assurance of your own salvation. There is no weapon like it. He that speaks doubtingly of what he would convince another, asks that other to doubt his testimony. Be positive in your experience and your assurance, for this will help you.

Andrew had power over Peter because he put the good news before him in an earnest fashion. He did not say to him, as though it were a commonplace fact, "The Messiah has come," but no, he communicated it to him as the most weighty of all messages with becoming tones and gestures, I doubt not, "We have found the Messiah, which is called Christ." Now then, brethren and sisters, to your own kinsfolk tell your belief, your enjoyments, and your assurance, tell all judiciously, with assurance of the truth of it, and who can tell whether God may not bless your work?

IV. My time is past, or I meant to have spoken of *the sweet reward* Andrew had.

His reward being that he won a soul, won his brother's soul, won such a treasure! He won no other than that Simon, who at the first cast of the gospel net, when Christ had made him a soul-fisherman, caught three thousand souls at a single haul! Peter, a very prince in the Christian church, one of the mightiest of the servants of the Lord in all his after usefulness, would be a comfort to Andrew. I should not wonder but what Andrew would say in days of doubt and fear, "Blessed be God that he has made Peter so useful! Blessed be God that ever I spoke to Peter! What I cannot do, Peter will help to do; and while I sit down in my helplessness, I can feel thankful that my dear brother Peter is honored in bringing souls to Christ." In this house today there may sit an unconverted Whitefield; in your class this afternoon there may be an unsaved John Wesley, a Calvin, and a Luther, mute and inglorious, yet who is to be called by grace through you. Your fingers are yet to wake to ecstasy the living lyre of a heart that up till now has not been tuned to the praise of Christ; you are to kindle the fire which shall light up a sacred sacrifice of a consecrated life to Christ. Only be up and doing for the Lord Jesus, be importunate and prayerful, be zealous and self-sacrificing. Unite with us, during this month, in your daily prayers; constantly, while in business, let your hearts go up for the blessing, and I make no doubt of it, that, when we have proved our God by prayer, he will pour us down such a blessing that we shall not have room to receive it. The Lord make it so, for his name's sake. Amen.

Nathanael: Under the Fig Tree

Delivered on Lord's Day morning, March 20, 1870, at the Metropolitan Tabernacle, Newington. No. 921.

> *Philip findeth Nathanael, and saith unto him, "We have found him, of whom Moses in the law, and the prophets, did write, Jesus of Nazareth, the son of Joseph." And Nathanael said unto him, "Can there any good thing come out of Nazareth?" Philip saith unto him, "Come and see." Jesus saw Nathanael coming to him, and saith of him, "Behold an Israelite, indeed, in whom is no guile!" Nathanael saith unto him, "Whence knowest thou me?" Jesus answered and said unto him, "Before that Philip called thee, when thou wast under the fig tree, I saw thee." Nathanael answered and saith unto him, "Rabbi, thou art the Son of God; thou art the King of Israel." Jesus answered and said unto him, "Because I said unto thee, I saw thee under the fig tree, believest thou? thou shalt see greater things than these." And he saith unto him, "Verily, verily, I say unto you, Hereafter ye shall see heaven open, and the angels of God ascending and descending upon the Son of man."*
> —JOHN 1:45–51

Very often we address the gospel to the chief of sinners. We believe it to be our duty to do this with the greatest frequency; for did not our Lord, when bidding his disciples to preach the good news in every place, use the words, "beginning at Jerusalem"? Where the chief of sinners lived, there was the gospel first to be preached. But at the same time it would show great lack of observation if we regarded all mankind as being equally gross, open offenders against God. It would not only show a want of wisdom, but it would involve a want of truthfulness; for though all have sinned, and deserve the wrath of God, yet all unconverted men are not precisely in the same condition of mind in reference to the gospel. In the parable of the sower, we are taught that before the good seed fell upon the field at all, there was a difference in the various soils; some of it was stony ground, another part was thorny, a third was trodden hard like a highway, while another plot is described by our Lord as "honest and good ground." Although in every case the carnal mind is enmity against God, yet are there influences at work which in many cases have mitigated, if not subdued, that enmity.

While many took up stones to kill our Lord, there were others who heard him gladly. While to this day thousands reject the gospel, there are others who receive the word with joy. These differences we ascribe to God's prevenient grace; we believe, however, that the subject of these differences is not aware that grace is at work upon him; neither is it precisely grace in the same form as saving grace, for the soul under its power has not yet learned its own need of Christ, or the excellency of his salvation. There is such a thing as a preparatory work of mercy on the soul, making it ready for the yet higher work of grace, even as the plowing comes before the sowing. We read in the narrative of the creation that before the divine voice said, "Let there be light," darkness was upon the face of the deep, yet it is added, "The Spirit of God moved upon the face of the waters"; even so in the darkness of human nature, whereas yet no ray of living light has shone, the Spirit of God may be moving with secret energy, making the soul ready for the hour when the true light shall shine. I believe that in our congregations there are many persons who have been mercifully restrained from the grosser vices, and exhibit everything that is pure and excellent in moral character, persons who are not maliciously opposed to the gospel, who are ready enough to receive it if they did but understand it, who are even anxious to be saved by Jesus Christ, and have a reverence for his name, though as yet it is an ignorant reverence. They know so little of the Redeemer that they are not able to find rest in him; but this slenderness of knowledge is the only thing that holds them back from faith in him. They are willing enough to obey if they understood the command. If they had but a clear apprehension of our Lord's person and work, they would cheerfully accept him as their Lord and God.

I have great hopes that the Lord of love may guide the word which is now to be spoken, so that it may find out such persons, and may make manifest the Lord's secretly chosen ones, those prisoners of hope who pine for liberty, but know not that the Son can make them free. O captive soul, abhorring the chains of sin, your day of liberty is come! The Lord, the liberator, who looseth the prisoners, is come at this very hour to snap thy bonds.

I. In dwelling on this narrative, I shall first say a few words concerning *Nathanael himself.*

We are told that he was a *guileless man,* "an Israelite, indeed, in whom is no guile," that is to say, like Jacob, "he was a plain man," and not like Esau, "a cunning hunter." Some minds are naturally serpentine, tortuous, slippery; they cannot think except in curves; their motives are involved and intricate, and they are of a double heart. These are the men who look one way and row the other; they worship the god Janus with two faces, and are of the same practice, if not of the same persuasion, as the Jesuits. They cannot speak a thing out plainly or look you in the face while they talk, for they are full of mental reservations and prudential cautions. They guard their speech; they dare not send abroad their own thoughts till they have mailed them up to the throat with double meanings.

Nathanael was just the very opposite of all this; he was no hypocrite and no crafty deceiver. He wore his heart upon his sleeve; if he spoke, you might know that he said what he meant and that he meant what he said. He was a childlike, simple-hearted man, transparent as glass. He was not one of those fools who believe everything, but on the other hand, he was not of that other sort of fools so much admired in these days, who will believe nothing, but who find it necessary to doubt the most self-evident truth in order to maintain their credit for profound philosophy. These "thinkers" of this enlightened age are great at quibbles, mighty in feigning or feeling mistrust concerning matters which common sense has no doubts about. They will profess to doubt whether there is a God, though that be as plain as the sun at noonday. No, Nathanael was neither credulous nor mistrustful; he was honestly ready to yield to the force of truth; he was willing to receive testimony and to be swayed by evidence. He was not suspicious, because he was not a man who himself would be suspected; he was truehearted and straightforward; a plain dealer and plain speaker. Cana had not within her gates a more thoroughly honest man. This Philip seems to have known, for he went to him directly, as to a man who was likely to be convinced and worth winning to the good cause.

In addition to being thus a simple-hearted man, Nathanael was *an earnest seeker*. Philip found him out because he felt that the good news would interest him. "We have found the Messiah," would be no gladsome news to anyone who had not looked for the Messiah; but Nathanael had been expecting the Christ, and perhaps had so well understood Moses and the prophets, that he had been led to look for his speedy coming. The time when Messiah would suddenly come in his temple had certainly arrived, and he was day and night with prayer, like all the faithful of the ten tribes, watching and waiting for the appearing of their salvation. He had not as yet heard that the glory of Israel had indeed come, but he was on the tiptoe of expectation. What a hopeful state of heart is yours, my dear hearer, if you are now honestly desirous to know the truth, and intensely anxious to be saved by it! It is well indeed for you if your soul is ready, like the photographer's sensitive plate, to receive the impression of the divine light, if you are anxiously desiring to be informed if there be indeed a Savior, if there be a gospel, if there be hope for you, if there be such a thing as purity and a way to reach it; it is well, I say, if you are anxiously, earnestly desiring to know how and when and where, and determinately resolved, by God's grace, that no exertion shall be spared on your part to run in the way that shall be marked out, and to submit yourself unto the will of God. This was the state of Nathanael, an honest-hearted lover of plain truth, seeking to find the Christ.

It is also true that he was *ignorant* up to a certain point. He was not ignorant of Moses and the prophets; these he had well considered, but he knew not that Christ as yet had come. There was some little distance between Nazareth and Cana, and the news of the Messiah's coming had not traveled thither; if it had been bad news, it would have flown on eagles' wings, but being good news, its flight was slower, for few persons are so anxious to tell out the good as the evil. He had not therefore heard of Jesus of Nazareth till Philip came to him. And how many there are even in this country who do not know yet what the gospel means, but are anxious to know it, and if they did but know it would receive it! "What," say you, "where there are so many places of worship and so many ministers?" Yes, just that. Yes, and in the very heart of our congregations and in the midst of our godly families, ignorance has its strongholds. These uninstructed ones may be Bible readers, they may be gospel hearers, but as yet they may not have been able to grasp the great truth that God was in Christ reconciling the world unto himself. They may never have seen what it is for Christ to stand in the sinner's place, and for that sinner by an act of trust to obtain the blessings which spring out of a substitutionary sacrifice. Yes, and here in this house where I have tried and labored to put the gospel in short Saxon words and sentences that cannot be misunderstood, there may be some who are still saying, "What is this all about? I hear much of believing, but what is it? Who is this Christ, the Son of God, and what is it to be saved from sin, to be regenerated, to be sanctified? What are all these things?" Well, dear friend, I am sorry you should be in the dark, yet am I glad at heart, that though you do not know what I would have you know, yet you are simple hearted, truth loving, and sincere in your seeking. I am persuaded that light will not be denied you, you shall yet know Jesus and be known of him.

In addition to this, however, Nathanael was prejudiced—we must modify that expression—he was somewhat *prejudiced*. As soon as Philip told him that he had found Jesus of Nazareth, the son of Joseph, Nathanael said, "Can any good thing come out of Nazareth?" Here let us remark that his prejudice is exceedingly excusable, for it arose out of the faulty testimony of Philip. Philip was a young convert; he had only found Jesus the day before, and the natural instinct of every truly gracious soul is to try and tell out the blessed things of Christ. So away went Philip to tell his friend Nathanael, but what a many blunders he made in the telling out the gospel! I bless God, blundering as it was, it was enough to bring Nathanael to Christ; but it was full of mistakes. Dear souls, if you know only a little about Christ, and if you would make a great many mistakes in telling out that little, yet do not hold it in, God will overlook the errors and bless the truth. Now observe what Philip said. He said, "We have found Jesus of Nazareth, the son of Joseph," which was our Lord's popular name, but was in no way correct. He was not Jesus of *Nazareth* at all; he was not a native of Nazareth, our Lord was of Bethlehem. He had dwelled at Nazareth certainly, but he was no more entitled to be called of Nazareth than of Jerusalem. Then Philip said, "son of Joseph," but he was only the reputed son of Joseph, he was in truth, the Son of the Highest. Philip gave to our Lord the common and erroneous titles which the unthinking many passed from hand to hand. He did not say, "We have found the Son of God," or, "the Son of David," but yet he uttered all he knew, and that is all God expects of you or me.

Oh, what a mercy it is that the imperfections of our ministry do not prevent God's saving souls by us! If it were not so, how little good would be done in the world! Mr. John Wesley preached most earnestly one view of the gospel, and William Huntingdon preached quite another view of it. The two men would have had a holy horror of each other, and censured each other most conscientiously; yet no rational man dare say that souls were not saved under John Wesley, or under William Huntingdon either, for God blessed them both. Both ministers were faulty, but both were sincere, and both made useful. So is it with all our testimonies. They are all imperfect, full of exaggerations of one truth, and misapprehensions of another; but as long as we witness to the true Christ foretold by Moses and the prophets, our mistakes shall be forgiven, and God will bless our ministry, despite every flaw.

So he did with Nathanael; but Nathanael's prejudice rose out of Philip's blundering way of talking. If Philip had not said, "of Nazareth," then Nathanael would not have said, "Can any good thing come out of Nazareth?" If Philip had said that Jesus was of Bethlehem, and of the tribe of Judah, and that God was his Father, then this prejudice would never have beclouded the mind of Nathanael, and it would have been easier for him to have acknowledged Jesus as the Messiah. We must, therefore, try to avoid mistakes, lest we cause needless prejudice. We should so state the gospel that if men be offended by it, it shall be the gospel which offends them, and not our way of putting it. It may be that you, my friend, are a little prejudiced against Christ's holy gospel, because of the imperfect character of a religious acquaintance, or the rough manners of a certain minister; but I trust you will not allow such things to bias you. I hope that, being candid and honest, you will come and see Jesus for yourself. Revise the report of the disciple by a personal inspection of the Master. Philip made up for his faults when he added, "Come and see." And I would try to prevent mine from injuring you by using the same exhortation,

Come and see Jesus and his gospel for yourself.

One other mark of Nathanael I would mention, he was in all respects a godly, sincere man, up to the measure of his light. He was not yet a believer in Jesus, but still he was an Israelite indeed. He was a man of secret prayer, he did not mock God as the Pharisees did by mere outward worship. He was a worshiper of God in his heart, his soul had private dealings with the God of heaven when no eye saw him. So it is, I trust, with you, dear hearer, you may not yet have found peace, but you do pray, you are desirous of being saved; you do not wish to be a hypocrite; you dread, above all things, falling into formality; you pray that if ever you become a Christian you may be a Christian indeed. Such is the character I am endeavoring to find out, and if it is your character, may you get the blessing that Nathanael did.

II. Now second, we have seen Nathanael, let us for a moment consider *Nathanael's sight of Jesus.*

"Philip saith unto him, Come and see"; and so Nathanael came to see the Savior, which implies, that although he was somewhat prejudiced against this new Messiah, yet he was candid enough to investigate his claims. Beloved friend, to whom I have already spoken, if you have any prejudice against the true gospel of Jesus Christ, whether it be occasioned by your birth and education, or previous profession of some other faith, be honest enough to give the gospel of Jesus Christ a fair hearing. You may hear it in this house; you may read it in these pages. Do not dismiss it until you have thoroughly examined it. All that we would ask of you is now, knowing you to be honest, knowing you to be earnest, seriously to sit down and weigh the doctrines of grace as you shall find them in the Scripture, and especially the life of Christ, and the blessings which he brings to those who believe in him. Look these things over carefully. They will commend themselves to your conscience, for God has already prepared your conscience to judge, righteously; and as you judge, you will perceive a peculiar beauty and a charm about the truths of the gospel which will surely win your heart. Latimer had preached a sermon against the doctrines of the gospel, and among his hearers there was a holy man who afterward became a martyr, who thought as he listened to Latimer that he perceived something in his tone which showed him to be an honest opponent, and, therefore, he hoped that if light were brought to him he would be willing to see by it. He sought him out, obtained an interview with him, and his explanations entirely won honest Hugh to the Reformed opinions, and you know what a valiant and popular minister of the new covenant he became. So, my honest friend, give to the gospel of salvation by faith in the precious blood of Jesus, a fair hearing, and we are not afraid of the result.

Nathanael came to Christ, again, with *great activity* of heart. As soon as he was told to "come and see," he did come and see. He did not sit still and say, "Well, if there is any light in this new doctrine, it will come to me," but he went to it. Do not believe in any teaching which bids men sit down and find peace in the idea that they need not strive to enter in at the strait gate of truth. No, brethren, if grace has ever come to you, it will arouse you from lethargy, and lead you to go to Christ, and you will be most earnest, with all the activity of your spirit, to search for him as for hid treasure. It is a delightful thing to see a soul on the wing. The mass of our population are, as regards religion, down on the ground, and unwilling to rise. They are indifferent to spiritual truth; you cannot get them to give earnest heed to eternal matters; but once get a mind on the wing with a holy earnestness and solemn thoughtfulness, and we do believe, with God's grace, that it will before long be brought to a saving faith in Christ. "Come and see," said Philip, and come and see Nathanael did. He does not appear to have expected to be converted to Christ by what he saw with his natural eyes; his judgment was formed from a mental view of him. It is true he saw the person of the Messiah, but he did not expect to see in the human form any lineaments that might guide his judgment. He waited until the lips of the Messiah had spoken, and then, when he had seen the omniscience of that mysterious person, and how he could read his thoughts and spy out his secret actions, then he believed. Now, I fear some of you live in darkness because you are expecting some kind of physical manifestation. You hope for a vivid dream, or some strange feeling in your flesh, or some very remarkable occurrence in your family; except you see signs and wonders you will not believe. No, but a saving sight of Christ is another matter; truth must impress your mental faculties, enlighten your understanding, and win your affections. The presence of Christ on earth is a spiritual one, and you will come to see him not with these mortal optics just now, but with the eyes of your soul. You will perceive the beauty of his character, the majesty of his person, the all-sufficiency of his atonement; and as you see these things, the Holy Spirit will lead you to believe in him and live. I pray God that such a sight as this may be granted to every honest seeker who may hear or read these words.

III. A far greater matter now demands our attention—*Christ's sight of Nathanael.*

As soon as Jesus saw the man, he said, "Behold an Israelite indeed," which shows us that Christ Jesus read Nathanael's heart. I do not suppose that our Lord had ever seen Nathanael with his own human eyes, but yet he understood Nathanael's character, not because he was a great judge of physiognomy and could perceive at once that he had a simple-hearted man before him, but because being Nathanael's Creator, being the searcher of hearts and the trier of the reins, he could read Nathanael as readily as a man reads a book which is open before his eyes. He saw at once all that was within the inquirer, and pronounced a verdict upon him that he was free from falsehood. And then to prove to Nathanael still further how clearly he knew all about him, he mentioned a little incident which I cannot explain, nor can you, nor do I suppose anybody could have explained it except Nathanael and Jesus—a special secret known only to them both. He said to him, "Before that Philip called thee, when thou wast under the fig tree, I saw thee." What he was doing under the fig tree we may guess, but we cannot know to a certainty. Perhaps it would be truest of all to believe that the fig tree was to Nathanael what the Hermonites and the hill Mizar had been to David. David says, "I will remember thee from the land of Jordan, and of the Hermonites, from the hill Mizar." What were those sacred recollections he does not tell us, and although we can form a shrewd guess, David and his God alone knew the full mystery. So between Christ and Nathanael there was a common knowledge connected with that fig tree which we cannot hope to discover, and the moment our Lord mentioned that hallowed spot, its remembrances were to Nathanael so secret and so sacred, that he felt that the omniscient One was before him. Here was evidence which he could not doubt for an instant, for one of the most private and special secrets of his life, which he had never whispered into any human ear, had been brought up as by a talismanic sign. A red-letter day in his private diary had been revived by the mention of the fig tree, and he who could touch so hidden a spring in his soul must be the Son of God.

But what was Nathanael doing under the fig tree, according to our best surmise? Well, as devout [Middle] Easterners are accustomed to have a special place for prayer, this may have been a shadowy fig tree under which Nathanael was accustomed to offer his devotions, and perhaps just before Philip came to him, he may have been engaged in personal and solitary *confession of sin*. He had looked around the garden, and fastened the gate that none might come in, and he had poured into the ear of his God some very tender confession, under the fig tree shade. When Christ said to him, "when thou wast under the fig tree," it brought to his recollection how he poured out his broken and his contrite spirit, and confessed sins unknown to all but God. That confession, it may be, the very look of Christ brought back to his remembrance, and the words and look together seemed to say, "I know your secret burden, and the peace you found in rolling it upon the Lord." He felt therefore that Jesus must be Israel's God.

It is very possible that in addition to his confession, he had under the fig tree made *a deliberate investigation of his own heart*. Good men generally mingle with their confessions self-examination. There it may be, that this man who was free from guile had looked into the tendencies of his nature, and had been enabled with holy surprise to see the fountains of the great deep of his natural depravity; he may have been taken like Ezekiel from chamber to chamber to see the idols in his heart, beholding greater abominations than he suspected to be there, and there humbled before the Lord; beneath that fig tree he may have cried with Job, "I abhor myself in dust and ashes." This also Jesus had seen.

Or under the fig tree he had been engaged in *very earnest prayer.* Was that fig tree to Nathanael what Peniel was to Jacob, a spot wherein he had wrestled till the break of day, pleading with God to fulfill his ancient promise, to send the promised One who should be a light to lighten the gentiles, and the glory of his people Israel? Was it so? We think it probable. That fig tree had been to him a Bethel, no other than the house of God and the very gate of heaven.

And what if we should suggest that, perhaps in addition to his prayer, Nathanael had vowed some solemn vow under the fig tree—if the Lord would but appear and give to him some sign and token for good, then he would be the Lord's, and spend and be spent for him; if the Lord would but send the Messiah, he would be among his first followers; if he would but speak to him by an angel or otherwise, he would obey the voice. Jesus now tells him that he shall see angels ascending and descending; and reveals himself as the Messiah to whom he had solemnly pledged himself. It may be so.

Once more, it may be that under that fig tree he had enjoyed the sweetest *communion* with his God. Beloved friends, do you not remember well certain hallowed spots? I have one or two in my own life too sacred to mention. If my memory should forget all the world besides, yet those spots will evermore be green in my memory, the truly holy place where Jesus my Lord has met with me and showed me his loves. One time it was "the king hath brought me into his chambers"; another time I got me to "the mountain of myrrh and to the hill of frankincense." Once he said, "Come, my beloved, let us go forth into the field; let us lodge in the villages," and anon he changed the scene and said, "Come with me from Lebanon, my spouse, with me from Lebanon: look from the top of Amana, from the top of Shenir and Hermon, from the lions' dens, from the mountains of the leopards." Have we not sometimes had special festivals when he has broached the spiced wine of his pomegranate? When our joy has been almost too much for the frail body to endure, for our joyous spirit like a sharp sword has well-nigh cut through its scabbard? Ah, it is sweetly true, he has baptized us in the fire of his love, and we shall forever remember those secret spots, those dear occasions. This then was a token, a secret token between Christ and Nathanael, by which the disciple recognized his divine Friend and future Master and Lord. He had met the Messiah in spirit before, and now he meets him in very flesh and blood, and by this token doth he know him. In spirit the Lord set his seal upon Nathanael's heart, and now by the sacred signet the Israelite indeed discerns his King.

Thus we see the Lord had seen Nathanael in his previous engagements, before he became actually a believer in Jesus. This fact suggests that each of you who have been sincerely seeking to be set right, and to know the truth, have been fully perceived in all your seekings and desirings by the God of grace. When you let fall a tear because you could not understand the Word, Jesus saw that tear; when you groaned because you could not get satisfaction of heart, he heard that groan. Never true heart seeks Christ without Christ's being well aware of it. Well may he know of it, for every motion of a trembling heart toward himself is caused by his own love. He is drawing you, though you perceive not the hands of a man which encircle you. He is the hidden lodestone by which your heart is moved. I know it is night with you, and you grope like a blind man for the wall; but if your heart says, "Oh, that I could but embrace him! Oh, that he were mine! If I could but find rest in him, I would give all that I have," then be assured that Jesus is close to you: your prayers are in his ear, your tears fall upon his heart; he knows all about your difficulties, all about your doubts and fears, and he sympathizes in the whole, and in due time he will break your snares, and you shall yet with joy draw water out of the wells of salvation. This truth is full of consolation to all who seek with sincerity, though as yet in the dark. Before the minister's voice spoke to you, when you were under the fig tree, when you were by the bedside, when you were in that inner chamber, when you were down in that saw-pit, when you were in the hayloft, when you were walking behind the hedge in the field, Jesus saw you; he knew your desires, he read your longings, he saw you through and through. Even from of old he has known you.

IV. So we have seen Nathanael's sight of Christ, and then Christ's sight of Nathanael; now the fourth thing is *Nathanael's faith*.

I must go over much the same ground again under this head. Nathanael's faith. Note *what it was grounded on*. He cheerfully accepted Jesus as the Messiah, and the ground of his acceptance lay in this, Jesus had mentioned to him a peculiar incident in his life which he was persuaded no one could have known but the omniscient God; thereon he concluded Jesus to be the omniscient God, and accepted him at once as his King. This was very frequently the way in which persons were brought to confidence in Christ. The same thing is recorded in this very gospel a few chapters further on. The Lord sat down on the well and talked to the Samaritan woman, and there was no kind of impression produced upon her until he said, "Thou hast had five husbands, and he whom thou now hast is not thine husband." Then it flashed upon her, "This stranger knows my private history! Then he is something more than he appears to be; he is the great Prophet"; and away she ran with this on her tongue, because it was in her heart, "Come, see a man which told me all things that ever I did: is not this the Christ?" The same was the case with Zacchaeus. You may perhaps think, however, that this mode of conversion was confined to the days of our Lord's flesh, and the age of miracles, but it is not so. The fact is, that at this very day, the discovery of the thoughts of men's hearts by the gospel is still a very potent means in the hands of the Holy Ghost of convincing them of the truth of the gospel. How often have I heard inquirers say, "It seemed to me, sir, as if that sermon was meant for me, there were points in it which were so exactly like myself, that I felt sure someone had told the preacher about me, and there were words and sentences so peculiarly descriptive of my private thought, that I was sure no one but God knew of them. I perceived that God was in the gospel speaking to my soul." Yes, and it always will be so. The gospel is the great revealer of secrets; it is a discerner of the thoughts and intents of the heart. Jesus Christ in the gospel knows all about your sin, all about your seeking, all about the difficulties which you are meeting with. This ought to convince you that the gospel is divine, since its teachings lay bare the heart, and its remedies touch every spiritual disease. The knowledge of human nature displayed in the simplest passage of the gospel is more profound than the productions of Plato or Socrates. The gospel, like a silken clue, runs through all the windings and twistings of human nature in its fallen state. Oh, that its voice may come home personally so to you; may it by the Spirit convince you of sin, of righteousness, and of judgment, and bring you to lay hold on eternal life.

Nathanael's faith, it must be mentioned, was peculiar not only in its ground, but *in its clear and comprehensive character.* He accepted Jesus at once as the Son of God; he was divine to him, and he adored him. He also accepted him as the King of Israel; he was a royal personage to him, and he tendered him his homage. May you and I receive Jesus Christ in this way, as a real man, but yet certainly God, a man who was despised and rejected, but yet the man anointed above his brethren, who is King of kings, and Lord of lords.

I admire Nathanael's faith again, because it was *so quick, unreserved, and decisive.* "Thou *art* the Son of God; thou *art* the King of Israel." Christ was glorified by the decision, the quickness of this faith. Delay in believing him dishonors him. O honest heart, O sincere mind, pray thou that you may as quickly come into the light and liberty of true belief. May the Holy Ghost work in you a ready satisfaction in the atoning sacrifice and divine person of the ever blessed Emmanuel.

V. This brings us to the last point of consideration. We have shown you Nathanael and his sight of Christ, and Christ's sight of him, and then the faith that Nathanael received; now notice *Nathanael's after sight.*

Some persons want to see all that there is in Christianity before they can believe in Jesus, that is to say, before they will go to the dame school [kindergarten] they must needs clamor for a degree at the university. Many want to know the ninth of Romans before they have read the third of John. They are all for understanding great mysteries before they understand that primary simplicity, "Believe and live." But those who are wiser and, like Nathanael, are content to believe at first what they are able to perceive, namely, that Christ is the Son of God and the King of Israel, shall go on to learn more. Let us read our Lord's words, "Thou shalt see greater things than these. Verily, verily, I say unto you, Hereafter ye shall see heaven opened, and the angels of God ascending and descending upon the Son of man." To full-grown disciples Jesus promises, "Greater things than these shall ye do"; to young converts he says, "Greater things than these shall ye see." He gives promises in proportion to our ability to receive them. The promise given to Nathanael was a most fitting one. He was all Israelite indeed—then he shall have Israel's vision. What was the great sight that Israel or Jacob saw? He saw the ladder whereon angels ascended and descended. Precisely this shall Nathanael see. He shall see Jesus Christ as the communication between an opened heaven and a blessed earth, and he shall see the angels ascending and descending upon the Son of man. If you bear the character of Israel, you shall enjoy the privileges of Israel. If you are an Israelite indeed, you shall have the blessing that made Israel glad. Nathanael had owned Jesus as the Son of God: here he is told that he shall see him in his glory as the Son of man. Note that last word of the chapter. It is not so much that Christ humbly called himself the Son of man—though that is true—as this, that to see the glory of Christ as God is a simple thing, but to see and understand the glory of Christ as man, this is a sight for faith, and probably a sight which, so far as our senses are concerned, is reserved for the day of his coming. When he shall appear, the very Man that suffered upon Calvary, upon the great white throne to judge the quick and the dead, if you believe in Jesus as the Son of God, you shall yet see him in his glory as man swaying the universal scepter, and enthroned as King of all the earth. He had called Jesus the King of Israel, if you remember, now he is to see his Lord as the King of the angels, to see the angels of God ascending and descending upon him. Believe, my dear brother in Christ, as far as you know him, and you shall know more of him. Open your eyes but to the candlelight of the law, and you shall soon behold the sunlight of the gospel.

The Lord is very gracious to fulfill the gospel rule, "To him that hath shall be given, and he shall have abundance." If you acknowledge the King of Israel, you shall see him as the Lord of hosts before whom archangels veil their faces, and to whom seraphim are servitors. The great sight, I suppose, Nathanael did see as the result of his faith was not the transfiguration, nor the ascension as some suppose, but a spiritual view of Christ in his mediatorial capacity as the great link between earth and heaven. This is indeed a sight transcending all others. We are not divided from the invisible, we are not separated from the infinite, the mortal has communion with immortal, the sinner speaks with the Holy One, prayers climb up to heaven, and benisons descend by way of the great Substitute. Can you see this, O soul? If so, the sight will make you glad. You are not exiled now, you are only at the foot of the stairs which lead to the upper chamber of your Father's house. Your God is above, and bright spirits traverse constantly the open gangway of the Mediator's person. Here is joy for all the saints, for this ladder can never be broken, our communion is abiding. No doubt, to Nathanael's view, the promise would be fulfilled as he perceived the providence of God as ruled by Christ Jesus, who orders all things for the good of the church. Was not this intended in the figure of angels ascending and descending upon the Son of man, that is, all agencies whether living or material, all subject to the law and the dominion of Christ; so that all things work together for good to them that love God?

Do not go fretting to your homes, and say, "Here are new doctrines springing up, and new gods that our fathers knew not, and ministers are slipping aside from the faith, and bad days have fallen upon the church, and Romanism is coming up, and infidelity with it." All this may be true, but it does not matter one fig for the great end that God has in view. He has a bit for the mouth of leviathan; he can do as he wills with his most powerful enemies; he rides upon the wings of cherubs and rules the storm; the clouds are but the dust of his feet. Never believe that Providence is out of joint; the wheels of this great engine may revolve some this way and some that, but the sure result will be produced, for the great Artist sees the final result to be secure. God's glory shall arise from it all. Angels descend, but they as much do the will of God as those which ascend. Some events seem disastrous, and even calamitous; but they shall all, in the end, prove to be for the best; for he—

> From seeming evil still educeth good,
> And better still, and better still, in infinite progression.

Until the crown shall come upon the head of him who was separated from his brethren, and all the glory shall roll in waves of mighty song at the foot of his throne, may you and I continue to see this great sight more and more clearly. Until the Lord shall descend from heaven with a shout, with the trump of the archangel, and the voice of God, and once for all shall we see heaven and earth blended, may we continue to see angels ascending and descending upon the Son of man. All this matchless glory will come to us through that little window by which we first saw the Savior. If we will not see him as our Lord until we can see all the future, we shall perish in darkness. If you will not believe, neither shall you be established, but if, with simple and true hearts, you have been seeking Jesus, and now come and accept him as the Lord, the King of Israel, then greater things than these shall be in store for you; your eyes shall see the King in his beauty and the land that is very far off, and the day of his pompous appearing, when heaven and earth shall hang out their streamers for overflowing joy, because the King hath come unto his own, and the crown is put upon the head of the Son of David; then shall you see it and see it all, for you shall be with him where he is, that you may behold his glory, the glory which the Father gave him before the foundation of the world.

Thomas: "My Lord and My God"

Delivered on Lord's Day morning, April 13, 1884, at the Metropolitan Tabernacle, Newington. No. 1775.

And Thomas answered and said unto him, "My Lord and my God."
—JOHN 20:28

When the apostles met on the first Lord's Day after Jesus had risen, Thomas was the only disciple absent out of the eleven; on the second Lord's Day, Thomas was there, and he was the only disciple doubting out of the eleven. How much the fact of his doubting was occasioned and helped by the fact of his former absence I cannot say; but still it looks highly probable that had he been there at the first, he would have enjoyed the same experience as the other ten, and would have been able to say as they did, "We have seen the Lord." Let us not forsake the assembling of ourselves together as the manner of some is, for we cannot tell what loss we may sustain thereby. Though our Lord may reveal himself to single individuals in solitude as he did to Mary Magdalene, yet he more usually shows himself to two or three, and he delights most of all to come into the assembly of his servants. The Lord seems most at home when, standing in the midst of his people, he says, "Peace be unto you." Let us not fail to meet with our fellow believers. For my part, the assemblies of God's people shall ever be dear to me. Where Jesus pays his frequent visits, there would I be found.

> *My soul shall pray for Zion still,*
> *While life or breath remains;*
> *There my best friends, my kindred dwell,*
> *There God my Savior reigns.*

I know that full many of you can most heartily say the same. Oh, that we may behold the Lord Jesus in the present assembly!

On the second occasion Thomas is present, and he is the only one out of the eleven who is vexed with doubts. He cannot think it possible that the Lord Jesus, who was nailed to the cross, and whose side was pierced, could have really risen from the dead. Observe joyfully the Lord's patience with him. All the others had been doubtful too, and the Lord had gently upbraided them for their unbelief and the hardness of their hearts; but Thomas is not convinced by the tenfold testimony of his brethren, who each one well deserved his implicit confidence. After the plain way in which the Lord had told his disciples that he should be crucified and would rise again from the dead, they ought to have expected the resurrection; and inasmuch as they did not they were to be blamed: what shall we say of him who in addition to all this had heard the witness of his ten comrades who had actually seen the Lord? Yet there he is, the one doubter, the one sturdy questioner who has laid down most stringent requirements as to the only way in which he will be brought to believe. Will not his Lord be provoked by his obstinacy? See how patient Jesus is! If we had been in that case, and had died for those people, and had passed through the grave, and risen again for them, we should have felt very greatly grieved and somewhat angered if they had refused to believe in what we had done, but our Lord shows no such sign. He is tender among them as a nursing father. He rebukes their unbelief: for that was needful for their sakes; but he manifests no vexation of spirit. Especially on this occasion he shows his tenderness toward Thomas, and addresses his first words to him. If Thomas will not be convinced except by what I must call the most gross and materialistic evidence, he will give him such evidence: if he must put his finger into the print of the nails, he shall put his finger there, if he must thrust his hand into his side, he shall be permitted to take that liberty. Oh, see how Jesus condescends to the weaknesses and even to the follies of his people! If we are unbelieving it is not his fault; for he goes out of his way to teach us faith, and sometimes he even gives what we have no right to ask, what we have no reason to expect, what it was even sin in us to have desired. We are so weak, so ignorant, so prone to unbelief that he will do anything to create, sustain, and strengthen our faith in him. He condescends to men of low estate. If through our own folly we are such babes that we cannot eat the meat which is fit food for men, our Lord will not grow weary of giving us milk, but he will even break the bread into morsels, and take away the hard crusts, that we may be able to feed thereon. It is not his will that one of his little ones should perish; and therefore he chases away unbelief, which is their deadliest foe.

Our Lord had special reasons for turning as he did to Thomas that day, and for taking so much trouble to bring Thomas out of his unbelieving condition. The reason must have been, surely, first, that he desired to make of Thomas a most convincing witness to the reality of his resurrection. Here is a man who is determined not to be deceived; let him come and use the tests of his own choice. If you tell me that the resurrection of our Lord from the dead was witnessed by men who were prepared to believe it, I reply that the statement is totally false. Not one among that company even knew the meaning of the Lord's prophecy that he would rise again from the dead. It was hard to make any of them catch the idea; it was so foreign to their thought, so far above their expectation. In Thomas we have a man who was specially hard to be convinced, a man who was so obstinate as to give the lie to ten of his friends with whom he had been associated for years. Now, if I had a statement to make which I wished to have well attested, I should like to place in the witness box a person who was known to be exceedingly cautious and wary. I should be glad if it were known that at the first he had been suspicious and critical, but had at length been overwhelmed by evidence so as to be compelled to believe. I am sure that such a man would give his evidence with the accent of conviction as indeed Thomas did when he cried, "My Lord and my God." We cannot have a better witness to the fact that the Lord is risen indeed than that this cool, examining, prudent, critical Thomas arrived at an absolute certainty.

Further, I conceive that our Lord thus personally dealt with Thomas, because he would have us see that he will not lose even one of those whom the Father has given him. The good Shepherd will leave the ninety and nine to seek the one wanderer. If Thomas is the most unbelieving, Thomas shall have the most care. He is only one, but yet he is one, and the Lord Jesus will not lose one whom he has ordained to save. You and I might have said, "Well, if he will not be convinced, we must let him alone; he is only one—we can do without his testimony; we cannot be forever seeking a solitary individual, let him go." Thus might we have done; but thus Jesus will not do. Our good Shepherd looks after the units; he is tenderly observant of each separate individual, and this is a ground of comfort to us all. If one sheep be lost, why not the whole flock? If one be thus cared for, all will be cared for.

This note is also to be heard in reference to this matter: after all, it is to be feared that the dull, the slow, the questioning, the anxious, the weak in faith, make up a very considerable part of the church: I do not know that they are in the majority, but they are certainly far too numerous. If all Christians were arranged and classified, I fear we could not many of us place ourselves in the front rank; but a large portion would have to go among the Little Faiths. Our Lord here shows us that he has a condescending care for those who lag behind. Thomas is a week behind everybody else, yet his Lord has not lost patience, but waits to be gracious. The other ten apostles have all seen the Lord, and been well assured of his resurrection for the last seven days; but that is no reason why the latecomer should be left out in the cold. Our Lord does not leave the rear rank to perish. We know that in the wilderness the

Amalekites slew the hindmost of the children of Israel; but when King Jesus heads the army, no Amalekites shall smite even the hindmost of his people, for the glory of the Lord shall bring up the rear. The walls of Zion enclose babes as well as veterans; the ark of our salvation preserves mice as well as bullocks; our Solomon speaks of the hyssop on the wall as well as of the cedar in Lebanon; and the glory of the Lord may be seen in the preservation of the glowworm's lamp as truly as in the sustenance of the furnace of the sun.

Now if there should be any in this assembly who honestly have to put themselves down in the sick list, I beg them to take comfort while I try and set forth the experience of Thomas and what came of it. First, I shall call your attention to the *exclamation of Thomas*, "My Lord and my God": second, we will consider, *how he came to it*; and third, *how we come to it*; for I trust many of us have also cried, "My Lord and my God."

I. Let us consider *the exclamation of Thomas*, "My Lord and my God."

This is a most plain and hearty confession of the true and proper deity of our Lord Jesus Christ.

It is much as a man could say if he wished to assert indisputably and dogmatically that Jesus is indeed God and Lord. We find David saying, "O Lᴏʀᴅ of hosts, my King, and my God," and in another place (Ps. 35:23) he says, "my God and my Lᴏʀᴅ," terms only applicable to Jehovah. Such expressions were known to Thomas, and he as an Israelite would never have applied them to any person whom he did not believe to be God. We are sure therefore that it was the belief of Thomas that the risen Savior was Lord and God. If this had been a mistake, the Lord Jesus would have rebuked him, for he would not have allowed him to be guilty of worshiping a mere man. No good man among us would permit a person to call him God and Lord; we should feel like Paul and Barnabas when they rent their clothes because the men of Lystra were ready to do sacrifice to them; how much more would the holy Jesus have felt a revolting of spirit against the idea of being worshiped and called "my Lord and my God," if he had not been of such a nature that he "thought it not robbery to be equal with God"! The perfect Jesus accepted divine homage, and therefore we are assured that it was rightly and properly given, and we do here at this moment offer him the like adoration.

To escape from the force of this confession, some who denied our Lord's deity in olden times had the effrontery to charge Thomas with breaking the Third Commandment by uttering such a cry of surprise as is common among profane talkers. Just as thoughtless persons take the Lord's name in vain and say, "Good God!" or, "O Lord!" when they are much astonished, so certain ancient heretics dared to interpret these words, "My Lord and my God." It is clear to any thoughtful person that this could not have been the case. For, in the first place, it was not the habit of a Jew to use any such exclamation when surprised or amazed. An irreligious gentile might have done so, but it was the last thing that would occur to a devout Israelite. If there is one thing about which the Jews in our Lord's times were particular beyond everything, it was about using the name of God. Why, even in their sacred books they have omitted the word *Jehovah*, and have only written *Adonai*, because of a superstitious reverence for the very letters of the divine name. How can we, then, believe that Thomas would have done what no Jew at that time would have dreamed of? Israel after the Babylonian captivity had many faults, but not that of idolatry or irreverence to the divine name. I do not know what an Israelite might have said under the influence of a great surprise, but I am absolutely certain that he would not have said, "My Lord and my God."

In the next place, it could not have been a mere *exclamation of surprise*, or an irreverent utterance, because it was not rebuked by our Lord, and we may be sure he would not have suffered such an unhallowed cry to have gone without a reprimand. Observe, too, that it was addressed to the Lord Jesus—"Thomas answered and said unto him, 'My Lord and my God.'" It was not a mere outburst of surprise addressed to no one, but it was an answer directed to the Lord who had spoken to him. It was also such a reply that our Lord Jesus Christ accepted it as an evidence of faith, for in the twenty-ninth verse he says, "Thou hast believed," and that confession was the only evidence of his believing which our Lord had received from Thomas. A mere outcry of confused astonishment in irreverent words would never have been received as a satisfactory proof of faith. Sin is no due evidence of faith. The slander proposed by the Arian must, therefore, be rejected with derision. I am almost ashamed to have mentioned it, but in these days, when every kind of error is rife, it is needful to bring to light and break in pieces many idols which we had rather have left with the moles and bats.

I regard this cry of Thomas, first, *as a devout expression of that holy wonder* which came upon him when his heart made the great discovery that Jesus was assuredly his Lord and God. It had flashed upon the mind of Thomas that this august person whom he had regarded as the Messiah was also God. He saw that the man at whose feet he had sat was more than man, and was assuredly God, and this amazed him so that he used broken speech. He does not say, "Thou art my Lord and my God," as a man would say who is making a doctrinal statement, but he brings it out in fragments, he makes adoration of it, he cries in ecstasy, "My Lord and my God." He is amazed at the discovery which he has made, and probably also at the fact that he has not seen it long before. Why, he might have known it, and ought to have perceived it years before! Had he not been present when Jesus trod the sea? When he hushed the winds, and bade the waters sleep? Had he not seen him open the blind eyes, and unstop the deaf ears? Why did he not cry, "My Lord and my God," then? Thomas had been slow to learn, and the Lord might have said to him, as he did to Philip, "Have I been so long time with you, and yet hast thou not known me?" Now on a sudden he does know his Lord—knows him to such a surprising extent that such knowledge is too wonderful for him. He had come to the meeting to prove whether he who appeared to his brethren was the same man who had died on Calvary, but now he seems to have forgotten that original question; it is more than answered, it has ceased to be a question; he is carried far further by the flood of evidence, he is landed in a full belief of the Godhead of Jesus. He spies out within that wounded body the indwelling Godhead, and at a leap he springs beyond the conviction that it is the same man to the firm assurance that Jesus is God, and consequently in broken accents, but with double assurance, he cries, "My Lord and my God." My brethren, how I wish you would all follow Thomas this morning! I will stop a minute that you may do so. Let us wonder and admire! He that had nowhere to lay his head, he that suffered scourging and spitting, and died on Calvary, is nevertheless God over all, blessed forever. He who was laid in the tomb lives and reigns, King of kings and Lord of lords. Hallelujah! Behold, he comes in the glory of the Father to judge the quick and the dead. Let your spirits drink in that truth and be amazed at it. If the fact that Jesus, the Son of God, suffered and bled, and died for you, never astonishes you, I fear that you do not believe it, or have no intelligent apprehension of the full meaning of it. Angels wonder, should not you? Oh, let us feel a holy surprise today, as we realize the truth that he who has redeemed us from our sins by his blood is the Son of the Highest!

Next, I believe that this was an expression of *immeasurable delight*; for you observe he does not say, "Lord and God," but, "My Lord and my God." He seems to take hold of the Lord Jesus with both hands, by those two blessed "my's"—"My Lord and my God." Oh, the joy that flashed from the eyes of Thomas at that moment! How quickly his heart beat! He had never known such joy as at that instant, and though he must have felt deeply humbled, yet in that humiliation there was an excessive sweetness of intense satisfaction as he looked at his divine Lord and gazed on him, from the pierced feet up to the brow so marred with the crown of thorns, and said, "My Lord and my God." There is in these few words a music akin to the sonnet of the spouse in the

Canticles when she sang, "My beloved is mine, and I am his." The enraptured disciple saw the friend of his heart standing before him, shining upon him in love, and knitting his heart to him. I pray you follow Thomas in this joy in Christ. I pause a minute that you may do so. Before you Jesus now stands, visible to your faith. Delight yourselves in him. Be always ravished with his love. He is altogether lovely and altogether yours. He loves you with all the infinity of his nature. The tenderness of his humanity and the majesty of his deity blend in his love to you. Oh, love the Lord, his saints, for he deserves your hearts! Therefore at this moment say, "My Lord and my God."

More than this, I believe that the words of Thomas indicate *a complete change of mind*—in other words, a most hearty repentance. He has not asked of the Lord Jesus to be permitted to put his finger into the print of the nails. No, all that has gone without debate. If you look at the chapter you will find no statement that he ever did handle the Lord as he had at first proposed. Whether he did put his finger into the print of the nails and his hand into the side, must forever be unknown to us until we see Thomas in heaven and ask him the question. If you read the Savior's words as commanding him to do so, then we may conclude that he did so; but if you read them as only permitting him to do it, then I think he did not do it. I put the question to a dear companion of mine; I read the passage, and then I asked, "What think you, did Thomas put his hand into Christ's side?" and the answer from a thoughtful mind and a gentle heart was this: "I do not think he could; after the Master had so spoken to him he would shrink from doing so, and would think it willful unbelief to attempt it." This reply coincided exactly with my own convictions. I feel sure that had it been my case, I should have felt so ashamed at ever having proposed such a test, and so overwhelmed to find the Lord yielding to it, that I could not have gone an inch further in the way of seeking tokens and proofs unless I had been absolutely commanded to do so. So, judging Thomas to be like ourselves, and indeed much better than any of us, notwithstanding his imperfection, I gather that he completely turned round, and instead of putting his finger into the print of the nails, he cried, "My Lord and my God." The Savior said to him, "Because thou hast seen me, thou hast believed." Now I lay no stress upon it; but it would seem probable that the Savior might have said, "Because thou hast touched me, thou hast believed," if Thomas had indeed touched him; but inasmuch as he only speaks of sight, it may be that sight was enough for Thomas. I do not insist upon it, but I think it right to suggest it; I feel it is not unreasonable to conclude that all Thomas did was to look at his Lord. He could do no more; the delicacy of his spirit would not permit him to accept the offered test; his reverence checked him; he saw and believed.

In him we see a complete change of feeling; from being the most unbelieving of the eleven, he came to believe more than any of them, and to confess Jesus to be God.

This exclamation is also *a brief confession of faith*, "My Lord and my God." Whosoever will be saved, before all things it is necessary that he be able to unite with Thomas heartily in this creed, "My Lord and my God." I do not go in for all the minute distinctions of the Athanasian Creed, but I have no doubt that it was absolutely needful at the time it was written, and that it materially helped to check the evasions and tricks of the Arians. This short creed of Thomas I like much better, for it is brief, pithy, full, sententious, and it avoids those matters of detail which are the quicksands of faith. Such a belief is needful; but no man can truly hold it unless he be taught by the Holy Ghost. He can say the words, but he cannot receive the spiritual truth. No man can call Jesus "Lord" but by the Holy Ghost. It is therefore a most needful and saving creed that we should cry to the Lord Jesus, "My Lord and my God." I ask you to do this now in your hearts. Renew your faith, and confess that he who died for you is your Lord and God. Socinians may call Jesus what they please; to me he is God over all, blessed forever. I know that you say, "Amen."

Further than this, do you not think that these words of Thomas were *an enthusiastic profession of his allegiance* to Christ? "My Lord and my God." It was as though he paid him lowliest homage and dedicated himself there and then in the entirety of his nature to his service. To him whom he had once doubted he now submits himself, for in him he fully believes. He does as good as say, "Henceforth, O Christ, you are my Lord, and I will serve you; you are my God, and I will worship you."

Finally, I regard it as a *distinct and direct act of adoration*. At the feet of the manifested Savior, Thomas cries, "My Lord and my God." It sounds like a rehearsal of the eternal song which ascends before that throne where cherubim and seraphim continually do cry, "Holy, holy, holy, Lord God of Sabaoth." It sounds like a stray note from those choral symphonies which day without night circle the throne of the Eternal. Let us in solemn silence now present our souls before the throne, bowing in reverent adoration unto him that was, and is, and is to come, even the Lamb that was slain, who is risen, and who liveth forever. "My Lord and my God." O Son of Mary, you are also Son of the Highest, and unto my heart and spirit you are my Lord and my God, and I worship you this day!

We have not time or else I would sit down and invite you to spend a few minutes in private, personal worship, following the example of Thomas in adoring our Lord and God.

II. Our next division is to be headed with the question: How *did he come to that exclamation?*

Have you ever thought what Thomas's feelings were when he went to the meeting that evening? His going needed a complicated explanation. Why did he mingle with men whose assertions he doubted? Could he have fellowship with them, and yet give them the lie? Suppose Jesus Christ to be dead and not risen, why does Thomas go? Is he going to worship a dead man? Is he about to renounce the faith of the last two years? How can he hold it if Jesus is not alive? Yet how can he give it up? Was Jesus Christ Lord and God to Thomas when he first entered that meeting? I suppose not. He did not, when he entered the room, believe him to be the same person who had died. The other disciples did believe, and Thomas was now the lone doubter, peculiar, positive, obstinate. Has it never happened to other disciples to drift into much the same condition? Thomas was a lot out of catalogue that evening: he was the odd person in the little gathering, and yet before service was over the Lord had completely altered him. "Behold, there are last which shall be first, and there are first which shall be last."

The first thing, I think, that led Thomas to this confession of his belief in Christ's deity was that *he had his thoughts revealed*. The Savior came into the room, the doors being shut; without opening the doors he suddenly appeared before them by his own divine power. There and then pointing to Thomas he repeated to him the very words which Thomas had said to his brethren. They had not been reported to the Savior, but the Savior had read Thomas's thoughts at a distance, and he was therefore able to bring before him his exact words. Notice that the Savior did not say, "Stoop down and put thy finger into the nail prints in my feet." Why not? Why, because Thomas had not said anything about his feet, and therefore the Savior did not mention them. Everything was exact. We in looking at it can see the exactness; but Thomas must have felt it much more. He was overwhelmed. To have his thoughts put in plain words and to hear his own words repeated by him whom they concerned, this was truly wonderful. "Oh," he said, "he who now speaks to me is none other than God, and he shall be my Lord and my God." This helped him to his assured conviction that one who had read his thoughts must be God.

He was aided still further, for as soon as he perceived that this was the same Jesus with whom he had conversed before, *all the past must have risen before his mind*, and he must have remembered the many occasions in which the Lord Jesus had exercised the attributes of Deity. That past intercourse thus revived before him must all have gone to support the conviction that Jesus was none other than Lord and God.

And then, I think, *the very air, and manner, and presence of the Savior* convinced the trembling disciple. They say there is a divinity that does hedge a king; that I am not prepared to believe; but I am sure there was a majesty about the look of our Lord, a more than human dignity in his manner and tone, and speech and bearing. Our Lord's personal presence convinced Thomas: so that he saw and believed.

But perhaps the most convincing arguments of all were *our Lord's wounds.* It seems a long way around to infer the deity of Christ from his wounds: yet it is good and clear argument. I shall not set it out in order before you, but leave you to think it out for yourselves, yet one little hint I would give you: here is a wound in his side more than sufficient to have caused death; it has gone right to the heart; the soldier with a spear pierced his side, and forthwith flowed there out blood and water, proving that the heart was pierced. The opening was still there, for the Lord invited Thomas to thrust his hand into his side, and yet Jesus lived. Heard you ever such a story as this—a man with a death wound gaping wide inviting another to thrust his hand therein. Had our Lord been living after the way in which we live, by the circulation of the blood, one can hardly see how this could have been possible. *Flesh and blood,* being subject to corruption, cannot inherit the kingdom of God; but the Savior's risen body came not under that description, as indeed his buried body did not, for he saw no corruption. I invite you to note well the distinction which may be seen in our Lord's words concerning his own body. He does not speak of his body as flesh and blood, but he says, "Handle me, and see; for a spirit has not flesh and bones as you see me have." It was a real body and a material body: for he took a piece of a broiled fish and of a honeycomb, and did eat before them; but still his resurrection body, living with an open wound in his side, reaching to the heart, was not after the manner of men. So even in the wounds of Christ, we read that he is man, but not mere man: his wounds in various ways were evidence to Thomas of his deity. Anyhow, the glorious fact rushed upon Thomas's astonished mind in a single moment, and therefore he cried out, "My Lord and my God."

III. Finally, let us see how *we may come to it.*

That is our final point, and the most practical of all. I doubt not that the Spirit of God was at work with Thomas at that time very mightily, and that the true cause of his enlightenment was heavenly illumination. If ever anyone of us shall cry in spirit and in truth, "My Lord and my God!" the Holy Spirit must teach us. Blessed are you who can call Jesus "Lord and God," for flesh and blood has not revealed this unto you, but the Father from heaven. But I will tell you when believers do cry, "My Lord and my God." I remember the first time it filled my heart. Burdened with guilt, and full of fears, I was as wretched as a man could be outside of hell-gate, when I heard the voice of the Lord saying, "Look unto me, and be ye saved, all the ends of the earth: for I am God, and there is none else." I did look there and then; I gave a faith-glance to him who suffered in my stead, and in an instant my peace was like a river. My heart leaped from despair to gladness, and I knew my Lord to be divine. If anyone had said to me then, "Jesus Christ is not God," I would have laughed him to scorn. He was beyond all question my Lord and my God, for he had worked a divine work in me.

It may not be an argument to anybody else, but forgiveness consciously known in the soul is a conclusive argument to the man who has ever felt it. If the Lord Jesus turns your mourning into dancing, brings you up out of the horrible pit and out of the miry clay, and sets your feet upon a rock and establishes your goings, he is sure to be your Lord and God henceforth and forever. In the teeth of all that deny it, in the teeth of all the devils in hell, the redeemed heart will assert the Godhead of its Savior. He that hath saved me is indeed God, and beside him there is none else.

This first avowal has proved to be only the beginning of these confessions. We remember many other acknowledgments of the same fact. We were severely tempted, and yet we did not slip, nor stain our garments, a wonder that we escaped! He that kept us from falling must be God. I know some moments in my life when I could stand and look back in the morning light upon the valley through which I had passed in the dark; and when I saw how narrow the pathway was, how a little step to the left or to the right must have been my total destruction, and yet I had never tripped, but had come straight through in perfect safety, I was astounded, and bowing my head, I worshiped, saying, "The Lord has been my refuge and my defense. He has kept my soul in life and preserved me from the destroyer, therefore will I sing songs unto him as long as I live." Oh, yes, dear children of God, when your heads have been covered in the day of battle, you have magnified the Keeper of Israel, saying, "My Lord and my God." We have felt that we could not doubt again and have joyfully committed ourselves to his keeping as to the guardian care of a faithful Creator.

Such, also, has been the case in time of trouble, when you have been comforted and upheld. A very heavy affliction has fallen upon you, and yet to your surprise it has not crushed you as you feared it would have done. Years before you had looked forward to the stroke with agonizing apprehension, and said, "I shall never bear it"; but you did bear it, and at this moment you are thankful that you had it to bear. The thing which you feared came upon you, and when it came it seemed like a featherweight compared with what you expected it to be, you were able to sit down and say, "The Lord gave, and the Lord hath taken away; blessed be the name of the Lord." Your friends were surprised at you: you had been a poor, wretchedly nervous creature before, but in the time of trial you displayed a singular strength such as surprised everybody. Most of all you surprised yourself, for you were full of amazement that in weakness you were made so strong. You said, "I was brought low, and he helped me." You could not doubt his deity then: anything which would rob him of glory you detested, for your heart said, "Lord, there is none that could have solaced my soul in this fashion save only the Lord God Almighty." Personally I have had to cry out, "It is the Lord's" when I have seen his wonders in the deep. "O my soul, thou hast trodden down strength." My soul shall magnify my Lord and my God, for "he sent from above, he took me; he drew me out of many waters. He brought me forth also into a large place: he delivered me, because he delighted in me."

There have been other occasions less trying. Bear with me if I mention one or two more. When we have been musing, the fire has burned. While studying the story of our Lord, our faith in his deity has been intensified. When the Spirit of God has revealed the Lord Jesus to us and in us, then we have cried, "My Lord and my God." Though not after the flesh, yet in very deed and truth we have seen the Lord. On a day which I had given lip to prayer, I sat before the Lord in holy peacefulness, wrapped in solemn contemplation, and though I did not see a vision, nor wish to see one, yet I so realized my Master's presence that I was borne away from all earthly things, and knew of no man save Jesus only. Then a sense of his Godhead filled me till I would fain have stood up where I was and have proclaimed aloud, as with the voice of a trumpet, that he was my Lord and my God. Such times you also have known.

Jesus is often known of us in the breaking of bread. At the communion table many a time we have seen and adored. It was very precious; we were ready to weep and laugh for joy. Our heart kept beating to the tune of "my Lord and my God." Perhaps it was not in any outward ordinance that your soul thus adored; but quite away in the country, or by the seaside, as you walked along and communed with your own heart, you were suddenly overpowered with a sense of Jesus' glorious majesty, so that you could only whisper to yourself as in a still, small voice, "My Lord and my God." Or perhaps it was when you were laid aside with illness that he made all your bed, and then you knew his power divine. It was a long and weary night to those who watched you, but to you it was all too short, and brimmed with sweetness, for the Lord was there, and he gave you songs in the night. When you awoke you were still with him and felt ready to faint with overwhelming delight because of the brightness of the manifestation. At such a time you could have sung,

> My Christ, he is the Lord of lords,
> He is the King of kings;
> He is the Sun of Righteousness,
> With healing in his wings.
>
> My Christ, he is the heaven of heavens,
> My Christ, what shall I call?
> My Christ is first, my Christ is last,
> My Christ is All in all.

I will tell you yet again when Jesus has been Lord and God both to me and to you, and that is in times when he has blessed our labors, and laid his arm bare in the salvation of men. When our report has been believed by those who rejected it before, and the Lord has sent us a happy season of revival, we have given to him the glory, and rejoiced in his omnipotent love. We prayed for our children, and when to our surprise—it is a shame to say to our surprise, for it ought not to have surprised us—the Lord heard our prayer, and first one and then another came to us and said, "Father, I have found the Lord," then we knew that the Lord he is God, and our God too. We looked up from our prayers with tears in our eyes to think the Lord Jesus could have heard such weak petitions, and we said in the depths of our hearts, "My Lord and my God." We went out and tried to teach a dozen or two in a cottage; poor, broken words were all that we could utter; but the Lord blessed it, and we heard a poor woman crying for mercy as we came out, and we said inwardly, "My Lord and my God." If you have been in the inquiry room after some brother whom God greatly honors has been proclaiming the word with power, and if you have seen the people falling right and left under the shafts of the divine Word, you must have cried, "This is no cunningly devised fable, no fiction, and no fancy," and your heart must have throbbed with all its life, "My Lord and my God." Have you not felt as if you would dare to go through the very streets of hell, and tell the grinning fiends that Christ is King and Lord forever and ever?

The time is very soon coming with some of us when we shall have our last opportunities in this life to find this true. How comforted and refreshed have I often been when visiting dying saints. Truly the Lord has prepared a table for them in the presence of the last enemy. I can truly say that no scenes that these eyes have ever beheld have so gladdened me as the sight of my dear brethren and sisters when they have been departing out of the world unto the Father. The saddest scene has been the happiest. I have known some of them in life as self-distrusting, trembling, lowly minded believers; and when they have come into the valley of death-shade they have displayed no fear, no doubt, but all has been full assurance. Placid, calm, beautiful, joyful, and even triumphant have been the last hours of timid believers. As I have heard their charming words I have been certain of the Godhead of him who gives us victory while we die. It is faith in his name that makes men strong in death. When heart and flesh fail us, only the living God can be the strength of our life, and our portion forever. How sweet to know Jesus as our living God in our dying moments! In him we rejoice with joy unspeakable and full of glory, as we say unto him in death, "My Lord and my God." Come, brothers and sisters, be of good cheer! A little further on we shall come to the narrow stream. This we shall cross in an instant, and then! It will be but a short, short time; twenty years is soon gone, a hundred years even fly as on eagles' wings, and then we shall be forever with the Lord in the glory land. How sweetly will we sing to his eternal praise, "My Lord and my God"! There shall be no doubters in heaven; no skeptics shall worry us there; but this shall be the unanimous voice of all the redeemed: "Jesus is our Lord and God." The united church, freed from every spot and wrinkle, and gloriously arrayed as the bride of Christ, shall be conducted to his throne, and acknowledged as the Lord's beloved, and then shall she with full heart exclaim, "My Lord and my God."

Zacchaeus: Must He?

Intended for reading on Lord's Day, December 1, 1901; delivered on Lord's Day evening, July 27, 1879, at the Metropolitan Tabernacle, Newington. No. 2755.

And when Jesus came to the place, he looked up, and saw him, and said unto him, "Zacchaeus, make haste, and come down; for today I must abide at thy house."—LUKE 19:5

I think this is the only instance in which our Lord invited himself to any-body's house. He often went when he was bidden; but this time, if I may use the expression, he did the bidding himself. Usually, we must seek the Lord if we want to find him. To the eye, at any rate, the apparent work of grace goes on in this way: a man begins to cry for mercy, as the blind man, who heard that Jesus of Nazareth was passing by, cried to him, "Thou Son of David, have mercy on me." But God is so rich in grace that he does not restrict himself to this usual method. Generally, he is found of them that seek him; but, some-times, he is found of them that seek him not. Yes, if I tell the whole *truth*, if you go down to the bedrock of actual fact, it is always God who seeks sinners. He always calls them a people who are not a people; and the first movement, between God and the sinner, is never on the sinner's part, but on God's part. Still, apparently, men begin to pray to God, and begin to seek the Lord; and this is the usual order in which salvation comes to them. The prodigal said, "'I will arise and go to my father.' . . . And he arose, and came to his father." The blind man cried, "Jesus, thou Son of David, have mercy on me."

Our text, however, describes a case which shows the freeness of divine mercy; for, although Zacchaeus did not invite Christ to his house, Christ invited himself. Though there was no asking him to be a guest, much less any pressing entreaty on the part of Zacchaeus, Christ pressed himself upon him, and said to him, "Make haste, and come down; for today I must abide at thy house." I reckon that there are some here who are on an errand something like that of Zacchaeus. They want, perhaps, to see the preacher, which is not nearly so good a thing as wanting to see the preacher's Master. Still, that curiosity has brought them into the place where Jesus of Nazareth is wont to come; and I do pray that he may find many to whom he will say, "Make haste, and come and receive me; for I must abide, this very night, with you, and dwell in your house and heart at this time and forever."

I. The first thing I am going to talk about is *the divine necessity which pressed upon the Savior*. He says, "I must." "Today I must abide at thy house."

I do not think of this so much as a necessity upon Zacchaeus as upon Christ. You know that he felt this "must" at other times. In John 4:4, we read, "He must needs go through Samaria." There was a sacred necessity that he should go that way. The most notable instance of all was when "Jesus began to show unto his disciples, how that he must go unto Jerusalem, and suffer many things of the elders and chief priests and scribes, and be killed, and be raised again the third day." In this case, the "must" was of another kind; he must abide in the house of Zacchaeus. What necessity was this which pressed so urgently upon our blessed Master? There were many other houses in Jericho besides that of the tax gatherer. I daresay there were other persons who would, apparently, have been more suitable hosts for the Lord Jesus Christ; yet it was not really so. There was a mighty pressure upon him, who is the omnipotent Lord of all. Necessity was laid upon him who is the blessed and only Potentate, the King of kings, and Lord of lords. He was his own Master, yet he must do something to which he was constrained by an urgent necessity; he must go and lodge that night nowhere else but at the house of Zacchaeus. What did this "must" mean?

I answer, first, it was *a necessity of love*. Our Lord Jesus wanted to bless somebody; he had seen Zacchaeus, and he knew what his occupation was, and what his sin was, and he felt that he must bless him. As he looked at him, he felt as a mother does concerning her child when it is ill, and she must nurse it; or as you might feel concerning a starving man, whom you saw to be ready to expire with hunger, and you felt that you must feed him; or as some men have felt when they have seen a fellow creature drowning, and they have plunged in to save him. They did not stop to think; they dared to do the brave deed without a thought, for they felt that they "must" do it. The compulsions of charity, the necessities of benevolence—these urgent things laid violent hands upon them, so they must do it. Thus Jesus felt—only in a much higher sense— that he must bless Zacchaeus. He must go to his house, that he might enter his heart, to abide there, and to make Zacchaeus holy and happy henceforth and forever. And he is the same Christ now that he was then; he is not less loving, he is the same gracious Savior, and he feels the same necessity, the same hunger after souls, the same thirst of love to bless the sons of men; and I, therefore, hopefully expect that there will be, even in this place and I hope in many other parts of the world, some of whom it will be true that the Lord Jesus Christ must come to their house and heart. So this was a necessity arising out of our Savior's divine benevolence and love.

Next, I think it *was a necessity of his sovereignty:* "*I* must abide at thy house." Here were scribes and Pharisees and all sorts of people round about him, who were saying, "*He* is a prophet; he has opened a blind man's eyes; and he must, therefore, as a prophet, be entertained by some notable Pharisee. Some very respectable person must find him a lodging tonight." But our Lord Jesus Christ seems to say, "I cannot be bound; I will not be fettered; I must exert my own will; I must display my sovereignty; and though these people will all murmur, I cannot help that. Zacchaeus, I will come and stay with you, just to show them that I will have mercy on whom I will have mercy, and I will have compassion on whom I will have compassion."

You see, this man was in bad odor. We are not very fond of tax gatherers here; but in the East they like them still less than we do; and among the Jews a tax gatherer, if he was himself a Jew who came to collect an obnoxious impost by a foreign power upon a people who thought that they were the people of God and ought to be free, was a man who was intensely hated for having stooped to become one of the farmers of taxes; and if he was the head farmer, the chief contractor of customs, as Zacchaeus was, he had a very bad name indeed. People did not cultivate his acquaintance; they seldom dropped in to tea at his house; and as a general rule they fought very shy of him. When they mentioned sinners, they always reckoned that Zacchaeus, who had made a fine thing out of the business they specially loathed and was reputed to be very rich, was one of the very worst; nobody thought much of him. I think, too, that he had been excommunicated by a law of the Sanhedrin, for the publicans were generally regarded as excommunicated persons—shut out, certainly, from the society of more respectable people.

Besides, to my mind, Zacchaeus was an eccentric sort of body. That running of his was a very strange action for such a man; wealthy men, even though they happen to be short of stature, do not generally take to running through the streets and climbing trees. I should think Zacchaeus was the sort of man who kept himself to himself; and who, when he meant to do a thing, would do it; and if it was to climb a tree, as a boy might, he did not mind that, for he had got beyond caring for public opinion. He was an oddity; he may have been a very good sort of fellow, in some respects; but it is quite clear that he was an odd sort of person. So our Lord Jesus Christ seemed to say, "I will show these people that, when I save men, it is not because they stand well in society, or because they enjoy an excellent repute, or because there are some beautiful points in their character. I will save this odd man, this Zacchaeus, this despised tax gatherer. I must have him; he is just the sort of man in whom I can best display the sovereignty of my grace." To this day, men cannot bear that doctrine. Free will suits them very well, but free grace does not. They would not let Christ choose his own wife; I say it with the utmost reverence. I mean, they would not let him have the choice of his own bride, his church; but say that must be left to the will of men. But Christ will have his way, whatever they may say. He has a sacred determination, in his blessed heart, that he will do as he pleases; and so, for that reason, he says to Zacchaeus, "I *must* abide at thy house."

Our Lord Jesus was also under another necessity: *he wanted someone in whom he could display the great power of his grace.* He needed a sinner, to begin with; that was to be the raw material out of which he was going to make a saint, and a saint of a very special character. Is there a Christian in this place who comes up to the standard of Zacchaeus after he was converted? I do not wish to be censorious, but I doubt if there is one. Is there anybody here who gives away half his income to the poor? I think that was going a long way in grace in the matter of almsgiving; and then remember that he was but a babe in grace when he did that; so what he did when he grew older, I do not know. But the first day he was born to Christ, he was a saint of that kind; so what kind of a saint he grew to be by and by, I can scarcely imagine. Lord, out of what material did you make such a generous soul as this? Why, out of a grasping, grinding tax gatherer, who sought to grab all he could lay his hands on! The mighty grace of God, better than a magic wand, opened his closed heart, and made it gush forth like a fountain flowing in a thousand generous streams. Jesus seems to say, "I must have Zacchaeus, so that the men of the world may see what I can make out of the most unlikely material; how I can take coarse pebbles from the brook and transmute them into diamonds; how I can bedeck my crown with jewels of the first water [highest quality], which were originally but as the common stones of the street." I wonder whether there is anybody here who feels that he has not anything at all in him that is any good whatever. If so, the Lord could say, "I will make something of that man that will cause all who know him to marvel. I will make his wife wonder what has changed him; I will make all his children say, 'What has come over father?' I will make the whole parish say, 'What a miracle! What a miracle!'" This was the kind of "must" that was laid upon our Savior, and I hope such a *"must"* is laid upon him now.

There was one more *"must"* upon him, namely, he must abide in the house of Zacchaeus *because Zacchaeus was to be his host at Jericho.* Even the Savior must be lodged somewhere; and, in most places, his Father had appointed some gracious spirit to entertain him, and Zacchaeus was to be his host that day; and if he ever came that way again, I feel certain that he would go to his old quarters. Blessed be my Master's dear name, he still has some hosts left where the guest chamber is always ready for him! In every town and village and hamlet, there is some house where there is a prophet's chamber; and if you were to ask, "Is there anybody here who will entertain the Lord Jesus Christ?" you would soon find people who would be glad to have his company. Perhaps there is a large upper room, furnished and prepared, where they might break bread together; or a little room, where two or three might meet with Jesus, a place that never seems so bright as when there are a few praying people met together in it. The Lord must be entertained in this world, and Zacchaeus was to be the man to entertain him in Jericho.

Who is the one here now who will take Jesus in? A stranger from the country, perhaps; there is no preaching place in your village, the gospel is not often proclaimed within miles of the place where you live, and few people go to hear it when it is preached. That is all the more reason why Jesus must come to your house, for he means to have your best room, or that old shed of yours, or that big barn, that the gospel may be preached there. There is a divine necessity laid upon him to have your heart for himself, so that he may come and dwell with you, and make your house his headquarters, whence his disciples may go forth to attack the enemy where you live; and that all in your region may know that the true salvation army has come there, and that the Captain of our salvation has himself come to make his abode in your house and your heart.

There is plenty of room for enlargement upon this point, but we must go on to the next one.

II. If so, second, *let us inquire whether there is such a necessity in reference to ourselves.*

Has the Lord Jesus Christ any necessity to come and stay at your house, to come and abide in your heart? I can answer that question best by putting to you a few inquiries.

First, *are you willing to receive Christ at once?* Then there is a necessity laid upon him to come to you, for he never sent the will into a man without also sending his grace with the will; indeed, the willingness be receive him is the proof of the working of his grace. Do you long and sigh that Christ might be yours? Then, you shall surely have him. Are you earnestly anxious to be reconciled to God by Jesus Christ? Then you may have that great blessing at once. Are you thirsting after righteousness? Then you shall be filled; for what says the Scripture? "Let him that is athirst come"; and lest anybody should say, "Oh! but there is some preparation implied in that word *thirst,* and I am afraid that I do not thirst enough," what does the Scripture further say? "And whosoever will—whosoever will—let him take the water of life freely."

Next, *will you heartily receive Jesus?* Zacchaeus "received him joyfully," and if you will do the same, then he must abide at your house. I think I hear somebody say, "Receive him joyfully? Ah! that I would if he would but come to me. I would give all I have to have Christ as my Savior, to have the new life implanted within me, and to have Jesus dwelling in my heart. I would be willing to live, or be willing to die, if I might but have him as mine." So you will receive him joyfully, will you? Ah, then he is bound to come to you. When the door of your heart is opened, Jesus will not be long before he enters. He will stand and knock even at a closed door; therefore I am sure that he will enter an open one. It is written of Lydia, "whose heart the Lord opened"; and her heart was not long open before the Lord entered it; and if yours is open to Christ, that is a proof that you are one of those in whom he must abide at this time.

Let me ask you another question. *Will you receive Christ, whatever the murmurers may say?* Suppose he comes to you, they will begin to murmur, as they did when he went to be the guest of Zacchaeus. I do not know where you live, but those around you will be sure to find fault both with you and with your Lord too. "They all murmured, saying, That he was gone to be guest with a man that is a sinner." So, you see, they were murmuring at Zacchaeus as well as at Christ, and you will have the same sort of treatment when you receive Christ. Those who used to say, "You are a fine fellow," when they find that you have become a Christian, will call you a mean-spirited wretch. As long as you give them something to drink, they will say what a jolly dog you are; but as soon as ever you have done with their ways, you will be literally like a dog to them, and they will have nothing for you but kicks and curses. In more respectable society, you know how they give a Christian the cold shoulder. Nothing is actually said, but there is a very clear intimation that your room is preferred to your company when you once become a Christian. Can you bear that? Can you dare that? Because, if Christ comes to your house and heart, you must expect that he will bring his cross with him. Are you willing to have Christ, cross and all, and say, "Let the murmurers say what they will, and do what they will, my mind is made up, Christ for me, Christ for me; I cannot give him up"?

Further, will you receive Jesus Christ as your Lord? Zacchaeus did so, for he said, "Behold, Lord." Now are you willing to give up all to Christ, and to let him be Lord over you? Are you willing to do what he bids you, as he bids you, when he bids you, and simply because he bids you? For, verily, I say unto you, you cannot have Christ for your Savior unless you also have him as your Lord. He must rule over us as well as forgive us; as one of our poets says—

> Yet know, nor of the terms complain,
> Where Jesus comes, he comes to reign;
> To reign, and with no partial sway;
> Thoughts must be slain that disobey.

Sins must be given up, evil practices must be forsaken, you must renew after holiness, and endeavor in all things to imitate your Savior, who has left you an example that you should follow his steps. Are you ready for that? Because, if you are, then Christ is ready to abide at your house, and to dwell in your heart.

Once more, *will you be prepared to defend him*? If Jesus comes to a house, it becomes the duty of the host to defend him. So Zacchaeus, not in boasting, but as a kind of answer to the sneers of the murmurers, when they said that Christ had gone to dwell with a sinner, seemed to say, "But I am no longer a sinner as I used to be. If I have wronged anybody, I will restore it fourfold; and, henceforth, the half of my income shall be given in alms to the poor." That was the best defense he could give, and Christ must be defended by the changed lives of his disciples. You must so live that, when men attempt to attack the Savior, they may be compelled to say, "Well, after all, that man is the better for being a Christian." Your children may rail at religion, but they will be compelled to say, "We could speak against Christ and Christians generally, but when we think of how our mother lived, and how she died, our tongues are silenced. Then, there is our old nurse, who feared the Lord; many a joke did we crack about her religion, but ah! there was something about her that was so heavenly that we were obliged to believe in the reality of it whether we would or not." Yes, dear friends, if the Lord Jesus Christ should come to your house, you must say, "It shall be my heart's ambition, as long as I live, to defend his cause by the holiness of the character which I trust his Holy Spirit will work in me." If this is the case with any of you, then he must abide at your house tonight. God grant that he may do so!

III. Now I must close by reminding you of *what will happen if Christ comes to abide in your house.*

First, *you must be ready to meet objections at home.* You who say that you are willing to receive my Master, are you quite sure that you know what that reception involves? Christ says that he wishes to abide at your house, and that he must do so; and you say, "Yes, my Lord, I gladly welcome you to my heart and my home." But stay a moment, my friend; have you asked your wife about that matter? You know that you must not bring home strangers; she will be down upon you if you do; have you counted the cost of your decision? And, my good woman, you say, "I want to bring Christ home with me." Have you asked your husband about it? Sometimes a dear child says, "Jesus Christ shall abide with me," but what will father say? For alas! often the father is at enmity against God. If that is the case in your home, are you prepared to endure hardness for Christ's sake? Our Lord himself said, "A man's foes shall be they of his own household," and it is often so. David said to Jonathan, "What if thy father answer thee roughly?" Suppose that is your experience, can you keep true to Christ under such circumstances? Can you say, "I love my wife; I love my child; I love my father; but I love Jesus more than all of them; and I must have Christ in my heart, and in my house, even if it brings war there"? Ah! then he will come to your house if that be your resolve; but if not, he will not come to take the second place. He will not come there if you turn coward at the first jest that is made against you, or the first hard thing that is spoken against your Lord; but he will come to your house if, despite all rebuffs and rebukes, you are determined that he shall make his abode with you.

But, next, *is your house fit for him to enter and abide there?* I know some houses where my Lord could not lodge for a single night, the table, the talk, the whole surroundings would be so uncongenial to him. Are you prepared, then, to put away everything that would displease him, and to have your house cleansed of all that is evil? You cannot expect the Lord Jesus to come into your house if you invite the devil to come too. Christ would not remain in the same heaven with the devil; as soon as ever Satan sinned, he hurled him out of the holy place; he could not endure to have a sinful spirit, the spirit of evil, there, and he will not come and live in your house if you make provision for the lusts of the flesh, the lust of the eyes, and the pride of life, and all those evil things that he abhors. Are you prepared, by his grace, to make a clean sweep of these things? He will not come to you on any other terms.

Further, *we must admit none who would grieve our Guest.* It is hard to lodge with some people because their children are so badly behaved. My Lord loves not to dwell in families where Eli is at the head of the household, and where the children and young people live as they like; but if he comes to your house, he will want you to be like Abraham, of whom he said, "I know him, that he will command his children and his household after him, and they shall keep the way of the Lord." If he comes to your house, you must ask him to come in the same way that he came to the house of the jailer at Philippi. How was that? I have often heard half of that passage quoted without the context: "'Sirs, what must I do to be saved?' And they said, 'Believe on the Lord Jesus Christ, and thou shalt be saved, *and thy house.'*" Many leave out those last three words, "and thy house," but what a mercy it is when all in the house, as well as the head of the family, have faith in the Lord Jesus Christ! Do you not wish that it may be so in your house? Do you not ardently desire it? I trust that you do.

Once more, *when the Lord Jesus Christ comes into your house, you must entertain him.* He wants no riches at your hands, yet he wants the best that you have. What is the best that you have? Why, your heart, your soul! Give him your heart, give him your life, give him your very self. If you had to entertain the queen—if she had promised to come and spend an evening with you—I will warrant that you would be fidgeting and worrying for weeks about what you should get for such an occasion; and if you have but little means, you would try to get the very best that you could.

I frequently used to go and preach in a country place, where I stayed at a farm; and the dear old man who lived there, used to have about a hundred pounds of beef, at the very least, on his table; and when, year after year, I noticed such enormous joints, I said to him one day, You must have a very curious idea of my appetite; it is not possible that I should ever get through these masses of meat that you put on your table." "Oh!" he replied, "we get through it all very easily after you are gone, for there are plenty of poor people, and plenty of farm laborers round about, and they soon clear it up." "But," I inquired, "why do you have so much when I come?" "Bless you, sir," he answered, "I would give you a piece as big as a house if I could get it—I would, indeed—just to show you how welcome you are to my home." I understood what he meant, and appreciated his kindness; and, in a far higher sense, let us all do as much as ever we possibly can to show the Lord Jesus how welcome he is to our heart and our home. How welcome he ought always to be when he comes, as our blessed Savior, to put away our sin and change our nature and honor us with his royal company, and keep and preserve us even to the end, that he may take us up, and our children too, to dwell at his right hand forever! Oh, there ought to be grand entertainment for such a Guest as he is! Where is the man who is going to ask him home tonight? Here stands my Master, and in his name I ask, Who will take him home tonight? With whom shall Jesus lodge tonight? "Oh!" says one, "if he would but come to me, I would he glad enough to welcome him." He is glad enough to come, for he delights to be entertained in human hearts. O you soldiers, over there, with the red coats on—I am always glad to see you here—shall Jesus Christ abide with you tonight? And you others, in black coats, or in colored dresses, shall Jesus Christ abide with you tonight? You good friends who are up from the country, if you have not taken Christ into your hearts, will you not take him in now? I cannot hear what you say, but he can; and if this be the reply, "God be merciful to me a sinner, and come and lodge with me tonight," it shall be done, and his shall be the praise.

Now the time has gone, but I must say just these few words more. I recollect that, when I was crying to God for mercy, and I could get no answer to my supplication, so that I feared I must really give up prayer as hopeless, the thought which kept me praying was this, "Well, if I do not get salvation, I shall perish." I seemed to fancy that the Lord had kept me waiting—that was only my foolish way of thinking, and it was not true—but I said to myself, "If the Lord keeps me waiting, I also kept him waiting a long while. Was I not for many years resisting him, and refusing him? So that, if he makes me wait for salvation, I must not complain." Then I thought, "Well, now, if I were to keep on praying, and I did not find Christ for twenty years, yet, if I found him at last, the blessing would be well worth having and worth waiting for, so I will never leave off praying for it." And then I thought, "Why should I expect that I must be heard the moment I choose to come to the mercy seat, when I would not hear God's call when he so often spoke to me?" So I still persevered in prayer, yet with this thought, "What can I do else?"—like a whip ever upon my back. I felt that this must be my resolve—

> *I can but perish if I go;*
> *I am resolved to try;*
> *For if I stay away, I know*
> *I must forever die.*

I like that plan which I have known to be followed by some who have gone to their room and shut the door, determined not to go out till they had found the Savior. They have read the Word, especially such passages as these, "Believe on the Lord Jesus Christ, and thou shalt be saved"; "He that believeth on the Son hath everlasting life"; and they have gone down on their knees and have said, "Lord, this is thy promise. Help me now to believe in Jesus, and give me salvation, for his sake, for I will not leave this place without thy blessing!" Such vehemence, such importunity, is sure to prevail. How dare any one of you continue to live unsaved?

How dare you, sir, again close your eyes in sleep while you are unreconciled to God? What if, instead of waking up in that bedroom of yours, you should lift up your eyes and say, "Where am I? What is this dreadful place? Where are the things I once loved? Where are the things I lived for? Where am I? Where is Christ? Where is the gospel? Where are Sabbath days? Where are the warning words I used to despise? Where is the power to pray? Is all this gone forever? And where am I? In dark, dark, dire despair; an enemy to thee, O God, and an enemy to you forever! Horror and dismay have taken hold upon me."

The very attempt to depict that awful scene makes me feel as though dread would stop my tongue. Oh, I pray you, go not there! There are some who deny the eternity of future punishment; but, for my part, I would not risk such suffering for an hour even if it should end then. What woe it would be to be only an hour in hell! Oh, how you would wish then that you had sought the Savior and had found him. But alas! there is no such thing as an hour in hell; once lost, you are lost forever! Therefore, seek the Lord now; cry, with Jeremiah, "O LORD our God, we will wait upon thee." You cannot brazen it out; you cannot escape from everlasting wrath unless you trust in Jesus, so let this be your cry—

> *Thou, O Christ, art all I want;*
> *More than all in thee I find!*
> *Other refuge have I none,*
> *Hangs my helpless soul on thee!*

So, Christ of God, we cast ourselves into your arms! Save us, save us, save us, for your sweet mercy's sake! Amen.

Joseph of Arimathaea

Preached on Lord's Day morning, July 6, 1884, at the Metropolitan Tabernacle, Newington. No. 1789.

Joseph of Arimathaea, an honorable counselor, which also waited for the kingdom of God, came, and went in boldly unto Pilate, and craved the body of Jesus. And Pilate marveled if he were already dead: and calling unto him the centurion, he asked him whether he had been any while dead. And when he knew it of the centurion, he gave the body to Joseph. And he bought fine linen, and took him down, and wrapped him in the linen, and laid him in a sepulcher which was hewn out of a rock, and rolled a stone unto the door of the sepulcher.—MARK 15:43–46

It was a very dark day with the church of God and with the cause of Christ, for the Lord Jesus was dead, and so the sun of their souls had set. "All the disciples forsook him, and fled." "Ye shall be scattered, every man to his own, and shall leave me alone," were the sad words of Jesus, and they had come true. He was dead upon the cross, and his enemies hoped that there was an end of him, while his friends feared that it was even so. A few women who had remained about the cross, true to the very last, were found faithful unto death, but what could they do to obtain his sacred body and give it honorable burial? That priceless flesh seemed to be in danger of the fate which usually awaited the bodies of malefactors: at any rate, the fear was that it might be hurled into the first grave that could be found to shelter it. At that perilous moment, Joseph of Arimathaea, a city of the Jews, of whom we never heard before, and of whom we never hear again, suddenly made his appearance. He was the very man needed for the occasion, a man of influence, a man possessing that kind of influence which was most potent with Pilate—a rich man, a counselor, a member of the Sanhedrin, a person of weight and character. Every Evangelist mentions him and tells us something about him, and from these we learn that he was a disciple, "a good man and a just; who also himself waited for the kingdom of God." Joseph had been retiring and probably cowardly before; but now he came to the cross and saw how matters stood, and then went in boldly unto Pilate, craved the body of Jesus, and obtained it. Let us learn from this that God will always have his witnesses. It matters not though the ministry should forsake the truth, though they that should be leaders should become recreant, the truth of God will not fail for lack of friends. It may be with the church as when a standard-bearer faints and the host is ready to melt with dismay; but there shall be found other standard-bearers, and the banner of the Lord shall wave over all. As the Lord lives, so shall his truth live: as God reigns, so shall the gospel reign, even though it be from the cross. "Tell it out among the heathen that the Lord reigneth from the tree." Such is a singular version of a verse in the Psalms, and it contains a glorious truth. Even while Jesus hangs on the cross in death, he is still keeping possession of the throne, and he shall reign forever and ever.

Let this be remembered for your encouragement in the cloudy and dark day. If you live in any place where the faithful fail from among men, do not wring your hands in grief and sit down in despair, as though it was all over with the cause you love. The Lord lives, and he will yet keep a faithful seed alive in the earth. Another Joseph of Arimathaea will come forward at the desperate moment: just when we cannot do without him, the man will be found. There was a Joseph for Israel in Egypt, and there was a Joseph for Jesus on the cross. A Joseph acted to him a father's part at his birth, and another Joseph arranged for his burial. The Lord shall not be left without friends. There was a dark day in the Old Testament history when the eyes of Eli, the servant of God, had failed him; and worse still, he was almost as blind mentally as physically; for his sons made themselves vile, and he restrained them not. It seemed as if God must forsake his Israel. But who is this little boy who is brought in by his mother? This tiny child who is to be left in the sanctuary to serve his God as long as he lives? This pretty little man who wears the little coat which his mother's hands have lovingly made for him? Look, you that have eyes of faith; for the prophet Samuel is before you, the servant of the Lord, by whose holy example Israel shall be led to better things, and delivered from the oppression which chastised the iniquities of Eli's sons.

God hath today somewhere, I know not where, in yon obscure cottage of an English village, or in a log hut far away in the backwoods of America, or in the slums of our backstreets, or in our palaces, a man who in maturer life shall deliver Israel, fighting the battles of the Lord. The Lord has his servant making ready, and when the time shall come, when the hour shall want the man, the man shall be found for the hour. The Lord's will shall be done, let infidels and doubters think what they please. I see in this advent of Joseph of Arimathaea exactly at the needed time, a well of consolation for all who have the cause of God laid upon their hearts. We need not worry our heads about who is to succeed the pastors and evangelists of today: the apostolic succession we may safely leave with our God.

Concerning this Joseph of Arimathaea, the honorable counselor, I want to speak this morning, praying that I may speak to your souls all along. As I have already said, we hear no more of Joseph than what is recorded here. He shines out when he is wanted, and anon he disappears: his record is on high. We need not mention the traditions about him, for I think that even the quotation of legends has an evil tendency, and may turn us aside from the pure, unadulterated Word of God. What have you and I to do with tradition? Is not the Scripture enough? There is probably no truth in the silly tales about Joseph and Glastonbury; and if there were, it could be of no consequence to us; if any fact had been worthy of the pen of inspiration, it would have been written, and because it is not written, we need not desire to know. Let us be satisfied to pause where the Holy Spirit stays his pen.

I shall use Joseph of Arimathaea this morning in four ways: first, as *our warning*—he was a disciple of Jesus, "but secretly for fear of the Jews"; second, for *our instruction*—he was at last brought out by the cross concerning which holy Simeon had declared that by the death of the Lord Jesus the thoughts of many hearts should be revealed; third, for *our arousing*—there was an occasion for Joseph to come forward, and there is occasion now for all the timid to grow brave; and last, for *our guidance*—that we may, if we have been at all bashful and fearful, come forward in the hour of need and behave ourselves as bravely as Joseph of Arimathaea did on the eve before the Paschal Sabbath.

I. First, then, I desire to look at Joseph of Arimathaea as *our warning*.

He was a disciple of Christ, but secretly, for fear of the Jews: we do not advise any one of you to imitate Joseph in that. Fear which leads us to conceal our faith is an evil thing. Be a disciple by all means, but not secretly; you miss a great part of your life's purpose if you are. Above all, do not be a disciple secretly because of the fear of man, for the fear of man brings a snare. If you are the slave of such fear it demeans you, belittles you, and prevents your giving due glory to God.

> Fear him, ye saints, and you will then
> Have nothing else to fear.

Be careful to give honor to Christ, and he will take care of your honor. Why was it that Joseph of Arimathaea was so backward? Perhaps it was owing to his natural disposition. Many men are by nature very bold; some are a little too much so, for they become intrusive, self-assertive, not to say impudent. I have heard of a certain class of persons who "rush in where angels fear to tread." They are fearless because they are brainless. Let us avoid fault in that direction. Many, on the other hand, are too retiring: they have to screw their courage up even to say a good word for the Savior whom they love. If they can do so they fall into the rear rank; they hope to be found among the victors when they divide the spoil, but they are not overambitious to be among the warriors while they are braving the foe. Some of these are truehearted notwithstanding their timidity. It was found in the martyr days that certain of those who endured most bravely at the stake were naturally of a fearful mind. It is noted by Foxe that some who boasted of how well they could bear pain and death for Christ turned tail and recanted; while others who in prison trembled at the thought of the fire played the man in death, to the admiration of all that were round about them. Still, dear friends, it is not a desirable thing if you are troubled with timidity to foster it at all. Fear of man is a plant to be rooted up, and not to be nurtured. I should set that plant, if I could, where it would get but little water, and no sunshine, and meanwhile I would beg a cutting from a better tree. Would it not be well often to brace ourselves with such a hymn as this—

> *Am I a soldier of the cross,*
> *A follower of the Lamb?*
> *And shall I fear to own his cause,*
> *Or blush to speak his name?*
>
> *Must I be carried to the skies*
> *On flowery beds of ease,*
> *While others fought to win the prize,*
> *And sailed through bloody seas?*

If you know that your temptation lies in the direction of fear, watch and strive against it, and school yourselves evermore to dauntless courage by the help of the Holy Spirit.

I am afraid, too, that what helped to intimidate Joseph of Arimathaea was the fact that he was a *rich man*. A sad truth lies within our Lord's solemn exclamation, "How hardly shall they that have riches enter into the kingdom of God." Riches do not strengthen the heart or make men daring for the good cause. Albeit wealth is a great talent which may be well used by the man who has entered into the kingdom of heaven, yet it brings with it snares and temptations, and when a man has not yet entered into the kingdom it is, in many ways, a terrible hindrance to his entrance. "It is easier for a camel to go through the eye of a needle, than for a rich man to enter into the kingdom." The fishermen of the Galilean lake readily left their bits of boats, and their fishing tackle; but Joseph of Arimathaea was a rich man, and was therefore slow to leave all for Christ's sake. The tendency of great possessions is seen in the case of the young man who turned away in sorrow from the Lord Jesus, when put to the unusual test of selling all he had. Strong swimmers have saved their lives when the ship has struck upon a rock, by casting aside every weight; while others have gone straight down to the bottom because they have bound their gold around their waists. Gold sinks men as surely as lead. Take care, any of you that are well-to-do in this world, that you do not permit the liberality of God to be a cause of disloyalty to him. Beware of the pride of life, the lust for rank, the desire to hoard, for any of these may prevent your service of your Lord. Riches puff men up, and prevent their stooping to find the pearl of great price. A poor man enters a humble village sanctuary where Christ is preached, and he finds eternal life; another man under concern of soul in the same village does not like to go down to the poor conventicle, and remains unblessed. He keeps away because he puts to himself the question, "What will the people say if the squire goes to hear the gospel? What a stir there will be if the son of a lord is converted!" Joseph of Arimathaea's wealth made him unduly cautious; and possibly, without his knowing it, prevented his casting in his lot with the common sort of people who followed the Lord Jesus. His heart was for the prize, but the heavy weight of his substance hindered him in his race; it was an instance of abounding grace that he was helped to run well at the last.

Possibly, too, he may have been checked by the fact that *he was in office, and that he was honorable in it.* It needs great grace to carry human honor; and, truth to tell, it is not particularly much worth carrying when you have it. For what is fame but the breath of men's nostrils? Poor stuff to feed a soul upon! If a man could so live as to gain universal plaudits, if he could write his name across the sky in letters of gold, what of it all? What is there in the applause of a thoughtless multitude? The approbation of good men, if it be gained by persevering virtue, is better to be desired than great riches; but even then it may become a temptation; for the man may begin to question rather, "What will people say?" than, "What will God say?" and the moment he falls into that mood he has introduced a weakening element into his life. The "well done, good and faithful servant" of the Master's own lip is worth ten thousand thunders of applause from senators and princes. Honor among men is, at best, a peril to the best. Joseph was honored in council, and this is apt to make a man prudently slow. The tendency of office is toward caution rather than enthusiasm. I would have those placed in high positions remember this, and candidly judge themselves as to whether their shrinking from the public avowal of Christ may not be a cowardice unworthy of the position in which the Lord has placed them.

It seems clear that all the earthly things which men covet may not be so desirable as they appear to be; and that which men would give their eyes to procure, they might, if their eyes were opened, think far less of.

I would lovingly inquire of you at this time (for the sermon is meant to be personal all the way through) if any of you who love my Lord and Master are doing so secretly because of the fear of men. You have never openly confessed your faith, and why not? What hinders your taking up a decided position on the Lord's side? Are you wealthy? Are you honorable? Do you occupy an enviable position in society? And are you such a mean-spirited creature that you have become proud of these glittering surroundings, like a child that is vain of its new frock? Are you so craven that you will not cast in your lot with the followers of truth and righteousness, because they are persons of low degree? Are you really so base? Is there no holy chivalry in you? Can it be so, that, because God has dealt so well with you, and trusted you so generously, you will repay him by denying his Son, violating your conscience, and turning your back on truth; and all for the sake of being in the fashion? I know it may seem hard to receive the cold shoulder in society, or to have the finger of scorn pointed at you; but to bow before this selfish dread is scarcely worthy of a man, and utterly disgraceful to a Christian man. "Oh, but I am so retiring in disposition." Yes, but do not indulge it, I pray you; for if all were of such a mind, where were the noble advances of truth, her reformations, her revivals? Where would have been our Luther or our Calvin or our Zwingli? Where would have been our Whitefield or our Wesley, if they had thought it to be the main object of desire to walk at ease along the cool sequestered vale of life? Come forth, my brother, for the truth and for the Lord. Recollect that what is right for you would be right for the rest of us: if you do not join the Christian church, for instance, every one of us might also neglect that duty, and where would be the visible church of Christ, and how would the ordinances of our holy faith be kept up as a witness among the sons of men? I charge all concealed believers to think over the inconsistency of their concealment and to quit that cowardly condition.

I feel sure that Joseph of Arimathaea was a great loser by his secrecy; for you see, he did not live with Jesus, as many other disciples did. During that brief but golden period in which men walked and talked, and ate and drank, with Jesus, Joseph was not with him. He was not among the twelve: as possibly he might have been if he had possessed more courage and decision. He lost many of those familiar talks with which the Lord indulged his own after the multitudes had been sent away. He missed that sacred training and strengthening which fitted men for the noble lives of primitive saints. How many opportunities he must have missed, too, of working for the Master and with the Master! Perhaps we hear no more of him because he had done no more. Possibly that one grand action which has redeemed his name from forgetfulness is all that is recorded because it really was all that was worth recording. Joseph must have been a weaker, a sadder, a less useful man for having followed Christ afar off. I would to God that such reflections as these would fetch out our beloved, truly faithful and honorable Christian men, who hitherto have hidden away among the stuff, and have not come to the front to stand up for Jesus.

II. Second, having viewed Joseph of Arimathaea as a warning, I shall go on to speak of him as a lesson for *our instruction.*

Joseph did come out after all; and so will you, my friends. If you are honest and sincere, you will have to avow your Lord sooner or later. Do you not think it would be better to make it sooner rather than later? The day will come when that shame which you are now dreading will be yours. As surely as you are a sincere believer, you will have to encounter that reproach and derision which now alarm you: why not face them at once and get it over? You will have to confess Christ before many witnesses; why not begin to do so at once? What is the hardship of it? It will come easier to you, and it will bring you a larger blessing, and it will be sweeter in the recollection afterward than if you keep on postponing it. What was it that fetched Joseph of Arimathaea out? *It was the power of the cross!* Is it not a remarkable thing that all the life of Christ did not draw out an open avowal from this man? Our Lord's miracles, his marvelous discourses, his poverty, and self-renunciation, his glorious life of holiness and benevolence, all may have helped to build up Joseph in his secret faith, but it did not suffice to develop in him a bold avowal of faith. The shameful death of the cross had greater power over Joseph than all the beauty of Christ's life.

Now let us see, you timid, backward ones, whether the cross will not have the same influence over you today. I believe it will, if you carefully study it. I am sure it will, if the Holy Spirit lays it home to your heart. I suppose that to Joseph of Arimathaea Christ's death on the cross seemed such *a wicked thing* that he must come out on behalf of one so evil-entreated. He had not consented to the deed of the men of the Sanhedrin when they condemned Jesus to death; probably he and Nicodemus withdrew themselves from the assembly altogether; but when he saw that the crime was actually committed, and that the innocent man had been put to death, then he said, "I cannot be a silent witness of such a murder. I must now side with the holy and the just." Therefore he came out and was found the willing servant of his crucified Master. Come what may of it, he felt that he must own himself to be on the right side, now that they had maliciously taken away the life of the Lord Jesus. It was late, it was sadly late, but it was not too late.

O secret disciple, will you not quit your hiding place? Will you not hasten to do so? You who are quiet and retiring, when you hear the name of Jesus blasphemed, as it is in these evil days, will you not stand up for him? When you hear his deity denied, when his headship in the church is given to another, when his very person is by lewd fellows of the baser sort set up as the target of their criticism, will you not speak up for him? Will you not be shocked by such evil conduct into an open avowal? His cause is that of truth and righteousness, and mercy and hope for the sons of men; therefore he must not be abused while you sit by in silence. Had others favored him you might, perhaps, have been somewhat excused for holding back; but you cannot keep back without grievous sin now that so many deride him. Jesus is worthy of all honor, and yet they heap scorn upon him: will you not defend him? He is your Savior and Lord; oh, be not slow to own that you are his. The cross laid bare the heart of Joseph; he loathed the wickedness which slew the holy and the just, and therefore he girded himself to become the guardian of his sacred body.

But, next, it may have been in part *the wonderful patience of the Master's death* which made Joseph feel he could not hide any longer. Did he hear him say, "Father, forgive them; for they know not what they do"? Did he mark him when those blessed lips said, "I thirst"? Do you think he observed the ribaldry and scorn which surrounded the dying Lord? And did he feel that the stones would cry out if he did not show kindness to his best friend? Since Jesus spoke not for himself, but was dumb as a sheep before her shearers, Joseph is bound to open his mouth for him. If Jesus answered not, but only breathed out prayers for his murderers, the honorable counselor must acknowledge him. The sun has owned him, and veiled his face in sackcloth! The earth has owned him, and trembled to her very heart at his sufferings! Death has owned him, and yielded up the bodies which the sepulcher had hitherto detained! The temple has owned him, and in its horror has rent its veil, like a woman that is utterly broken in heart by the horrors she has seen! Therefore Joseph must own him, he cannot resist the impulse. O brethren, if you have been backward, let some such motive lead you unto the vanguard of the host.

Then there were all *the wonders of that death* which he saw, and to which I have already alluded. They sufficed to convince the centurion that this was a righteous man. They convinced others that he was the Son of God; and he who was already a disciple of Christ must have been greatly confirmed in that conviction by what he saw around the cross. The time was come when he must boldly act as Christ's disciple. Have there been no wonders of conversion around you? No answers to prayer? No providential deliverances? Should not these lead the secret ones to declare themselves?

I do not suppose he fully understood the design of our Lord's death; he had some knowledge of it, but not such a knowledge as we have now that the Spirit of God has appeared in all his fullness and taught us the meaning of the cross. Oh, listen, sirs, you that are not upon his side openly, you that have never worn his livery, nor manifestly entered on his service. He died for you! Those wounds were all for you; that bloody sweat, of which you still may see the marks upon the countenance of the crucified, was all for you. For you the thirst and fever, for you the bowing of the head, and the giving up of the ghost, and can you be ashamed to own him? Will you not endure rebuke and scorn for his dear sake who bore all this for you? Now speak from your soul and say, "He loved me, and gave himself for me." If you cannot say that, you cannot be happy; but if you can, then what follows? Must you not love him and give your-self for him? The cross is a wondrous magnet, drawing to Jesus every man of the true metal. It is as a banner lifted on high, to which all who are loyal must rally. This fiery cross, carried through all lands, will rouse the valiant and speed them to the field. Can you see your Lord suffering to the death for you, and then turn your backs? I pray you may no longer hesitate, but may at once cry, "Set down my name among his followers; for I will fight it out even to the end, till I hear him say—

> Come in, come in;
> Eternal glory thou shalt win.

Thus much by way of instruction taken from the life of Joseph of Arimathaea. If the cross does not bring a man out, what will? If the spectacle of dying love does not quicken us into courageous affection for him, what can?

III. So I have to mention, in the third place, something for *our arousing*.

Perhaps you are saying in your heart that the season in which Joseph lived was one which imperatively demanded that he should leave his hiding place and should go in to Pilate, but that you are under no such constraint. Hearken, friends, many people are not true to their occasions, whatever they may be; they do not consider that they have come to the kingdom for such a time as this. The Lord Jesus is not hanging on a cross today needing to be buried; but other stern necessities exist and call for your exertions. This hour's necessities imperiously demand that every man who is right at heart should acknowledge his Lord and do him service. Every man that loves Christ should at this hour prove it by his actions. A buoy off the Mumbles in South Wales bears a bell which is meant to warn mariners of a dangerous rock. This bell is quiet enough in ordinary weather; but when the winds are out, and the great waves rush in toward the shore, its solemn tones are heard for miles around as it swings to and fro in the hands of the sea. I believe there are true men who are silent when everything is calm, who will be forced to speak when the wild winds are out. Permit me to assure you that a storm is raging now, and it is growing worse and worse. If I rightly read the signs of the times, it is meet that every bell should ring out its warning note lest souls be lost upon the rocks of error. You that have fallen behind, because the fighting did not seem to require you, must quit your positions of ease. I summon you in the Master's name to the war. The Lord hath need of you. If you come not to his help against the mighty, a curse will light upon you. You must either be written across the back as *craven cowards*, or else you will today solemnly espouse the cause of Jesus. Shall I tell you why?

I will tell you why Joseph was wanted, and that was, just because *Christ's enemies had at last gone too far.* When they hunted him about and took up stones to stone him, they went a very long way; when they said he had a devil and was mad, they went much too far; when they asserted that he cast out devils by Beelzebub, the prince of the devils, that was a piece of blasphemy; but now, now they have overstepped the line most fatally; they have actually taken the King of Israel and nailed him up to a cross, and he is dead; and therefore Joseph cannot stand it any longer. He quits their company and joins himself to the Lord Jesus. See how far men are going in these days. In the outside world we have infidelity of so gross, so brutish, a character, that it is unworthy of the civilization, much less of the Christianity, of our age.

Now, you fearful ones, come out, and refuse to be numbered with the unbelieving world. Besides, in the outward Christian church we see men who, having already taken away every doctrine that we hold dear, are now assailing the inspiration of God's own Word. They tell us plainly that they do not believe what the Scriptures say further than they choose to do. The Bible to them is a fine book, but rather out of date. Now if you can be quiet, I cannot. The citadel of Christendom is now attacked. Let no brave man shrink from its defense. If you can hold your tongues and see the faith rent to pieces, I cannot. Why, it is enough to make every man gird on his weapon and rush to the fight.

Years ago, when they talked of the French invading England, an old lady grew very indignant and threatened deadly resistance. When she was asked what the women of England could do, she said they would rise to a man. I have no doubt whatever that they would do their best in any such emergency. Every iron in the fireplace, whether it be poker or shovel, would be grasped to defend our hearths and homes, and just so now, when error knows no bounds, we must stand up for the defense of the truth. Since they push error to extremes, it becomes us to hold by every particle of the faith. I will not, for my own part, give up a corner of my creed for any man. Even if we might have been prepared to modify expressions had the age been different, we are not in that mood now. A generation of vipers shall have a naked [iron] file to bite at. We will modify nothing. If truth bears a stern aspect, we will not veil it. If there be an offense in the cross, we will not conceal it. This shall be my answer to those who would have us attune ourselves to the spirit of the age: I know no Spirit but one, and he is unchanging in every age. Your extravagance of doubt shall have no influence over us except to make us bind the gospel more closely to our hearts. If we gave you an inch, you would take a mile, and so no inch shall be given you. Our resolve is to live for the Book as we read it, for the gospel as we rest in it, for the Lord as he made atonement, for the kingdom as it rules over all. I beg every trembling Christian to take heart, put on his Lord's livery, and advance to the fray. Come out now, if you never did before! Come out, if there is any manliness in you, in these days of blasphemy and rebuke.

> *Ye that are men, now serve him,*
> *Against unnumbered foes;*
> *Your courage rise with danger,*
> *And strength to strength oppose.*

When Joseph of Arimathaea revealed himself as our Lord's disciple, *our Lord's friends had mostly fled*—we might almost say they had all departed. Then Joseph said, "I will go in and beg for the body." When everybody else runs away, then the timid man grows brave; and often have I noticed it, that when there has been a wide desertion from the faith, then the feeble have become strong. Those poor souls who had said, "You hardly know whether we are the people of God at all, we are so unworthy," have crept out of their dens and have waxed valiant in fight, putting to flight the armies of the aliens. A sister was asked to tell her experience before the church, and she could not do it; but as she went away, she turned around and said, "I cannot speak for Christ, but I could die for him." "Come back," said the minister, "you are welcome here!" They do gloriously, those hidden ones, in days whereof we are apt to fear that no witness for the truth will remain alive. O that you who live where religion is declining may be all the more resolved to serve the Lord Jesus faithfully!

And then, you know, in Joseph's time *the people that were true to the Lord Jesus were such a feeble company*. Those that were not absolutely poor—the women that could minister to him of their substance—were nevertheless unable to go in unto Pilate and beg for the Lord's body. He would not have received them, and if he would they were too timid to have sought an interview; but Joseph is rich, and a counselor, and therefore he seemed to say, "These dear good women need a friend; they cannot get that precious body down from the cross alone. I will go to the Roman governor. Together with Nicodemus, I will provide the linen and the spices, and the women shall help us take Jesus down from the tree and lay him in my new tomb, and swathe his limbs in linen and spices, so as to embalm him honorably." Some of you live in country towns where those who are faithful to God are very poor, and have not much ability among them. If anything should move you to be the more decided, it should be that fact. It is a brave thing to help a feeble company; any common people will follow at the heels of success, but the true man is not ashamed of a despised cause when it is the cause of truth. You who have talent and substance should say, "I will go and help them now. I cannot leave the Master's cause to this feeble folk. I know they do their best, and as that is little, I will join them and lay myself out to aid them for my great Master's sake."

Can you not see my drift? My only desire this morning is to induce any of you who have for a moment faltered to "stand up, stand up for Jesus," and everywhere, in every place as wisdom may suggest, avow his dear and sacred name. Perhaps you are flowers that cannot bloom till the light is darkened, like the night-blooming cereus or the evening primrose. Now is your hour. The evening is already come; bloom, my dear friends, and fill the air with the delightful fragrance of your love. When other flowers are closed, take care to open to the dew. In these dark hours shine out, you stars! The sun has gone, else you might lie hid; but now let us see you! Joseph and Nicodemus had never been seen in the daylight when Jesus was alive; but when the sun was set through his death, then their radiance beamed at its full. O my hesitating brother, now is your time and your hour: boldly avail yourself of it, for our great Master's sake!

IV. Last, there is something in this subject for *our guidance.*

Somebody says, "Well, what do you mean by my coming out? I can see what Joseph did. What am I to do? I do not live at Arimathaea, and there is no Pilate in these days."

Joseph in owning his Lord *put himself under personal risk.* A Christian slave, whose master was executed for being a Christian, went to the judge and begged the body of his master that he might bury it. The judge replied, "Wherefore do you wish for your master's body?" "Because he was a Christian, and I am one." Upon this confession he was himself condemned to die. It might have been so with Pilate; for the Jewish rulers must have hated Joseph and longed for his death. He had been backward a long time, but now he put his life in his hand, and went in boldly to Pilate. We read, "He craved the body of Jesus"; but, as a commentator well says, he was not a craven, though he craved the body. He simply asked for it, begged for it, implored to have it, and the procurator yielded to his wish. Now do you think that if it were needful for you to jeopardize your best earthly interests for Christ, you could do it? Could you lose your character for culture and courage by avowing the old faith in these apostate days? Can you leave all for Jesus? Should it rend the fondest connection, should it break up the brightest prospects, could you take up the cross and follow your Lord? It is due to him who died for you that you should count the cost, and reckon it little enough for his dear sake, if you may but do him honor.

Remember, again, that this good man, Joseph of Arimathaea, when he took the body of Jesus, brought upon himself *ceremonial pollution.* It may seem little enough to you, but to a Jew it was a great deal, especially during the Passover week. He handled that blessed body and defiled himself in the judgment of the Jews. But, oh, I warrant you he did not think it any defilement to touch the blessed person of his Lord, even when the life was gone out of that matchless frame. Nor was it any pollution. It was an honor to touch that holy thing, that body prepared of God. Yet they will say to you, if you come out for Christ and unite with his people, that you lower yourself. They will point at you, give you some opprobrious name, and charge you with fanaticism. Take upon yourself this blessed shame, and say, as David did, "I will be yet more vile." Dishonor for Christ is honor, and shame for him is the very top of all glory. You will not stand back, I trust, but you will come forward and avow your faith, though you thus become as the offscouring of all things.

And then, this man having risked his life, and given up his honor was content to be *at great cost for the burial of Christ.* He went and bought the fine linen, and that rock-hewn sepulcher which it was the ambition of every Israelite to possess, he cheerfully resigned, that the Lord might lie there. Now, whenever you do own Christ, own him practically. Do not keep back your purse from him, or think that you are to say, "I am his," and do nothing for him. I was reading the story of a good old deacon in Maine, in America, who came into a meeting after there had been a missionary collection. The minister there and then asked "our good brother Sewell" to pray. Sewell did not pray, but thrust his hand in his pocket and stood fumbling about. "Bring the box," he said; and when the box came, and he had put his money into it, the minister said, "Brother Sewell? I did not ask you to give anything. I only wished you to pray." "Oh," said he, "I could not pray till I had first given something." He felt obliged first to do something for the great mission work, and having done that he could pray for it. Oh, that all Christ's people felt the justice of that course of conduct! Is it not most natural and proper? Joseph could not, when the Savior wanted burying, have been true to him without burying him. And now that the Savior does not want burying, but wants in all his living power to be preached among the sons of men, if we love him we must do all that lies in us to spread the knowledge of his name. Come out then, come out then, you that are hidden among the stud! Some of you strangers from the country, who have lived in the village and attended the services but never joined the church, do not let another Sunday dawn till you have sent in your name to be classed with the people of God. And any of you that have come often to the tabernacle, and say that nobody has spoken to you, just you speak to somebody and own what the Lord has done for you. Joseph of Arimathaea, where are you? Come forward, man! Come forth; your time has come! Come forth now! If you have followed Christ secretly, throw secrecy to the winds! Henceforth be bravest of the brave, among the bodyguard of Christ, who follow him whithersoever he goeth. Have no fear nor thought of fear, but count it all joy if you fall into manifold trials for his name's sake, who is King of kings and Lord of lords, to whom be glory forever and ever. Amen.

Simon of Cyrene: Up from the Country, and Pressed into the Service

◄♦►

Delivered on Lord's Day morning, August 2, 1885, at the Metropolitan Tabernacle, Newington. No. 1853.

And they compel one Simon a Cyrenian, who passed by, coming out of the country, the father of Alexander and Rufus, to bear his cross.—MARK 15:21

John tells us that our Savior went forth bearing his cross (John 19:17). We are much indebted to John for inserting that fact. The other Evangelists mention Simon the Cyrenian as bearing the cross of Christ; but John, who often fills up gaps which are left by the other three, tells us that Jesus set out to Calvary carrying his own cross. Our Lord Jesus came out from Pilate's palace laden with his cross, but he was so extremely emaciated and so greatly worn by the night of the bloody sweat, that the procession moved too slowly for the rough soldiers, and therefore they took the cross from their prisoner and laid it upon Simon; or possibly they laid the long end upon the shoulder of the strong countryman, while the Savior still continued to bear in part his cross till he came to the place of doom.

It is well that we should be told that the Savior bore his cross; for if it had not been so, objectors would have had grounds for disputation. I hear them say, "You admit that one of the most prominent types, in the Old Testament, of the sacrifice of the Son of God, was Abraham's offering up his son Isaac; now Abraham laid the wood upon Isaac his son, and not upon a servant. Should not therefore the Son of God bear the cross himself?" Had not our Lord carried his cross, there would have been a flaw in his fulfillment of the type; therefore the Savior must bear the wood when he goes forth to be offered up as a sacrifice. One of the greatest of English preachers has well reminded us that the fulfillment of this type appeared to have been in eminent jeopardy, since, at the very first, our Lord's weakness must have been apparent, and the reason which led to the laying of the cross upon the Cyrenian might have prevented our Lord's carrying the cross at all. If the soldiers had a little earlier put the cross upon Simon, which they might very naturally have done, then the prophecy had not been fulfilled; but God has the minds of men so entirely at his control, that even in the minutest circumstance he can order all things so as to complete the merest jots and tittles of the prophecy. Our Lord was made to be, in all points, an Isaac, and therefore we see him going forth bearing the wood of the burnt offering. Thus you see that it was important that Jesus should for a while bear his own cross.

But it was equally instructive that someone else should be made a partaker of the burden; for it has always been part of the divine counsel that for the salvation of men from sin the Lord should be associated with his church. So far as atonement is concerned, the Lord has trodden the winepress alone, and of the people there was none with him; but as far as the conversion of the world is concerned, and its rescue from the power of error and wickedness, Christ is not alone. We are workers together with God. We are ourselves to be in the hands of God part-bearers of the sorrow and travail by which men are to be delivered from the bondage of sin and Satan, and brought into the liberty of truth and righteousness. Hence it became important that in the bearing of the cross, though not in the death upon it, there should be yoked with the Christ one who should follow close behind him. To bear the cross after Jesus is the office of the faithful. Simon the Cyrenian is the representative of the whole church of God, and of each believer in particular. Often had Jesus said, "Except a man take up his cross daily and follow me, he cannot be my disciple"; and now at last he embodies that sermon in an actual person. The disciple must be as his Master: he that would follow the Crucified must himself bear the cross: this we see visibly set forth in Simon of Cyrene with the cross of Jesus laid upon his shoulder.

> Shall Simon bear the cross alone,
> And all the rest go free?
> No, there's a cross for every one,
> And there's a cross for me.

The lesson to each one of us is to take up our Lord's cross without delay, and go with him—without the camp, bearing his reproach. That many among this vast and mixed congregation may imitate Simon is the anxious desire of my heart. With holy expectancy I gaze upon this throng collected from all parts of the earth, and I long to find in it some who will take my Lord's yoke upon them this day.

I. I will begin with this first remark, that *unexpected persons are often called to cross bearing*.

Like Simon, they are impressed into the service of Christ. Our text says: "They compel one Simon a Cyrenian, who passed by, coming out of the country, the father of Alexander and Rufus, to bear his cross." Simon did not volunteer, but was forced into this work of cross bearing. It would seem from another Evangelist that he speedily yielded to the impressment, and lifted the burden heartily; but at first he was compelled. A rude authority was exercised by the guard, who being upon the governor's business acted with high-handed rigor and forced whomsoever they pleased to do their bidding. By the exercise of such irresponsible power, they compelled a passing stranger to carry Christ's cross. It was specially singular that the man to have this honor was not Peter nor James nor John nor any one of the many who had for years listened to the Redeemer's speech; but it was a stranger from Northern Africa, who had been in no way connected with the life or teachings of Jesus of Nazareth.

Notice, first, that *he was an unknown man*. He was spoken of "as one Simon." Simon was a very common name among the Jews, almost as common as John in our own country. This man was just "one Simon"—an individual who need not be further described. But the providence of God had determined that this obscure individual, this certain man, or I might better say, this uncertain man, should be selected to the high office of cross bearer to the Son of God. I have an impression upon my mind that there is "one Simon" here this morning, who has to bear Christ's cross from this time forward. I feel persuaded that I am right. That person is so far unknown that most probably he does not recognize a single individual in all this throng, neither does anybody in this assembly know anything of him: certainly the preacher does not. He is one John, one Thomas, or one William; or perhaps, in the feminine, she is one Mary, one Jane, one Maggie. Friend, nobody knows you save our Father who is in heaven, and he has appointed you to have fellowship with his Son. I shall roughly describe you as "one Simon," and leave the Holy Spirit to bring you into your place and service. But this "one Simon" was a very particular "one Simon." I lay the emphasis where there might seem to be no need of any: he was one whom God knew and chose and loved and set apart for this special service. In a congregation like the present, there may be somebody whom our God intends to use for his glory during the rest of his life. That person sits in the pew and listens to what I am saying, and perhaps as yet he does not begin to inquire whether he is that "one Simon," that one person; and yet it is so, and before this sermon is ended, he shall know that the call to bear the cross is for him. Many more unlikely things than this have happened in this house of prayer. I pray that many a man may go out from this house a different man from the man he was when he entered it an hour ago.

That man Saul, that great persecutor of the church, afterward became such a mighty preacher of the gospel that people exclaimed with wonder, "There is a strange alteration in this man." "Why," said one, "when I knew him he was a Pharisee of the Pharisees. He was as bigoted a man as ever wore a phylactery, and he hated Christ and Christians so intensely that he could never persecute the church sufficiently." "Yes," replied another, "it was so; but he has had a strange twist. They say that he was going down to Damascus to hunt out the disciples, and something happened; we do not know exactly what it was, but evidently it gave him such a turn that he has never been himself since. In fact, he seems turned altogether upside down, and the current of his life is evidently reversed: he lives enthusiastically for that faith which once he destroyed." This speedy change happened to "one Saul of Tarsus." There were plenty of Sauls in Israel, but upon this one Saul electing love had looked in the counsels of eternity; for that Saul redeeming love had shed its heart's blood, and in that Saul effectual grace worked mightily. Is there another Saul here today? The Lord grant that he may now cease to kick against the pricks, and may we soon hear of him, "Behold, he prayeth." I feel convinced the counterpart of that "one Simon" is in this house at this moment, and my prayer goes up to God, and I hope it is attended with the prayers of many thousands besides, that he may at once submit to the Lord Jesus.

It did not seem likely that Simon should bear the cross of Christ, for he was a stranger who had newly come up from the country. He probably knew little or nothing of what had been taking place in Jerusalem; for he had come from another continent. He was "one Simon a Cyrenian"; and I suppose that Cyrene could not have been less than eight hundred miles from Jerusalem. It was situated in what is now called Tripoli, in Northern Africa, in which place a colony of Jews had been formed long before. Very likely he had come in a Roman galley from Alexandria to Joppa, and there had been rowed through the surf, and landed in time to reach Jerusalem for the Passover. He had long wanted to come to Jerusalem; he had heard the fame of the temple and of the city of his fathers; and he had longed to see the great assembly of the tribes, and the solemn Paschal feast. He had traveled all those miles, he had hardly yet got the motion of the ship out of his brain, and it had never entered into his head that he should be impressed by the Roman guard, and made to assist at an execution. It was a singular providence that he should come into the city at the moment of the turmoil about Jesus, and should have crossed the street just as the sad procession started on its way to Golgotha. He passed by neither too soon nor too late; he was on the spot as punctually as if he had made an appointment to be there; and yet, as men speak, it was all by mere chance. I cannot tell how many providences had worked together to bring him there at the nick of time, but so the Lord would have it, and so it came about. He, a man there in Cyrene, in Northern Africa, must at a certain date, at the tick of the clock, be at Jerusalem, in order that he might help to carry the cross up to Mount Calvary; and he was there. Ah! my dear friend, I do not know what providences have been at work to bring you here today; perhaps very strange ones. If a little something had occurred, you had not taken this journey; it only needed a small dust to turn the scale, and you would have been hundreds of miles from this spot, in quite another scene from this. Why you are here you do not yet know, except that you have come to listen to the preacher, and join the throng. But God knows why he has brought you here. I trust it will be read in the annals of the future:

> *Thus the eternal mandate ran,*
> *Almighty grace arrest that man.*

God has brought you here, that on this spot, by the preaching of the gospel, you may be compelled to bear the cross of Jesus. I pray it may be so. "One Simon a Cyrenian . . . coming out of the country," is here after a long journey, and this day he will begin to live a higher and a better life.

Further, notice, *Simon had come for another purpose.* He had journeyed to Jerusalem with no thought of bearing the cross of Jesus. Probably Simon was a Jew far removed from the land of his fathers, and he had made a pilgrimage to the Holy City to keep the Passover. Every Jew loved to be present at Jerusalem at the Paschal feast. So, to put it roughly, it was holiday time; it was a time for making an excursion to the capital; it was a season for making a journey and going up to the great city which was "beautiful for situation, the joy of the whole earth." Simon from far-off Cyrene must by all means keep the feast at Jerusalem. Maybe he had saved his money for months, that he might pay his fare to Joppa; and he had counted down the gold freely for the joy which he had in going to the city of David, and the temple of his God.

He was come for the Passover, and for that only; and he would be perfectly satisfied to go home when once the feast was over, and once he had partaken of the lamb with the tribes of Israel. Then he could say throughout the rest of his life, "I, too, was once at the great feast of our people, when we commemorated the coming up out of Egypt." Brethren, we propose one way, but

God has other propositions. We say, "I will step in and hear the preacher," but God means that the arrows of his grace shall stick fast in our hearts. Many and many a time with no desire for grace, men have listened to the gospel, and the Lord has been found of them that sought him not. I heard of one who cared little for the sermon till the preacher chanced to use that word eternity, and the hearer was taken prisoner by holy thoughts, and led to the Savior's feet. Men have stepped into places of worship even with evil designs, and yet the purpose of grace has been accomplished; they came to scoff, but they remained to pray. Some have been cast by the providence of God into positions where they have met with Christian men, and a word of admonition has been blessed to them. A lady was one day at an evening party, and there met with Caesar Malan, the famous divine of Geneva, who, in his usual manner, inquired of her whether she was a Christian. She was startled, surprised, and vexed, and made a short reply to the effect that it was not a question she cared to discuss; whereupon, Mr. Malan replied with great sweetness, that he would not persist in speaking of it, but he would pray that she might be led to give her heart to Christ, and become a useful worker for him. Within a fortnight she met the minister again, and asked him how she must come to Jesus. Mr. Malan's reply was, "Come to him just as you are." That lady gave herself up to Jesus: it was Charlotte Elliott, to whom we owe that precious hymn—

> *Just as I am—without one plea*
> *But that thy blood was shed for me*
> *And that thou bidd'st me come to thee—*
> *O Lamb of God, I come.*

It was a blessed thing for her that she was at that party, and that the servant of God from Geneva should have been there, and should have spoken to her so faithfully. Oh, for many a repetition of the story "of one Simon a Cyrenian," coming, not with the intent to bear the cross, but with quite another mind, and yet being enlisted in the cross-bearing army of the Lord Jesus!

I would have you notice, once more, that this man was at this particular time not thinking upon the subject at all, for *he was at that time merely passing by.* He had come up to Jerusalem, and whatever occupied his mind he does not appear to have taken any notice of the trial of Jesus, or of the sad end of it. It is expressly said that he "passed by." He was not even sufficiently interested in the matter to stand in the crowd and look at the mournful procession. Women were weeping there right bitterly—the daughters of Jerusalem to whom the Master said, "Weep not for me, but weep for yourselves, and for your children"; but this man passed by. He was anxious to hurry away from so unpleasant a sight, and to get up to the temple. He was quietly making his way through the crowd, eager to go about his business, and he must have been greatly surprised and distressed when a rough hand was laid upon him, and a stern voice said, "Shoulder that cross." There was no resisting a Roman centurion when he gave command, and so the countryman meekly submitted, wishing, no doubt, that he were back in Cyrene tilling the ground. He must needs stoop his shoulder and take up a new burden, and tread in the footsteps of the mysterious personage to whom the cross belonged. He was only passing by, and yet he was enlisted and impressed by the Romans, and, as I take it, impressed by the grace of God for life; for whereas Mark says he was the father of Alexander and Rufus, it would seem that his sons were well known to the Christian people to whom Mark was writing. If his son was the same Rufus that Paul mentions, then he calls her [his mother] "his mother and mine"; and it would seem that Simon's wife and his sons became believers and partakers of the sufferings of Christ. His contact with the Lord in that strange compulsory way probably worked out for him another and more spiritual contact which made him a true cross bearer. O you that pass by this day, draw nigh to Jesus! I have no wish to call your attention to myself, far from it; but I do ask your attention to my Lord. Though you only intended to slip into this tabernacle and slip out again, I pray that you may be arrested by a call from my Lord. I speak as my Lord's servant, and I would constrain you to come to him. Stand where you are a while, and let me beg you to yield to his love, which even now would cast the bands of a man around you. I would compel you, by my Lord's authority, to take up his cross and bear it after him. It would be strange, say you. Yes, so it might be, but it would be a glorious event. I remember Mr. Knill, speaking of his own conversion, used an expression which I should like to use concerning one of you. Here it is: "It was just a quarter past twelve, August 2, when twang went every harp in paradise; for a sinner had repented." May it be so with you. Oh, that every harp in paradise may now ring out the high praises of sovereign grace, as you now yield yourself to the great Shepherd and Bishop of souls! May that divine impressment which is imaged in the text by the compulsion of the Roman soldier take place in your case at this very moment; and may it be seen in your instance that unexpected persons are often called to be cross bearers!

II. My second observation is—*cross bearing can still be practiced*. Very briefly let me tell you in what ways the cross can still be carried.

First, and chiefly, *by your becoming a Christian*. If the cross shall take you up, you will take up the cross. Christ will be your hope, his death your trust, himself the object of your love. You never become a cross bearer truly till you lay your burdens down at his feet who bore the cross and curse for you.

Next, you become a cross bearer *when you make an open avowal of the Lord Jesus Christ*. Do not deceive yourselves; this is expected of each one of you if you are to be saved. The promise as I read it in the New Testament is not to the believer alone, but to the believer who confesses his faith. "He that with his heart believeth and with his mouth maketh confession of him shall be saved." He says, "He that confesseth me before men, him will I confess before my Father; but he that denieth me"—and from the connection it should seem to mean, *he that does not confess me*—"him will I deny before my Father which is in heaven." To quote the inspired Scripture, "He that believeth and is baptized shall be saved." There should be, there must be, the open avowal in Christ's own way of the secret faith which you have in him. Now this is often a cross. Many people would like to go to heaven by an underground railway—secrecy suits them. They do not want to cross the channel; the sea is too rough; but when there is a tunnel made they will go to the fair country. My good people, you are cowardly, and I must quote to you a text which ought to sting your cowardice out of you: "But the fearful and unbelieving shall have their part in the lake which burneth with fire and brimstone." I say no more, and make no personal applications; but, I beseech you, run no risks. Be afraid to be afraid. Be ashamed of being ashamed of Christ. Shame on that man who counts it any shame to say before assembled angels, and men, and devils, "I am a follower of Christ." May you who have been secret followers of the crucified Lord become manifest cross bearers! Do you not even now cry out, "Set down my name, sir"?

Further, some have to take up their cross by *commencing Christian work*. You live in a village where there is no gospel preaching: preach yourself. You are in a backwoods town where the preaching is very far from being such as God approves of: begin to preach the truth yourself. "Alas!" say you, "I should make a fool of myself." Are you ashamed to be a fool for Christ? "Oh, but I should break down." Break down: it will do you good, and perhaps you may break somebody else down. There is no better preaching in the world than that of a man who breaks down under a sense of unworthiness: if that breakdown communicates itself to other people, it may begin a revival. If you are choked by your earnestness, others may become earnest too. Do you still murmur, "But I should get the ill will of everybody"? For Christ's sake could you not bear that? When the good monk said to Martin Luther, "Go home to your cell and keep quiet," why did not Martin take the advice? Why, indeed?

"It is very bad for young people to be so forward; you will do a great deal of mischief, therefore be quiet, you Martin. Who are you to interfere with the great authorities? Be holy for yourself, and don't trouble others. If you stir up a reformation thousands of good people will be burned through you. Do be quiet." Bless God, Martin did not go home, and was not quiet, but went about his Master's business, and raised heaven and earth by his brave witness bearing. Where are you, Martin, this morning? I pray God to call you out, and as you have confessed his name and are his servant, I pray that he may make you bear public testimony for him, and tell out the saving power of the Savior's precious blood. Come, Simon, I see you shrink; but the cross has to be carried; therefore bow your back. It is only a wooden cross, after all, and not an iron one. You can bear it: you must bear it. God help you.

Perhaps, too, some brother may have to take up his cross by *bearing witness against the rampant sin which surrounds him*. "Leave all those dirty matters alone; do not say a word about them. Let the people go to the devil, or else you will soil your white kid gloves." Sirs, we will spoil our hands as well as our gloves, and we will risk our characters, if need be; but we will put down the devilry which now defiles London. Truly the flesh does shrink, and the purest part of our manhood shrinks with it, when we are compelled to bear open protest against sins which are done of men in secret. But Simon, the Master may yet compel you to bear his cross in this respect, and if so, he will give you both courage and wisdom, and your labor shall not be in vain in the Lord.

Sometimes, however, the cross bearing is of another and more quiet kind, and may be described as *submission to providence*. A young friend is saying, "For me to live at home I know to be my duty; but father is unkind, and the family generally imposes upon me. I wish I could get away." Ah! dear sister, you must bear Christ's cross, and it may be the Lord would have you remain at home. Therefore bear the cross. A servant is saying, "I should like to be in a Christian family. I do not think I can stop where I am." Perhaps, good sister, the Lord has put you where you are to be a light in a dark place. All the lamps should not be in one street, or what will become of the courts and alleys? It is often the duty of a Christian man to say, "I shall stop where I am and fight this matter through. I mean by character and example, with kindness and courtesy and love, to win this place for Jesus." Of course the easy way is to turn monk and live quietly in a cloister, and serve God by doing nothing; or to turn nun and dwell in a convent, and expect to win the battle of life by running out of it. Is not this absurd? If you shut yourself away from this poor world, what is to become of it? You men and women that are Christians must stand up and stand out for Jesus where the providence of God has cast you: if your calling is not a sinful one, and if the temptations around you are not too great for you, you must "hold the fort" and never dream of surrender. If your lot is hard, look upon it as Christ's cross, and bow your back to the load. Your shoulder may be raw at first, but you will grow stronger before long, for as your day, your strength shall be. "It is good for a man that he bear the yoke in his youth"; but it is good for a man to bear the cross in his old age as well as in his youth; in fact, we ought never to be quit of so blessed a burden. What wings are to a bird, and sails to a ship, that the cross becomes to a man's spirit when he fully consents to accept it as his life's beloved load. Truly did Jesus say, "My yoke is easy, and my burden is light." Now, Simon, where are you? Shoulder the cross, man, in the name of God!

III. Third, *to cross bearing there are noble compulsions.*

Simon's compulsion was the rough hand of the Roman legionary, and the gruff voice in the Latin tongue, "Shoulder that cross"; but we hear gentler voices which compel us this day to take up Christ's cross.

The first compulsion is this: *"the love of Christ constraineth us."* He has done all this for you; therefore by sweet but irresistible compulsion you are made to render him some return of love. Does not Jesus appear to you in a vision as you sit in this house? Do you not see that thorn-crowned head, that visage crimsoned with the bloody sweat, those hands and feet pierced with the nails? Does he not say to you pointedly, "I did all this for thee; what hast thou done for me"? Startled in your seat, you cover your face, and inwardly reply, "I will answer that question by the rest of my life. I will be first and foremost a servant of Jesus: not a trader first and a Christian next, but a Christian first and a businessman afterward." You, my sister, must say, "I will live for Christ as a daughter, a wife, or a mother. I will live for my Lord; for he has given himself for me, and I am not my own, but bought with a price."

The true heart will feel a compulsion arising from a second reflection, namely, *the glory of a life spent for God and for his Christ.* What is the life of a man who toils in business, makes money, becomes rich, and dies? It winds up with a paragraph in the *Illustrated London News*, declaring that he died worth so much: the wretch was not worth anything himself; his estate had value, he had none. Had he been worth anything he would have sent his money about the world doing good; but as a worthless steward he laid his Master's stores in heaps to rot. The life of multitudes of men is self-seeking. It is ill for a man to live the life of swine. What a poor creature is the usual ordinary man! But a life spent for Jesus, though it involve cross bearing, is noble, heroic, sublime.

The mere earthworm leads a dunghill life. A life of what is called pleasure is a mean, beggarly business. A life of keeping up respectability is utter slavery—as well be a horse in a pug mill. A life wholly consecrated to Christ and his cross is life indeed; it is akin to the life of angels; yes, higher still, it is the life of God within the soul of man. O you that have a spark of true nobility, seek to live lives worth living, worth remembering, worthy to be the commencement of eternal life before the throne of God.

Some of you ought to feel the cross coming upon your shoulders this morning when you think of *the needs of those among whom you live*. They are dying, perishing for lack of knowledge, rich and poor alike ignorant of Christ; multitudes of them wrapped up in self-righteousness. They are perishing, and those who ought to warn them are often dumb dogs that cannot bark. Do you not feel that you ought to deliver the sheep from the wolf? Have you no bowels of compassion? Are your hearts turned to steel? I am sure you cannot deny that the times demand of you earnest and forceful lives. No Christian man can now sit still without incurring awful guilt. Whether you live in London or in any other great town amid reeking sin, or dwell in the country amid the dense darkness which broods over many rural districts, you are under bonds to be up and doing. It may be a cross to you, but for Jesus' sake you must uplift it, and never lay it down till the Lord calls you home.

Some of you should bear the cross of Christ *because the cause of Christ is at a discount where you dwell*. I delight in a man in whom the lordlier chivalry has found a congenial home. He loves to espouse the cause of truth in the cloudy and dark day. He never counts heads, but weighs arguments. When he settles down in a town, he never inquires, "Where is the most respectable congregation? Where shall I meet with those who will advantage me in business?" No, he studies his conscience rather than his convenience. He hears one say, "There is a Nonconformist chapel, but it is down a back street. There is a Baptist church, but the members are nearly all poor, and no gentlefolk are among them. Even the evangelical church is down at the heel: the best families attend the high church." I say he hears this, and his heart is sick of such talk. He will go where the gospel is preached, and nowhere else. Fine architecture has scant charms for him, and grand music is no part of his religion: if these are substitutes for the gospel, he abhors them. It is meanness itself for a man to forsake the truth for the sake of respectability. Multitudes who ought to be found maintaining the good old cause are recreant to their convictions, if indeed they ever had any. For this cause the true man resolves to stick to truth through thick and thin, and not to forsake her because her adherents are poor and despised. If ever we might temporize, that time is past and gone. I arrest yonder man this morning, who has long been a Christian, but has concealed half his Christianity in order to be thought respectable, or to escape the penalties of faithfulness. Come out from those with whom you are numbered, but with whom you are not united in heart. Be brave enough to defend good cause against all comers; for the day shall come when he shall have honor for his guerdon [reward] who accepted dishonor that he might be true to his God, his Bible, and his conscience. Blessed be he that can be loyal to his Lord, cost him what it may—loyal even in those matters which traitors call little things. We would compel that Simon the Cyrenian this day to bear the cross, because there are so few to bear it in these degenerate days.

Besides, I may say to some of you, you ought to bear the cross because you know you are not satisfied; *your hearts are not at rest.* You have prospered in worldly things, but you are not happy; you have good health, but you are not happy; you have loving friends, but you are not happy. There is but one way of getting rest to the heart and that is, to come to Jesus. That is his word: "Come unto me, all ye that labor and are heavy laden, and I will give you rest." If after this you need a further rest for other and higher longings, then you must come again to the same Savior, and hearken to his next word: "Take my yoke upon you, and learn of me; for I am meek and lowly in heart: and ye shall find rest unto your souls. For my yoke is easy, and my burden is light." Some of you professors have not yet found perfect rest, and the reason is because you have looked to the cross for pardon, but you have never taken to cross bearing as an occupation. You are hoping in Christ but not living for Christ. The finding of rest unto your soul will come to you in having something to do or to bear for Jesus. "Take my yoke upon you: and ye shall find rest unto your souls."

There are many ways, then, of bearing the cross for Christ, and there are many reasons why some here present should begin at once to carry the load.

IV. To close: bear with me a minute or two while I say that *cross bearing is a blessed occupation.*

I feel sure that Simon found it so. Let me mention certain blessings which must have attended the special service of Simon. First, *it brought him into Christ's company.* When they compelled him to bear his cross, he was brought close to Jesus. If it had not been for that compulsion, he might have gone his way, or might have been lost in the crowd; but now he is in the inner circle, near to Jesus. For the first time in his life he saw that blessed form, and as he saw it I believe his heart was enamored with it. As they lifted the cross on his shoulders, he looked at that sacred Person, and saw a crown of thorns about his brow; and as he looked at his fellow sufferer, he saw all down his cheeks the marks of bloody sweat, and black and blue bruises from cruel hands. As for those eyes, they looked him through and through! That face, that matchless face, he had never seen its like. Majesty was therein blended with misery, innocence with agony, and love with sorrow. He had never seen that countenance so well, nor marked the whole form of the Son of man so clearly if he had not been called to bear that cross. It is wonderful how much we see of Jesus when we suffer or labor for him. Believing souls, I pray that this day you may be so impressed into my Lord's service, that you may have nearer and dearer fellowship with him than in the past. If any man will do his will he shall know of the doctrine. They see Jesus best who carry his cross most.

Besides, *the cross held Simon in Christ's steps*. Do you catch it? If Jesus carried the front part of the cross and Simon followed behind, he was sure to put his feet down just where the Master's feet had been before. The cross is a wonderful implement for keeping us in the way of our Lord. As I was turning this subject over, I was thinking how of often I had felt a conscious contact between myself and my Lord when I have had to bear reproach for his sake; and how at the same time I have been led to watch my steps more carefully because of that very reproach. Brethren, we do not want to slip from under the cross. If we did so, we might slip away from our Lord and from holy walking. If we can keep our shoulder beneath that sacred load, and see our Lord a little on before, we shall be making the surest progress. This being near to Jesus is a blessed privilege, which is cheaply purchased at the price of cross bearing. If you would see Jesus, bestir yourselves to work for him. Boldly avow him, cheerfully suffer for him, and then you shall see him, and then you shall learn to follow him step by step. A blessed cross, which holds us to Jesus and to his ways!

Then Simon had this honor, that *he was linked with Christ's work*. He could not put away sin, but he could assist weakness. Simon did not die on the cross to make expiation, but he did live under the cross to aid in the accomplishment of the divine purpose. You and I cannot interfere with Jesus in his passion, but we can share with him in his commission; we cannot purchase liberty for the enslaved, but we can tell them of their emancipation. To have a finger in Christ's work is glory. I invite the man that seeks honor and immortality, to seek it thus. To have a share in the Redeemer's work is a more attractive thing than all the pomp and glitter of this world and the kingdoms thereof. Where are the men of heavenly mind who will covet to be joined unto the Lord in this ministry? Let them step out and say, "Jesus, I my cross have taken. Henceforth I will follow thee. Come life or death, I will carry thy cross till thou shalt give me the crown."

While Simon was carrying the cross through the crowd, I doubt not that the rough soldiery would deal him many a kick or buffet—but I feel equally sure that the dear Master sometimes stole a glance at him. *Simon enjoyed Christ's smile.* I know the Lord so well, that I feel sure he must have done so: he would not forget the man who was his partner for the while. And oh, that look! How Simon must have treasured up the remembrance of it. "I never carried a load that was so light," says he, "as that which I carried that morning; for when the blessed One smiled at me amid his woes, I felt myself to be strong as Hercules." Alexander, his firstborn, and that red-headed lad Rufus, when they grew up both felt it to be the honor of the family that their father carried the cross after Jesus. Rufus and Alexander had a patent of nobility in being the sons of such a man. Mark recorded the fact that Simon carried the cross, and that such and such persons were his sons. I think when the old man came to lie upon his deathbed, he said: "My hope is in him whose cross I carried. Blessed burden! Lay me down in my grave. This body of mine cannot perish, for it bore the cross which Jesus carried, and which carried *him.* I shall rise again to see him in his glory, for his cross has pressed me, and his love will surely raise me." Happy are we if we can while yet we live be coworkers together with him, that when he cometh in his kingdom we may be partakers of his glory. "Blessed is the man that endureth temptation: for when he is tried, he shall receive the crown of life, which the Lord hath promised to them that love him." God bless you, and especially you who have come out of the country. God bless you. Amen and amen.

Dismas: The Dying Thief in a New Light

✦✦✦

Intended for reading on Lord's Day, January 31, 1886, delivered on Lord's Day evening, August 23, 1885, at the Metropolitan Tabernacle, Newington. No. 1881.

> *But the other answering rebuked him, saying, "Dost not thou fear God, seeing thou art in the same condemnation? And we indeed justly; for we receive the due reward of our deeds: but this man hath done nothing amiss." And he said unto Jesus, "Lord, remember me when thou comest into thy kingdom."*
> —Luke 23:40–42

A great many persons, whenever they hear of the conversion of the dying thief, remember that he was saved in the very article of death, and they dwell upon that fact, and that alone. He has always been quoted as a case of salvation at the eleventh hour; and so, indeed, he is. In his case it is proven that as long as a man can repent, he can obtain forgiveness. The cross of Christ avails even for a man hanging on a gibbet, and drawing near to his last hour. He who is mighty to save was mighty, even during his own death, to pluck others from the grasp of the destroyer, though they were in the act of expiring.

But that is not everything which the story teaches us; and it is always a pity to look exclusively upon one point, and thus to miss everything else—perhaps miss that which is more important. So often has this been the case that it has produced a sort of revulsion of feeling in certain minds, so that they have been driven in a wrong direction by their wish to protest against what they think to be a common error. I read the other day that this story of the dying thief ought not to be taken as an encouragement to deathbed repentance. Brethren, if the author meant—and I do not think he did mean—that this ought never to be so used as to lead people to postpone repentance to a dying bed, he spoke correctly. No Christian man could or would use it so injuriously: he must be hopelessly bad who would draw from God's longsuffering an argument for continuing in sin. I trust, however, that the narrative is not often so used, even by the worst of men, and I feel sure that it will not be so used by any one of you. It cannot be properly turned to such a purpose: it might be used as an encouragement to thieving just as much as to the delay of repentance. I might say, "I may be a thief because this thief was saved," just as rationally as I might say, "I may put off repentance because this thief was saved when he was about to die." The fact is, there is nothing so good but men can pervert it into evil, if they have evil hearts: the justice of God is made a motive for despair, and his mercy an argument for sin. Wicked men will drown themselves in the rivers of truth as readily as in the pools of error. He that has a mind to destroy himself can choke his soul with the Bread of life, or dash himself in pieces against the Rock of ages. There is no doctrine of the grace of God so gracious that graceless men may not turn it into licentiousness.

I venture, however, to say that if I stood by the bedside of a dying man tonight, and I found him anxious about his soul, but fearful that Christ could not save him because repentance had been put off so late, I should certainly quote the dying thief to him, and I should do it with good conscience, and without hesitation. I should tell him that, though he was as near to dying as the thief upon the cross was, yet, if he repented of his sin, and turned his face to Christ believingly, he would find eternal life. I should do this with all my heart, rejoicing that I had such a story to tell to one at the gates of eternity. I do not think that I should be censured by the Holy Spirit for thus using a narrative which he has himself recorded, recorded with the foresight that it would be so used. I should feel, at any rate, in my own heart, a sweet conviction that I had treated the subject as I ought to have treated it, and as it was intended to be used for men *in extremis* whose hearts are turning toward the living God. Oh, yes, poor soul, whatever your age, or whatever the period of life to which you have come, you may now find eternal life by faith in Christ!

> *The dying thief rejoiced to see*
> *That fountain in his day;*
> *And there may you, though vile as he,*
> *Wash all your sins away.*

Many good people think that they ought to guard the gospel; but it is never so safe as when it stands out in its own naked majesty. It wants no covering from us. When we protect it with provisos, and guard it with exceptions, and qualify it with observations, it is like David in Saul's armor: it is hampered and hindered, and you may even hear it cry, "I cannot go with these." Let the gospel alone, and it will save; qualify it, and the salt has lost its savor. I will venture to put it thus to you. I have heard it said that few are ever converted in old age; and this is thought to be a statement which will prove exceedingly arousing and impressive for the young. It certainly wears that appearance; but, on the other hand, it is a statement very discouraging to the old. I demur to the frequent repetition of such statements, for I do not find their counterpart in the teaching of our Lord and his apostles. Assuredly our Lord spoke of some who entered the vineyard at the eleventh hour of the day; and among his miracles he not only saved those who were dying, but even raised the dead. Nothing can be concluded from the words of the Lord Jesus against the salvation of men at any hour or age. I tell you that, in the business of your acceptance with God, through faith in Christ Jesus, it does not matter what age you now are at. The same promise is to every one of you, "Today if ye will hear his voice, harden not your hearts"; and whether you are in the earliest stage of life, or are within a few hours of eternity, if now you fly for refuge to the hope set before you in the gospel, you shall be saved. The gospel that I preach excludes none on the ground either of age or character. Whoever you may be, "Believe on the Lord Jesus Christ, and thou shalt be saved" is the message we have to deliver to you. If we address to you the longer form of the gospel, "He that believeth and is baptized shall be saved," this is true of every living man, be his age whatever it may. I am not afraid that this story of the dying and repenting thief, who went straight from the cross to the crown, will be used by you amiss; but if you are wicked enough so to use it, I cannot help it. It will only fulfill that solemn Scripture which says that the gospel is a savor of death unto death to some, even that very gospel which is a savor of life unto life to others.

But I do not think, dear friends, that the only specialty about the thief is the lateness of his repentance. So far from being the only point of interest, it is not even the chief point. To some minds, at any rate, other points will be even more remarkable. I want to show you very briefly that there was a specialty in his case as to the means of his conversion; second, a specialty in his faith; third, a specialty in the result of his faith which he was here below; and, fourth, a specialty in the promise won by his faith—the promise fulfilled to him in paradise.

I. First, then, I think you ought to notice very carefully *the singularity and specialty of the means by which the thief was converted.*

How do you think it was? Well, we do not know. We cannot tell. It seems to me that the man was an unconverted, impenitent thief when they nailed him to the cross, because one of the Evangelists says, *"The thieves also,* which were crucified with him, *cast the same in his teeth."* I know that this may have been a general statement, and that it is reconcilable with its having been done by one thief only, according to the methods commonly used by critics; but I am not enamored of critics even when they are friendly. I have such respect for revelation that I never in my own mind permit the idea of discrepancies and mistakes, and when the Evangelist says "they" I believe he meant "they," and that both these thieves did at their first crucifixion rail at the Christ with whom they were crucified. It would appear that by some means or other this thief must have been converted while he was on the cross. Assuredly nobody preached a sermon to him, no evangelistic address was delivered at the foot of his cross, and no meeting was held for special prayer on his account. He does not even seem to have had an instruction, or an invitation, or an expostulation addressed to him; and yet this man became a sincere and accepted believer in the Lord Jesus Christ.

Dwell upon this fact, if you please, and note its practical bearing upon the cases of many around us. There are many among my hearers who have been instructed from their childhood, who have been admonished and warned and entreated and invited, and yet they have not come to Christ; while this man, without any of these advantages, nevertheless believed in the Lord Jesus Christ and found eternal life. O you that have lived under the sound of the gospel from your childhood, the thief does not comfort you, but he accuses you! What are you doing to abide so long in unbelief? Will you never believe the testimony of divine love? What more shall I say to you? What more can anyone say to you?

What do you think must have converted this poor thief? It strikes me that it may have been—it must have been—*the sight of our great Lord and Savior.* There was, to begin with, our Savior's wonderful behavior on the road to the cross. Perhaps the robber had mixed up with all sorts of society, but he had never seen a man like this. Never had cross been carried by a cross bearer of his look and fashion. The robber wondered who this meek and majestic personage could be. He heard the women weep, and he wondered in himself whether anybody would ever weep for him. He thought that this must be some very singular person that the people should stand about him with tears in their eyes. When he heard that mysterious sufferer say so solemnly, "Daughters of Jerusalem, weep not for me, but for your children," he must have been struck with wonder. When he came to think, in his death pangs, of the singular look of pity which Jesus cast on the women, and of the self-forgetfulness which gleamed from his eyes, he was smitten with a strange relenting: it was as if an angel had crossed his path and opened his eyes to a new world, and to a new form of manhood, the like of which he had never seen before. He and his companion were coarse, rough fellows: this was a delicately formed and fashioned Being, of superior order to himself; yes, and of superior order to any other of the sons of men. Who could he be? What must he be? Though he could see that he suffered and fainted as he went along, he marked that there was no word of complaining, no note of execration, in return for the revilings cast upon him. His eyes looked love on those who glared on him with hate. Surely that march along the Via Dolorosa was the first part of the sermon which God preached to that bad man's heart. It was preached to many others who did not regard its teaching; but upon this man, by God's special grace, it had a softening effect when he came to think over it, and consider it. Was it not a likely and convincing means of grace?

When he saw the Savior surrounded by the Roman soldiery—saw the executioners bring forth the hammers and the nails, and lay him down upon his back, and drive the nails into his hands and feet, this crucified criminal was startled and astonished as he heard him say, "Father, forgive them; for they know not what they do." He himself, probably, had met his executioners with a curse; but he heard this man breathe a prayer to the great Father; and, as a Jew, as he probably was, he understood what was meant by such a prayer. But it did astound him to hear Jesus pray for his murderers. That was a petition the like of which he had never heard, nor even dreamed of. From whose lips could it come but from the lips of a divine Being? Such a loving, forgiving, Godlike prayer proved him to be the Messiah. Who else had ever prayed so? Certainly not David and the kings of Israel, who, on the contrary, in all honesty and heartiness imprecated the wrath of God upon their enemies. Elijah himself would not have prayed in that fashion, rather would he have called fire from heaven on the centurion and his company. It was a new, strange sound to him. I do not suppose that he appreciated it to the full; but I can well believe that it deeply impressed him, and made him feel that his fellow sufferer was a being about whom there was an exceeding mystery of goodness.

And when the cross was lifted up, that thief hanging up on his own cross looked around, and I suppose he could see that inscription written in three languages: "Jesus of Nazareth, the King of the Jews." If so, that writing was his little Bible, his New Testament, and he interpreted it by what he knew of the Old Testament. Putting this and that together—that strange person, incarnate loveliness, all patience and all majesty, that strange prayer, and now this singular inscription, surely he who knew the Old Testament, as I have no doubt he did, would say to himself, "Is this he? Is this truly the King of the Jews? This is he who worked miracles, and raised the dead, and said that he was the Son of God; is it all true, and is he really our Messiah?" Then he would remember the words of the prophet Isaiah, "He was despised and rejected of men, a man of sorrows, and acquainted with grief. Surely, he hath borne our griefs, and carried our sorrows." "Why," he would say to himself, "I never understood that passage in the prophet Isaiah before, but it must point to him. The chastisement of our peace is upon him. Can this be he who cried in the Psalms, 'they pierced my hands and my feet'?" As he looked at him again, he felt in his soul, "It must be he. Could there be another so like to him?" He felt conviction creeping over his spirit. Then he looked again, and he marked how all men down below rejected and despised and hissed at him and hooted him, and all this would make the case the more clear. "All they that see me laugh me to scorn: they shoot out the lip, they shake the head, saying, 'He trusted on the Lord that he would deliver him: let him deliver him, seeing he delighted in him.'"

Peradventure, *this dying thief read the gospel out of the lips of Christ's enemies.* They said, "He saved others." "Ah!" thought he, "did he save others? Why should he not save me?" What a grand bit of gospel that was for the dying thief, "He saved others!" I think I could swim to heaven on that plank, "He saved others"; because, if he saved others, he can of a surety save me.

Thus the very things that the enemies disdainfully threw at Christ would be gospel to this poor dying man. When it has been my misery to read any of the wretched prints that are sent us out of scorn, in which our Lord is held up to ridicule, I have thought, "Why, perhaps those who read these loathsome blasphemies may, nevertheless, learn the gospel from them!" You may pick a jewel from a dunghill and find its radiance undiminished; and you may gather the gospel from a blasphemous mouth, and it shall be nonetheless the gospel of salvation. Peradventure this man learned the gospel from those who jested at our dying Lord; and so the servants of the devil were unconsciously made to be the servants of Christ.

But, after all, surely that which won him most must have been *to look at Jesus again,* as he was hanging upon the cruel tree. Possibly nothing about the physical person of Christ would be attractive to him, for his visage was more marred than that of any man, and his form more than the sons of men; but yet there must have been in that blessed face a singular charm. Was it not the very image of perfection? As I conceive the face of Christ, it was very different from anything that any painter has yet been able to place upon his canvas. It was all goodness and kindness and unselfishness; and yet it was a royal face. It was a face of superlative justice and unrivaled tenderness. Righteousness and uprightness sat upon his brow; but infinite pity and goodwill to men had also there taken up their abode. It was a face that would have struck you at once as one by itself, never to be forgotten, never to be fully understood. It was all sorrow, yet all love; all meekness, yet all resolution; all wisdom, yet all simplicity; the face of a child, or an angel, and yet peculiarly the face of a man. Majesty and misery, suffering and sacredness, were therein strangely combined; he was evidently the Lamb of God, and the Son of man. As the robber looked, he believed. Is it not singular, the very sight of the Master won him? The sight of the Lord in agony and shame and death! Scarcely a word; certainly no sermon, no attending worship on the Sabbath; no reading of gracious books; no appeal from mother or teacher or friend; but the sight of Jesus won him. I put it down as a very singular thing, a thing for you and for me to recollect, and dwell upon, with quite as much vividness as we do upon the lateness of this robber's conversion.

Oh, that God of his mercy might convert everybody in this tabernacle! Oh, that I could have a share in it by the preaching of the word! But I will be equally happy if you get to heaven anyhow; yes, if the Lord should take you there without outward ministries, leading you to Jesus by some simple method such as he adopted with this thief. If you do but get there, he shall have the glory of it, and his poor servant will be overjoyed! Oh, that you would now look to Jesus and live! Before your eyes he is set forth, evidently crucified among you. Look to him and be saved, even at this hour.

II. But now I want you to think with me a little upon *the specialty of this man's faith,* for I think it was a very singular faith that this man exerted toward our Lord Jesus Christ.

I greatly question whether the equal and the parallel of the dying thief's faith will be readily found outside the Scriptures, or even in the Scriptures.

Observe, that this man believed in Christ *when he literally saw him dying the death of a felon,* under circumstances of the greatest personal shame. You have never realized what it was to be crucified. None of you could do that, for the sight has never been seen in our day in England. There is not a man or woman here who has ever realized in their own mind the actual death of Christ. It stands beyond us. This man saw it with his own eyes, and for him to call *him* "Lord" who was hanging on a gibbet, was no small triumph of faith. For him to ask Jesus to remember him when he came into his kingdom, though he saw that Jesus bleeding his life away and hounded to the death, was a splendid act of reliance. For him to commit his everlasting destiny into the hands of One who was, to all appearance, unable even to preserve his own life, was a noble achievement of faith. I say that this dying thief leads the vanguard in the matter of faith, for what he saw of the circumstances of the Savior was calculated to contradict rather than help his confidence. What he saw was to his hindrance rather than to his help, for he saw our Lord in the very extremity of agony and death, and yet he believed in him as the King shortly to come into his kingdom.

Recollect, too, that at that moment when the thief believed in Christ, *all the disciples had forsaken him and fled.* John might be lingering at a little distance, and holy women may have stood farther off, but no one was present bravely to champion the dying Christ. Judas had sold him, Peter had denied him, and the rest had forsaken him; and it was then that the dying thief called him "Lord," and said, "Remember me when thou comest into thy kingdom." I call that splendid faith. Why, some of you do not believe, though you are surrounded with Christian friends, though you are urged on by the testimony of those whom you regard with love; but this man, all alone, comes out, and calls Jesus his Lord! No one else was confessing Christ at that moment: no revival was around him with enthusiastic crowds: he was all by himself as a confessor of his Lord. After our Lord was nailed to the tree, the first to bear witness for him was this thief. The centurion bore witness afterward, when our Lord expired; but this thief was a lone confessor, holding onto Christ when nobody would say "Amen" to what he said. Even his fellow thief was mocking at the crucified Savior, so that this man shone as a lone star in the midnight darkness. O sirs, dare you be Daniels? Dare you stand alone? Would you dare to stand out amidst a ribald crew, and say, "Jesus is my King. I only ask him to remember me when he comes into his kingdom"? Would you be likely to avow such a faith when priests and scribes, princes and people, were all mocking at the Christ, and deriding him? Brethren, the dying robber exhibited marvelous faith, and I beg you to think of this next time you speak of him.

And it seems to me that another point adds splendor to that faith, namely, that *he himself was in extreme torture.* Remember, he was crucified. It was a crucified man trusting in a crucified Christ. Oh, when our frame is racked with torture, when the tenderest nerves are pained, when our body is hung up to die by we know not what great length of torment, then to forget the present and live in the future is a grand achievement of faith! While dying, to turn one's eye to another dying at your side, and trust your soul with him, is very marvelous faith. Blessed thief, because they put you down at the bottom, as one of the least of saints, I think that I must bid you come up higher and take one of the uppermost seats among those who by faith have glorified the Christ of God!

Why, see, dear friends, once more, the specialty of this man's faith was that *he saw so much,* though his eyes had been opened for so short a time! He saw the future world. He was not a believer in annihilation or in the possibility of a man's not being immortal. He evidently expected to be in another world and to be in existence when the dying Lord should come into his kingdom. He believed all that, and it is more than some do nowadays. He also believed that Jesus would have a kingdom, a kingdom after he was dead, a kingdom though he was crucified. He believed that he was winning for himself a kingdom by those nailed hands and pierced feet. This was intelligent faith, was it not? He believed that Jesus would have a kingdom in which others would share, and therefore he aspired to have his portion in it. But yet he had fit views of himself, and therefore he did not say, "Lord, let me sit at thy right hand"; or, "Let me share of the dainties of thy palace"; but he said only, "Remember me. Think of me. Cast an eye my way. Think of your poor dying comrade on the cross at your right hand. Lord, remember me. Remember me." I see deep humility in the prayer and yet a sweet, joyous, confident exaltation of the Christ at the time when the Christ was in his deepest humiliation.

O dear sirs, if any of you have thought of this dying thief only as one who put off repentance, I want you now to think of him as one that did greatly and grandly believe in Christ; and, oh, that you would do the same! Oh, that you would put a great confidence in my great Lord! Never did a poor sinner trust Christ too much. There was never a case of a guilty one, who believed that Jesus could forgive him, and afterward found that he could not—who believed that Jesus could save him on the spot, and then woke up to find that it was a delusion. No, plunge into this river of confidence in Christ. The waters are waters to swim in, not to drown in. Never did a soul perish that glorified Christ by a living, loving faith in him. Come, then, with all your sin, whatever it may be, with all your deep depression of spirit, with all your agony of conscience. Come along with you, and grasp my Lord and Master with both the hands of your faith, and he shall be yours, and you shall be his.

> *Turn to Christ your longing eyes,*
> *View his bloody sacrifice:*
> *See in him your sins forgiven;*
> *Pardon, holiness, and heaven;*
> *Glorify the King of kings,*
> *Take the peace the gospel brings.*

I think that I have shown you something special in the means of the thief's conversion, and in his faith in our dying Lord.

III. But now, third, as God shall help me, I wish to show you another specialty, namely, in *the result of his faith*.

"Oh," I have heard people say, "well, you see, the dying thief was converted; but then he was not baptized. He never went to communion and never joined the church!" He could not do either; and that which God himself renders impossible to us he does not demand of us. He was nailed to the cross; how could he be baptized? But he did a great deal more than that; for if he could not carry out the outward signs, he most manifestly exhibited the things which they signified, which, in his condition, was better still.

This dying thief first of all confessed the Lord Jesus Christ; and that is the very essence of baptism. He confessed Christ. Did he not acknowledge him to his fellow thief? It was as open a confession as he could make it. Did he not acknowledge Christ before all that were gathered around the cross who were within hearing? It was as public a confession as he could possibly cause it to be. Yet certain cowardly fellows claim to be Christians, though they have never confessed Christ to a single person, and then they quote this poor thief as an excuse. Are they nailed to a cross? Are they dying in agony? Oh no; and yet they talk as if they could claim the exemption which these circumstances would give them. What a dishonest piece of business!

The fact is, that our Lord requires an open confession as well as a secret faith; and if you will not render it, there is no promise of salvation for you, but a threat of being denied at the last. The apostle puts it, "If thou shalt confess with thy mouth the Lord Jesus, and shalt believe in thine heart that God hath raised him from the dead, thou shalt be saved." It is stated in another place upon this wise: "He that believeth and is baptized shall be saved"; that is Christ's way of making the confession of him. If there be a true faith, there must be a declaration of it. If you are candles, and God has lit you, "Let your light so shine before men, that they may see your good works, and glorify your Father which is in heaven." Soldiers of Christ must, like Her Majesty's soldiers, wear their regimentals; and if they are ashamed of their regimentals, they ought to be drummed out of the regiment. They are not honest soldiers who refuse to march in rank with their comrades. The very least thing that the Lord Jesus Christ can expect of us is that we do confess him to the best of our power. If you are nailed up to a cross, I will not invite you to be baptized. If you are fastened up to a tree to die, I will not ask you to come into this pulpit and declare your faith, for you cannot. But you are required to do what you can do, namely, to make as distinct and open an avowal of the Lord Jesus Christ as may be suitable in your present condition.

I believe that many Christian people get into a deal of trouble through not being honest in their convictions. For instance, if a man goes into a workshop, or a soldier into a barrack room, and if he does not fly his flag from the first, it will be very difficult for him to run it up afterward. But if he immediately and boldly lets them know, "I am a Christian man, and there are certain things that I cannot do to please you, and certain other things that I cannot help doing, though they displease you"—when that is clearly understood, after a while the singularity of the thing will be gone, and the man will be let alone; but if he is a little sneaky, and thinks that he is going to please the world and please Christ too, he is in for a rough time, let him depend upon it. His life will be that of a toad under a harrow, or a fox in a dog kennel, if he tries the way of compromise. That will never do. Come out. Show your colors. Let it be known who you are, and what you are; and although your course will not be smooth, it will certainly be not half so rough as if you tried to run with the hare and hunt with the hounds, a very difficult piece of business that.

This man came out, then and there, and made as open an avowal of his faith in Christ as was possible.

The next thing he did was to rebuke his fellow sinner. He spoke to him in answer to the ribaldry with which he had assailed our Lord. I do not know what the unconverted convict had been blasphemously saying, but his converted comrade spoke very honestly to him. "Dost not thou fear God, seeing thou art in the same condemnation? And we indeed justly; for we receive the due reward of our deeds: but this man hath done nothing amiss." It is more than ever needful in these days that believers in Christ should not allow sin to go unrebuked; and yet a great many of them do so. Do you not know that a person who is silent when a wrong thing is said or done may become a participator in the sin? If you do not rebuke sin—I mean, of course, on all fit occasions, and in a proper spirit—your silence will give consent to the sin, and you will be an aider and abettor in it. A man who saw a robbery and who did not cry, "Stop thief!" would be thought to be in league with the thief; and the man who can hear swearing or see impurity, and never utter a word of protest may well question whether he is right himself. Our "other men's sins" make up a great item in our personal guilt unless we in anywise rebuke them. This our Lord expects us to do. The dying thief did it, and did it with all his heart; and therein far exceeded large numbers of those who hold their heads high in the church.

Next, *the dying thief made a full confession of his guilt.* He said to him who was hanged with him, "Dost not thou fear God, seeing thou art in the same condemnation? *And we indeed justly.*" Not many words, but what a world of meaning was in them: "we indeed justly." "You and I are dying for our crimes," said he, "and we deserve to die." When a man is willing to confess that he deserves the wrath of God—that he deserves the suffering which his sin has brought upon him—there is evidence of sincerity in him. In this man's case, his repentance glittered like a holy tear in the eye of his faith, so that his faith was bejeweled with the drops of his penitence. As I have often told you, I suspect the faith which is not born as a twin with repentance; but there is no room for suspicion in the case of this penitent confessor. I pray God that you and I may have such a thorough work as this in our own hearts as the result of our faith.

Then, see, *this dying thief defends his Lord right manfully.* He says, "We indeed justly, but this man hath done nothing amiss." Was not that beautifully said? He did not say, "this man does not deserve to die," but, "this man hath done nothing amiss." He means that he is perfectly innocent. He does not even say, "he has done nothing wicked," but he even asserts that he has not acted unwisely or indiscreetly: "this man hath done nothing amiss." This is a glorious testimony of a dying man to one who was numbered with the transgressors, and was being put to death because his enemies falsely accused him. Beloved, I only pray that you and I may bear as good witness to our Lord as this thief did. He outruns us all. We need not think much of the coming of his conversion late in life; we may far rather consider how blessed was the testimony which he bore for his Lord when it was most needed. When all other voices were silent, one suffering penitent spoke out, and said, "this man hath done nothing amiss."

See, again, another mark of this man's faith. He prays, and *his prayer is directed to Jesus.* "Lord, remember me when thou comest into thy kingdom." True faith is always praying faith. "Behold, he prayeth" is one of the surest tests of the new birth. O friends, may we abound in prayer, for thus we shall prove that our faith in Jesus Christ is what it ought to be! This converted robber opened his mouth wide in prayer; he prayed with great confidence as to the coming kingdom, and he sought that kingdom first, even to the exclusion of all else. He might have asked for life or for ease from pain; but he prefers the kingdom, and this is a high mark of grace.

In addition to thus praying, you will see that *he adores and worships Jesus,* for he says, "Lord, remember me when thou comest into thy kingdom." The petition is worded as if he felt, "Only let Christ think of me, and it is enough. Let him but remember me, and the thought of his mind will be effectual for everything that I shall need in the world to come." This is to impute Godhead to Christ. If a man can cast his all upon the mere memory of a person, he must have a very high esteem of that person. If to be remembered by the Lord Jesus is all that this man asks or desires, he pays to the Lord great honor. I think that there was about his prayer a worship equal to the eternal hallelujahs of cherubim and seraphim. There was in it a glorification of his Lord which is not excelled even by the endless symphonies of angelic spirits who surround the throne. Thief, you have well done!

Oh, that some penitent spirit here might be helped thus to believe, thus to confess, thus to defend his Master, thus to adore, thus to worship; and then the age of the convert would be a matter of the smallest imaginable consequence.

IV. Now the last remark is this: There was something very special about the dying thief as to *our Lord's word to him about the world to come.*

He said to him, "Today shalt thou be with me in paradise." He only asked the Lord to remember him, but he obtained this surprising answer, "Today shalt thou be with me in paradise."

In some respects I envy this dying thief; for this reason: that when the Lord pardoned me, and pardoned the most of you, who are present, he did not give us a place in paradise that same day. We are not yet come to the rest which is promised to us. No, you are waiting here. Some of you have been waiting very long. It is thirty years with many of us. It is forty years, it is fifty years, with many others since the Lord blotted out your sins, and yet you are not with him in paradise. There is a dear member of this church who, I suppose, has known the Lord for seventy-five years, and she is still with us, having long passed the ninetieth year of her age. The Lord did not admit her to paradise on the day of her conversion. He did not take any one of us from nature to grace, and from grace to glory, in a day. We have had to wait a good while. There is something for us to do in the wilderness, and so we are kept out of the heavenly garden. I remember that Mr. Baxter said that he was not in a hurry to be gone to heaven; and a friend called upon Dr. John Owen, who had been writing about the glory of Christ, and asked him what he thought of going to heaven. That great divine replied, "I am longing to be there." "Why," said the other, "I have just spoken to holy Mr. Baxter, and he says that he would prefer to be here, since he thinks that he can be more useful on earth." "Oh!" said Dr. Owen, "my brother Baxter is always full of practical godliness, but for all that I cannot say that I am at all desirous to linger in this mortal state. I would rather be gone." Each of these men seems to me to have been the half of Paul. Paul was made up of the two, for he was desirous to depart, but he was willing to remain because it was needful for the people. We would put both together, and, like Paul, have a strong desire to depart and to be with Christ, and yet be willing to wait if we can do service to our Lord and to his church. Still, I think he has the best of it who is converted and enters heaven the same night. This robber breakfasted with the devil, but he dined with Christ on earth, and supped with him in paradise. This was short work, but blessed work. What a host of troubles he escaped! What a world of temptation he missed! What an evil world he quitted! He was just born, like a lamb dropped in the field, and then he was lifted into the Shepherd's bosom straight away. I do not remember the Lord ever saying this to anybody else. I daresay it may have happened that souls have been converted and have gone home at once; but I never heard of anybody that had such an assurance from Christ as this man had: "Verily, I say unto thee"; such a personal assurance: "Verily I say unto thee, Today shalt thou be with me in paradise." Dying thief, you were favored above many, "to be with Christ, which is far better," and to be with him so soon!

Why is it that our Lord does not thus imparadise all of us at once? It is because there is something for us to do on earth. My brethren, are you doing it? *Are you doing it?* Some good people are still on earth: but why? But why? What is the use of them? I cannot make it out. If they are indeed the Lord's people, what are they here for? They get up in the morning and eat their breakfast, and in due course eat their dinner, and their supper, and go to bed and sleep; at a proper hour they get up the next morning, and do the same as on the previous day. Is this living for Jesus? Is this life? It does not come to much. Can this be the life of God in man? O Christian people, do justify your Lord in keeping you waiting here! How can you justify him but by serving him to the utmost of your power? The Lord help you to do so! Why, you owe as much to him as the dying thief! I know I owe a great deal more. What a mercy it is to have been converted while you were yet a boy, to be brought to the Savior while you were yet a girl! What a debt of obligation young Christians owe to the Lord! And if this poor thief crammed a life full of testimony into a few minutes, ought not you and I, who are spared, for years after conversion, to perform good service for our Lord? Come, let us wake up if we have been asleep! Let us begin to live if we have been half dead. May the Spirit of God make something of us yet: so that we may go as industrious servants from the labors of the vineyard to the pleasures of the paradise! To our once crucified Lord be glory forever and ever! Amen.

Stephen: Stephen's Death

Delivered on Lord's Day morning, May 24, 1874, at the Metropolitan Tabernacle, Newington. No. 1175.

> *And they stoned Stephen, calling upon God, and saying, "Lord Jesus, receive my spirit." And he kneeled down, and cried with a loud voice, "Lord, lay not this sin to their charge." And when he had said this, he fell asleep.*
> —ACTS 7:59–60

It is of the greatest service to us all to be reminded that our life is but a vapor, which appears for a little while and then vanishes away. Through forgetfulness of this, worldlings live at ease, and Christians walk carelessly. Unless we watch for the Lord's coming, worldliness soon eats into our spirit as does a canker. If you have this world's riches, believer, remember that this is not your rest, and set not too great a store by its comforts. If, on the other hand, you dwell in straitness, and are burdened with poverty, be not too much depressed thereby, for these light afflictions are but for a moment, and are not worthy to be compared with the glory which shall be revealed in us. Look upon the things that are as though they were not. Remember you are a part of a great procession which is always moving by; others come and go before your own eyes, you see them, and they disappear, and you yourself are moving onward to another and more real world. "'Tis greatly wise to talk with our last hours," to give a rehearsal of our departure, and to be prepared to stand before the great tribunal of the judgment. Our duty is to trim our lamps against the time when the Bridegroom comes; we are called upon to stand always ready, waiting for the appearing of our Lord and Savior Jesus Christ, or else for the summons which shall tell us that the pitcher is broken at the fountain, and the wheel broken at the cistern, that the body must return to the earth as it was, and the spirit unto God who gave it.

This death scene of Stephen's may aid our meditations while, by the help of the Holy Spirit, we cast our minds forward to the time when we also must fall asleep. This is the only martyrdom which is recorded in the New Testament in detail, the Holy Ghost foreseeing that there would be martyrdoms enough before the church's history would end, and that we should never lack memorials such as those with which Foxe's martyrology and works of the like order supply us. It is equally remarkable that this is the only death scene in the New Testament which has been described at length, with the exception of our Lord's. Of course we are told of the deaths of other saints, and facts relating thereto are mentioned, but what they said when they died, and how they felt in passing out of the world, are left unrecorded, probably because the Holy Spirit knew that we should never lack for holy deathbeds and triumphant departures. These he well knew would be everyday facts to the people of God. Perhaps, moreover, the Holy Spirit would have us gather from his silence that he would not have us attach so much importance to the manner of men's deaths as to the character of their lives. To live like Jesus most nearly concerns us; a triumphant death may be the crown, but a holy life is the head that must wear it. To obey our Lord's commands during our life is our most pressing business; we may leave the testimony of death to be given us in the selfsame hour. We shall have dying grace in dying moments, and at this present our chief business is to obtain the grace which will enable us to adorn the doctrine of God our Savior in all things. However, as we have this one case of Stephen given us at full length, we should prize it the more highly, and study it the more carefully, because it is the only one. Let us do so this morning.

There are three things upon which I shall speak: *The general character of Stephen's death*; second, *its most notable peculiarity*; and third, *things desirable in reference to death suggested to us by Stephen's departure*.

I. Let us look at Stephen's death, and notice *its general character*.

It strikes us at once that it happened in the very midst of his service. He had been appointed an officer of the church at Jerusalem, to see that the alms were distributed properly among the poor, especially among the Grecian widows. He discharged his duty to the satisfaction of the whole church, and thereby he did most useful service, for it gave the apostles opportunity to give themselves wholly to their true work, namely, that of preaching and prayer, and it is no small matter to be able to bear a burden for another if he is thereby set free for more eminent service than we could ourselves perform. If it be so that I cannot preach myself, yet if I can take away from one who does preach certain cares which burden him, if I thus enable him to preach the more and the better, I am virtually preaching myself. The care which Stephen exercised over the poor tended also to prevent heart burning and division, and this was a result of no mean order. But, not content with being a deacon, Stephen began to minister in holy things as a speaker of the word, and that with great power, for he was full of faith and of the Holy Ghost. He stands forth on the page of the church's history, for the time being, as quite a leading spirit; so much so, indeed, that the enemies of the gospel recognized his prominent usefulness and made him the object of their fiercest opposition, for they generally rage most against those who are doing most good. Stephen stood in the front rank of the Lord's host, and yet he was taken away! "A mystery," say some. "A great privilege," say I. My brethren, who desires to be removed at any other time? Is it not well to die in harness while yet you are useful? Who wants to linger till he becomes a burden rather than a help? If we are called to depart in the middle of service, we must submit to it thankfully, and may even wish to have it said of us, he did—

> *His body with his charge lay down,*
> *And ceased at once to work and live.*

He was removed in the very prime of his usefulness, just when many were being converted by his ministry, when, through his faith, miracles were being worked on all sides, when he seemed, indeed, to be necessary to the church. And is not this well? Well, first, that God should teach his people how much he can do by a man whom he chooses; well, next, that he should show them that he is not dependent upon any man, but can do his work even without the choicest laborer in his vineyard. If our life can teach one lesson, and when that is taught, if our death can teach another, it is well to live and well to die, and far more desirable than to tarry long and take one's flight in the dreary winter of declining influence. Let me be reaped, if I may venture on a choice, when my ministry shall be like the wheat in Pharaoh's dream, with seven ears rank and good, and not in a time when the east wind has shriveled me into barrenness. If God be glorified by our removal, is it not well? And may he not be more than ordinarily glorified when he lays us aside in order to show his church that he can do without his servants, or can raise up others in their stead? Happy is that messenger whose absence as well as his presence fulfills his Master's will.

But *Stephen's death was painful, and attended with much that flesh and blood would dread.* He died not surrounded by weeping friends, but by enemies who gnashed their teeth; no holy hymn made glad his death chamber, but the shouts and outcries of a maddened throng rang in his ears. For him no downy pillow, but the hard and cruel rocks; battered and bruised by a whirlwind of stones he laid him down to sleep, and woke up in the bosom of his Lord. Now brethren, this is all the more for our comfort, because if he died in perfect peace, no, in joy and triumph, how much more may we hope to depart in peace! Since we shall not have these grim attendants upon our departing hours, may we not hope that we shall be sustained and buoyed up by the presence of our Lord and Master even as he was, and grace will be made perfect in our weakness? Every circumstance tells on our side by way of comfort. If he slept amid a storm of stones, how may we hope to fall asleep right peacefully, in the same faith in Jesus, when the saints are gathered around our bed to bid us farewell!

More particularly, however, I want to call your attention to the fact that *Stephen's departing moments were calm, peaceful, confident, joyous.* He never flinched while he was addressing that infuriated audience. He told them the plain truth, with as much quiet deliberation as if he had been gratifying them with a pleasing discourse. When they grew angry he was not afraid; his lip did not quiver; he did not retract or soften down a single expression, but cut them to the heart with even more fidelity. With the courage of a man of God, his face was set as a flint. Knowing that he was now preaching his last sermon, he used the sharp two-edged sword of the Word, piercing into their very souls. Little cared he how they frowned; nothing was he abashed when they gnashed their teeth. He was as calm as the opened heaven above him, and continued so though they hurried him out of the city. When they had dragged him outside the gate, and stripped off their clothes to carry out his execution, he did not let fall a single timorous word or trembling cry; he stood up and committed his soul to God with calmness, and when the first murderous stones felled him to the earth he rose to his knees, still not to ask for pity, nor to utter a craven cry, but to plead with his Lord for mercy upon his assailants; then, closing his eyes like a child tired out with the sport of a long summer's day, and drops asleep upon its mother's lap, "he fell asleep."

Believe, then, O Christian, that if you abide in Christ, the like will be the case with you. You shall be undisturbed at the premonitions of decay; when the physician shakes his head your heart shall not fail; when friends look sad you will not share their sorrow. We wept when we were born though all around us smiled; so shall we smile when we die while all around us weep. The dying Christian is often the only calm and composed person in all the group which fills the chamber from which he ascends to heaven. Talking of what he enjoys and expects, he glides gently into glory. Why should we expect it to be otherwise? Stephen's God is our God; Stephen's faith we already possess in its germ, and we may have it in the same degree; the Holy Spirit dwells in us even as he did in Stephen, and if he puts not forth the same energy, what hinders him but our unbelief? Getting more faith we shall enjoy the same tranquil repose of spirit when our appointed hour shall come. Brethren, let us not fear death, but descend Jordan's shelving bank without the slightest dismay.

Some other points about Stephen's departure I beg you to notice, points relating to the state of his mind. *His mind was in a very elevated condition.* Here let us first remark *his intense sympathy with God.* All through that long speech of his you see that his soul is taken up with his God, and the treatment which he had received from Israel. He does not speak against his countrymen from any ill will, but he seems to take them very little into consideration. His God absorbs all his thoughts; and he tells how his God had sent Joseph, but his brethren persecuted him; his God had sent Moses, but they rebelled against him; his God had now sent Jesus, and they had been his betrayers and murderers. He had pity upon them in his heart, that is clearly seen in his dying prayer for them, but still his main feeling is sympathy with God in the rebellions which he had endured from the ungodly. Surely this is the mind which possesses the saints in heaven. I see, as I read Stephen's speech, that he regarded impenitent sinners from the standpoint of the saints above, who will be so taken up in sympathy with God, and the righteousness of his government, that the doom of the finally rebellious will cause them no pain. The triumph of right over willful wrong, of holiness over the foulest and most wanton sin, of justice over the ingratitude which made light of redeeming love, will clear the soul of all emotion but that which rejoices in every act of the most High, because it is and must be right. I know how easily this remark may be misrepresented; still it is true, and let it stand.

Notice, too, how *Stephen's mind clung only to that which is purely spiritual.* All ritualism was clean gone from him. I daresay at one time Stephen felt a great reverence for the temple; the first Jewish Christians still continued to feel a measure of that awe of the temple which, as Jews, they had formerly indulged; but Stephen says, "Howbeit the most High dwelleth not in temples made with hands; as saith the prophet, 'heaven is my throne and earth is my footstool: what house will ye build me? saith the Lord; or what is the place of my rest?'" It is noteworthy how the saints, when they are near to die, make very little of what others make a great deal of. What is ritual to a dying man— a man with his eyes opened, looking into the future, and about to meet his God? Sacraments are poor supports in the dying hour. Priestcraft, where is it? The reed has snapped beneath the weight of a burdened conscience, and the tremendous realities of death and judgment. The peculiar form of worship which a man contended for in health, and the little specialties of doctrines which he made much of aforetime, will seem little in comparison with the great spiritual essentials, when the soul is approaching the presence chamber of the Eternal. The saint in death is growingly spiritual, for he is nearing the land of spirits, and that city of which John said, "I saw no temple therein."

Brethren, it is a grand thing to grow in spiritual religion till you break the eggshell of form, and shake it off, for the outward fashion of ceremonies, and even of simplicities, is too often to men what the eggshell is to the living bird; and when the soul awakens into the highest forms of life, we chip and break that shell and leave our former bondage. Stephen came right away from those superstitious reverences, which still cast their blight over many Christians, and worshiped God, who is a Spirit, in spirit and in truth.

It is most clear *that he rose beyond all fear of men.* They grin at him, they howl at him, but what matters that to him? He will be put to a blasphemer's death outside the city by the hands of cruel men; but that daunts him not. His face glows with joy unspeakable; he looks not like a man hurried to his execution, but as one on the way to a wedding. He looks like an immortal angel rather than a man condemned to die. Ah, brethren, and so will it be with all the faithful! Today we fear man, who is but a worm; today we are so weak as to be swayed by the estimation of our fellows, and we listen to kindly voices, which counsel us to speak with bated breath upon certain points, lest we grieve this one or that; but the fitter we are for heaven, the more we scorn all compromise, and feel that for truth, for God, for Christ, we must speak out, even if we die, for who are we that we should be afraid of a man that shall die, and the son of man that is but a worm? It is a blessed thing if this shall be growingly our condition.

At the same time *Stephen was free from all cares.* He was a deacon, but he does not say, "What will those poor people do? How will the widows fare? Who will care for the orphans?" He does not even say, "What will the apostles do now that I can no longer take the labor from off their shoulders?" Not a word of it. He sees heaven opened, and thinks little of the church below, love it though he does with all his heart. He trusts the church militant with her Captain: he is called to the church triumphant. He hears the trumpet sound, "Up and away," and lo, he answers to the summons. Happy men who can thus cast off their cares and enter into rest. Why should it not be thus with us? Why, like Martha, do we allow our much serving to cumber us? Our Lord managed his church well enough before we were born; he will not be at a loss because he has called us home, and therefore we need not trouble ourselves as though we were all-important, and the church would pine for lack of us.

At the same time, *Stephen had no resentments.* That was a sweet prayer of his, "Lay not this sin to their charge." Just as Daniel before Belshazzar saw the scale and saw Belshazzar weighed in it and found wanting, so Stephen saw the balances of justice, and this murder of his, like a great weight, about to be placed in the scale against the raging Jews, and he cried, "Lord, cast not this sin into the balance." He could not say, as the Savior did, "They know not what they do," for they did know it and had been troubled by his speech, so that they stopped their ears, to hear no more; but he pleads for them as far as truth would permit him, while breathing out his soul. Every child of God ought to lay aside all resentments at once, or rather he should never have any. We are to carry in our hearts no remembrance of ills, but to live every day freely forgiving, as we are every day freely forgiven; but as we get nearer to heaven there must be growing love to those who hate us, for so shall we prove that we have been made ready for the skies.

To close up this description of his death, *Stephen died like a conqueror.* His name was *Stephanos,* or crown, and truly that day he not only received a crown, but he became the crown of the church as her first martyr. *He* was the conqueror, not his enemies. They stoned his body, but his soul had vanquished them. It was not in their power to move him; his quiet look defied their fury. He went home to his God to hear it said, "Servant of God, well done," and in nothing had his foes despoiled him on the way there. He was more than a conqueror through him that loved him. These are some of the characteristics of Stephen's departure, and I trust that in our measure they may be ours. God grant them to us, and we will give him all the glory.

II. Now I call your attention to a very interesting point—*the most notable peculiarity of Stephen's death.*

It was notable for this one point, that it was full of Jesus, and full of Jesus in four ways: Jesus was *seen, invoked, trusted,* and *imitated.*

First, *the Lord Jesus was seen.* The martyr looked up steadfastly into heaven and saw the glory of God, and Jesus standing on the right hand of God. At first he was probably in the council hall of the Sanhedrin, but the vision seemed to divide the roof, to roll away the firmament, and set open the gates of heaven, so that into its innermost chambers the anointed eye was able to gaze. It is said he saw *the Son of man.* Now this is the only place in Scripture where Jesus is called the Son of man by anyone but himself. He frequently called himself the Son of man, that was indeed a common name for himself, but his disciples did not call him so. Perhaps the glory of the rejected Messiah as man was the peculiar thought which was to be conveyed to Stephen's mind, to assure him that as the despised Lord had at length triumphed, so also should his persecuted servant. At all times it is a gladsome sight to see the representative man exalted to the throne of God, but it was peculiarly suitable for this occasion, for the Lord himself had warned his enemies, "Hereafter shall ye see the Son of man sitting on the right hand of power."

He had spoken those words to the very men who now heard Stephen bear witness that it was even so.

Stephen saw his Lord *standing*; now our Lord is generally described as sitting, but it was as if the sympathizing Lord had risen up to draw near to his suffering servant, eager both to sustain him and to receive him when the conflict was over. Jesus rose from the throne to gaze upon himself suffering again in the person of one of his beloved members. The place occupied by the Lord was "at the right hand of God." Stephen distinctly saw the ineffable brightness of eternal glory, which no human eye can see until strengthened by superior grace, and amid that glory he saw the Son of man in the place of love, power, and honor, worshiped and adored.

Now when we come to die, dear friends, we may not, perhaps, expect with these eyes to see what Stephen saw, but faith has a grand realizing power. The fact that Jesus is enthroned is always the same, and so long as we are sure that he is at the right hand of God, it little matters whether we see him with our natural eyes, for faith is the substance of things hoped for, and the evidence of things not seen. Brethren, if your faith shall be strong when you come to die, as doubtless it will be, you will have a sight and sense of Jesus in his manhood at the right hand of God, and this will effectually take away from you all fear of death; for you will feel, "If the man Christ is there, I, being already represented by him, shall also be there; I shall rise from the dead; I shall sit at the right hand of the Father; his eternal power and Godhead will raise me up to be where he is, for has he not said, "I will that they also whom thou hast given me be with me where I am"? I will, however, venture further. I am convinced, from my own observation, that not to a few but to many dying saints, something more is given than the realizations of faith. Much more frequently than we suppose, supernatural glimpses of the divine splendor are vouchsafed to the saints in the hour of their departure. I have heard persons comparatively uninstructed and certainly unimaginative speak of what they have seen in their last hour, in such a way that I am certain they never borrowed the expressions from books, but must have seen what they described. There has been a freshness about their descriptions which has convinced me they did see what they assured me they beheld; and, moreover, the joy which has resulted from it, the acquiescence in the divine will, the patience with which they have borne suffering, have gone far to prove that they were not under the influence of an idle imagination, but were really enabled to look within the veil. The flesh in its weakness becomes, if I may so say, a rarefied medium; the mists are blown away, the obscuring veil grows thinner, disease makes rents in it, and through the thin places and the rents the heavenly glory shines. Oh, how little will a man fear death, or care about pain, if he expects to breathe out his soul on a better Pisgah than Moses ever climbed! Well did we sing just now—I am sure I sang it with all my heart—

> *Oh, if my Lord would come and meet,*
> *My soul would stretch her wings in haste,*
> *Fly fearless through death's iron gate,*
> *Nor fear the terror as she passed.*

Now this model departure, which is given in Scripture as a type of Christian deaths, has this for its ensign, that Christ was visible; and such shall be the character of our departure, if through faith we are one with Jesus; therefore, let us not fear.

Next, notice that *Jesus was invoked*, for that is the meaning of the text. "They stoned Stephen, calling upon," or invoking, "and saying, 'Lord Jesus, receive my spirit.'" Dying Christians are not troubled with questions as to the deity of Christ. Dear friends, Unitarianism may do to live with, but it will not do to die with, at least for us. At such a time we need an almighty and divine Savior; we want "God over all, blessed forever" to come to our rescue in the solemn article. So Stephen called upon Jesus, and worshiped him. He makes no mention of any other intercessor. O martyr of Christ, why did you not cry, "Ave Maria! Blessed virgin, succor me"? Why did you not pray to St. Michael and all angels? Ah no! The abomination of saint and angel worship had not been invented in his day, and if it had been he would have scorned it as one of the foul devices of hell. There is "one mediator between God and men, the man Christ Jesus." He invoked Christ, and no one else.

Neither do we find him saying a word as to his good works and alms-deeds and sermons and miracles. No, he invoked the Lord Jesus and leaned on him wholly. Ah, brethren, it is well to live and to die resting wholly upon Jesus. If you lie down tonight and quietly think of your departure, and inquire whether you are ready to die, you will not feel at your ease till your heart stands at the foot of the cross, looking up and viewing the flowing of the Savior's precious blood, believing humbly that he made your peace with God. There is no right living, or joyful dying, except in invoking Christ.

What next did Stephen do? *He trusted Jesus* and confided in him only; for we find him saying, "Lord Jesus, receive my spirit." He felt that his spirit was about to leave the body to fly into the unknown world. Perhaps a shiver came over him of natural awe at the great mystery, even as it comes over us when we think of being disrobed of the familiar garment of our body; but he placed his unclothed spirit in the hands of Jesus, and his fear and care were over. See, he has quite done with it now! He prays no more for himself, but intercedes for his enemies; and then closes his eyes and falls asleep. This is the simple and sublime art of dying. Once more we take our guilty soul and place it in the dear pierced hand of him who is able to keep it; and then we feel assured that all is safe. The day's work is done, the doors are fastened, the watchman guards the streets; come, let us fall asleep. With Jesus seen, invoked, and trusted, it is sweet to die.

Notice, once again, that in Stephen we see *Jesus imitated*, the death of Stephen is a reproduction of the death of Jesus; let us hope that ours will be the same. It was so, even in little circumstances. Jesus died without [outside] the gate, so did Stephen; Jesus died praying, so did Stephen; Jesus died saying, "Father, into thy hands I commit my spirit"; Stephen cannot approach God absolutely, but he approaches him through the Mediator, and he says, "Lord Jesus, receive my spirit." Christ dies pleading for his murderers, so does Stephen: "Lord, lay not this sin to their charge." Now, if our death shall be a reproduction of the death of Jesus, why need we fear? It has hitherto been sweet to be made like him, and it will still be sweet: even to suffer with him has been delightful; surely it will be joyful to die with him. We are willing to sleep in Jesus' bed and lie as he did in the bosom of the earth, to arise in his likeness at the resurrection.

Thus you see, dear brethren, that Stephen's death was radiant with the glow of his Lord's brightness. Christ was glorified and reflected in him. None could question whose image and superscription he bore. If our lives shall be of that order, our deaths also shall be of the like character. Let your life be looking unto Jesus, pleading with Jesus, trusting in Jesus, copying Jesus, and then your departing moments will be attended by visions of Jesus and reproductions of his dying behavior. As you have been with him in the trials of life, he will be with you in the closing scenes of death. Happy they whose deathbed Jesus makes, and who sleep in Jesus, to be brought with him when he returns to take the kingdom.

III. From Stephen's departure we gather something as to *the kind of death which we may wisely desire*.

First, it is very desirable that *our death should be of a piece with our life*. Stephen was full of faith and of the Holy Ghost in life, and so was he full of the Holy Ghost in death. Stephen was bold, brave, calm, and composed in life; he is the same amid the falling stones. It is very sad when the reported account of a man's death does not fit in with his life. I am afraid that many funeral sermons have done great mischief by their flattery, for persons have very naturally said, "This is very strange, I never knew that the departed person was a saint until I heard this account of his end. Really, when I hear these wonderful things about him—well, I should not have thought it." No, it will not do to have no character for piety but that which is hurriedly run up in a few days of sickness and death. It is ill to die with a jerk, getting as it were upon another line of rails all on a sudden. It is better to glide from one degree of grace to another, and so to glory. We ought to die daily, die every morning before we go down to breakfast, that is to say, we should rehearse it all, so that when we come to die it will be no new thing to us. Death may be the fringe or border of life, but it should be made out of the same piece. A life of clay is not to be joined to a death of gold. We cannot hope to dine with the world and sup with God. We ought to dwell in the house of the Lord every day.

Again, it is most desirable that *death should be the perfecting of our whole career*, the putting of the cornerstone upon the edifice, so that when nothing else is wanted to complete the man's labors he falls asleep. Dear brethren, is it so with you? Suppose you were to die this morning in the pew; would your life be a complete life, or would it be like a broken column snapped off in the center? Why, there are some who even in their business lives have left many needful things undone; for instance, they have not made their wills yet and will cause much sorrow to wife and children through their neglect. Some Christian people do not keep their worldly affairs in proper order, but are lax, disorderly, and slovenly, so that if they were to die, there would be many things because of which they would feel loathe to die. Mr. Whitefield used to say when he went to bed at night, "I have not left even a pair of gloves out of their place: if I die tonight, all my affairs, for time and eternity, are in order." That is the best way to live; so that, let death come when it may, at midnight, cock-crowing, or midday, it will be a desirable *finis* to a book of which we have written the last line; we have finished our course, and served our generation, and our falling asleep is the fit conclusion of the matter.

May our death not be one of a kind which needs flurry and hot haste to make the man ready. There are people in the world who, if they were going off by train and knew of it a month beforehand, would be all in a fever an hour before they started; though they know the time the train starts, they cannot arrive a few minutes before by any means, but rush in just as the bell rings, and leap into a carriage only in time to save the train. Some die in that fashion, as if they had so much to do and were in such a hurry; and besides, had so little grace that they could be only saved so as by fire. When worldly Christians die, there is a deal to be done to pack up and get ready for departing; but a true Christian stands with his loins girded, he knows he has to travel; he does not know exactly when, but he stands with his staff in his hand. He knows the Bridegroom is soon coming, and he therefore keeps his lamp well trimmed. That is the way to live and the way to die. May the Holy Spirit put us in such a condition, that the angel of death may not summon us unawares, or catch us by surprise; then will going home be nothing out of the common way, but a simple matter. Bengel, the famous commentator, did not wish to die in spiritual parade, with a sensational scene, but to pass away like a person called out to the street door from the midst of business. His prayer was granted. He was revising the proof sheets of his works almost to the moment when he felt the death stroke. Is not this well? Equally desirable was the end of the Venerable Bede, who died as he completed his translation of the gospel of John. "Write quickly," said he, "for it is time for me to return to him who made me." "Dear master," said the pupil, "one sentence is still wanting." "Write quickly," said the venerable man. The young man soon added, "It is finished"; and Bede replied, "Thou hast well said, all is now finished," and he fell asleep. So would I desire to depart, so might every Christian desire; we would make no stir from our daily holiness, we would change our place but not our service; having waited on our Lord at this end of the room, we are called up higher, and we go.

It must be a dreadful thing for a professing Christian to die full of regrets for work neglected and opportunities wasted. It is sad to have to say, "I must leave my Sunday school class before I have earnestly warned those dear children to flee from the wrath to come." It would be wretched for me to go home today and say, "I have preached my last sermon, but it was not earnest nor calculated either to glorify God or benefit my fellowmen." Can the end of a wasted life be other than unhappy? Will it not be sorrowful to be called away with work undone and purposes unfulfilled? O my brethren, do not live so as to make it hard to die.

It must also be a sad thing to be taken away unwillingly, plucked like an unripe fruit from the tree. The unripe apple holds fast to its place, and so do many hold hard to their riches and cleave so fondly to worldly things that it needs a sharp pull to separate them from the world. The ripe fruit adheres but lightly, and when a gentle hand comes to take it, it yields itself freely, as if willing to be gathered, like an apple of gold into a basket of silver. God make you unworldly, and forbid that you should cleave so resolutely to things below as to make death a violence and departure a terror.

Brethren, we would not wish to die so that it should be a matter of question, especially to ourselves, to which place we are going, and yet you will die in that way if you live in that way. If you have no assurance of salvation, do you expect it to come to you on your dying bed? Why, my dear friend, when the pain increases and the brain becomes weary, you are very likely to suffer depression, and therefore you need strong faith to begin with for your own comfort then. Would you like friends to go out of your death chamber saying, "We hope he is saved, but we stand in doubt concerning him"? Your life should prevent that. Holy Mr. Whitefield, when someone observed, "I should like to hear your dying testimony," said, "No, I shall, in all probability bear no dying testimony." "Why not?" said the other. "Because I am bearing testimony every day while I live, and there will be the less need of it when I die." That seraphic apostle preached up to the last afternoon, and then went upstairs to bed and died. There was no need for anyone to ask, "What did he say when he was dying?" Ah no; they knew what he said when he was living, and that was a great deal better. Let your testimony in life be such that, whether you speak or not in your last moments, there shall be no question about whose you were nor whom you served.

In conclusion, one would desire to die so that *even our death should be useful*. I feel persuaded that Stephen's death had a great deal to do with Saul's conversion. Have you ever observed the evident influence of Stephen upon Paul? Augustine says, "If Stephen had never prayed, Saul had never preached." I do not say that the death of Stephen converted Saul; far from it; that change was worked by a divine interposition when Saul was on the road to Damascus; but what he saw in Stephen's martyrdom had made the soil ready to receive the good seed. Saul, in after life, seems to me to be always taking his text from Stephen's sermon. Read that sermon through at home, and see if it is not so. Stephen spoke about the covenant of circumcision, and that was a very favorite topic with Paul. When Paul stood at Athens on Mars' Hill and addressed the Areopagites he said to them, "God that made heaven and earth dwelleth not in temples made with hands," almost the identical words which Stephen had quoted, and surely the remembrance of Stephen before the Sanhedrin must have rushed over the apostle's mind at the time. There is yet another passage—and indeed I might carry on the parallel a very long way—where Stephen used the expression, "They received the law by the disposition of angels," an idea peculiar to Paul. Paul is the child of Stephen; Stephen dying is the seed out of which Paul springs up. What a privilege so to die that a phoenix may rise out of our ashes! If we have been useful ourselves up to the measure of a moderate ability, we may, as we die, call forth greater workers than ourselves; our expiring spark may kindle the divine light in some flaming beacon, which far across the seas shall scatter the beams of gospel light. And why not? God grant that we may, both in life and in death, serve him well. I would that even in our ashes might live our former lives, that being dead we yet may speak.

It was a happy thought of an earnest divine, who asked that when he was dead he might be placed in his coffin where all his congregation might come and see him, and that on his bosom should be placed a paper bearing this exhortation, "Remember the words which I have spoken to you, being yet present with you." Yes, we will go on telling of Jesus and winning souls in life and death, if God so helps us. Beloved believers, love the souls of men, and pray God to save them. As for you who are not saved yourselves, I implore you think of what your condition will be when you come to die; or, if a seared conscience should cause you to die in peace, think what you will do at the judgment, when that conscience will become tender. What will you do when the lips of the dear Redeemer shall say, "Depart, ye cursed, into everlasting fire in hell"?

Ye sinners, seek his grace,
Whose wrath ye cannot bear;
Look to the dying Savior's face,
And find salvation there.

Paul: As Pattern Convert

Published on Thursday, August 14, 1913; delivered at the Metropolitan Tabernacle, Newington. No. 3367.

> *Howbeit for this cause I obtained mercy, that in me first Jesus Christ might show forth all longsuffering, for a pattern to them which should hereafter believe on him to life everlasting.*—1 TIMOTHY 1:16

It is a vulgar error that the conversion of the apostle Paul was an uncommon and exceptional event, and that we cannot expect men to be saved nowadays after the same fashion. It is said that the incident was an exception to all rules, a wonder altogether by itself. Now my text is a flat contradiction to that notion, for it assures us that, instead of the apostle as a receiver of the longsuffering and mercy of God being at all an exception to the rule, he was a model convert, and is to be regarded as a type and pattern of God's grace in other believers. The apostle's language in the text, "for a pattern," may mean that he was what printers call a first proof, an early impression from the engraving, a specimen of those to follow. He was the typical instance of divine longsuffering, the model after which others are fashioned. To use a metaphor from the artist's studio, Paul was the ideal sketch of a convert, an outline of the work of Jesus on mankind, a cartoon of divine longsuffering. Just as artists make sketches in charcoal as the basis of their work, which outlines they paint out as the picture proceeds, so did the Lord in the apostle's case make, as it were, a cartoon or outline sketch of his usual work of grace. That outline in the case of each future believer he works out with infinite variety of skill, and produces the individual Christian, but the guiding lines are really there. All conversions are in a high degree similar to this pattern conversion. The transformation of persecuting Saul of Tarsus into the apostle Paul is a typical instance of the work of grace in the heart.

We will have no other preface, but proceed at once to two or three considerations. The first is that—

I. *In the conversion of Paul, the Lord had an eye to others, and in this Paul is a pattern.*

In every case the individual is saved, not for himself alone, but with a view to the good of others. Those who think the doctrine of election to be harsh should not deny it, for it is scriptural; but they may to their own minds soften some of its hardness by remembering that elect men bear a marked connection with the race. The Jews, as an elect people, were chosen in order to preserve the oracles of God for all nations and for all times. Men personally elected unto eternal life by divine grace are also elected that they may become chosen vessels to bear the name of Jesus unto others. While our Lord is said to be the Savior specially of them that believe, he is also called the Savior of all men; and while he has a special eye to the good of the one person whom he has chosen, yet through that person he has designs of love to others, perhaps even to thousands yet unborn.

The apostle Paul says, "I obtained mercy, that in me foremost Jesus Christ might show forth all longsuffering, for a pattern to them which should hereafter believe." Now, I think I see very clearly that *Paul's conversion had an immediate relation to the conversion of many others.* It had a tendency, had it not, to excite an interest in the minds of his brother Pharisee? Men of his class, men of culture, who were equally at home with the Greek philosophers and with the Jewish rabbis, men of influence, men of rank, would be sure to inquire, "What is this new religion which has fascinated Saul of Tarsus? That zealot for Judaism has now become a zealot for Christianity; what can there be in it?" I say that the natural tendency of his conversion was to awaken inquiry and thought, and so to lead others of his rank to become believers. And, my dear friend, if you have been saved, you ought to regard it as a token of God's mercy to your class. If you are a workingman, let your salvation be a blessing to the men with whom you labor. If you are a person of rank and station, consider that God intends to bless you to some with whom you are on familiar terms. If you are young, hope that God will bless the youth around you, and if you have come to older years, hope that your conversion, even at the eleventh hour, may be the means of encouraging other aged pilgrims to seek and find rest unto their souls. The Lord, by calling one out of any society of men, finds for himself a recruiting officer, who will enlist his fellows beneath the banner of the cross. May not this fact encourage some seeking soul to hope that the Lord may save him, though he be the only thoughtful person in all his family, and then make him to be the means of salvation to all his kindred.

We notice that *Paul often used the narrative of his conversion as an encouragement to others.* He was not ashamed to tell his own life story. Eminent soul winners, such as Whitefield and Bunyan, frequently pleaded God's mercy to themselves as an argument with their fellowmen. Though great preachers of another school, such as Robert Hall and Chalmers, do not mention themselves at all, and I can admire their abstinence, yet I am persuaded that if some of us were to follow their example, we should be throwing away one of the most powerful weapons of our warfare. What can be more affecting, more convincing, more overwhelming than the story of divine grace told by the very man who has experienced it? It is better than a score of tales of converted Africans, and infinitely more likely to win men's hearts than the most elaborate essays upon moral excellence. Again and again, Paul gave a long narrative of his conversion, for he felt it to be one of the most telling things that he could relate.

Whether he stood before Felix or Agrippa, this was his plea for the gospel. All through his epistles there are continual mentions of the grace of God toward himself, and we may be sure that the apostle did right thus to argue from his own case: it is fair and forcible reasoning, and ought by no means to be left unused because of a selfish dread of being called egotistical. God intends that we should use our conversion as an encouragement to others, and say to them, "Come and hear, all you that fear God, and I will tell you what he has done for my soul." We point to our own forgiveness and say, "Do but trust in the living Redeemer, and you shall find, as we have done, that Jesus blots out the transgressions of believers."

Paul's conversion was an encouragement to him all his life long to have hope for others. Have you ever read the first chapter of the epistle to the Romans? Well, the man who penned those terrible verses might very naturally have written at the end of them, "Can these monsters be reclaimed? It can be of no avail whatever to preach the gospel to people so sunken in vice." That one chapter gives as daring an outline as delicacy would permit of the nameless, shameful vices into which the heathen world had plunged, and yet, after all, Paul went forth to declare the gospel to that filthy and corrupt generation, believing that God meant to save a people out of it. Surely one element of his hope for humanity must have been found in the fact of his own salvation; he considered himself to be in some respects as bad as the heathen, and in other respects even worse: he calls himself the *foremost* of sinners (that is the word); and he speaks of God having saved him foremost, that in him he might show forth all longsuffering. Paul never doubted the possibility of the conversion of a person however infamous, after he had himself been converted. This strengthened him in battling with the fiercest opponents—he who overcame such a wild beast as I was, can also tame others and bring them into willing captivity to his love.

There was yet another relation between Paul's conversion and the salvation of others, and it was this: *It served as an impulse,* driving him forward in his life-work of bringing sinners to Christ.

"I obtained mercy," said he, "and that same voice which spoke peace to me said, 'I have made thee a chosen vessel unto me to bear my name among the gentiles.'" And he did bear it, my brethren. Going into regions beyond that, he might not build on another man's foundation, he became a master builder for the church of God. How indefatigably did he labor! With what vehemence did he pray! With what energy did he preach! Slander and contempt he bore with the utmost patience. Scourging or stoning had no terrors for him. Imprisonment, yes, death itself, he defied; nothing could daunt him. Because the Lord had saved him, he felt that he must by all means save some. He could not be quiet. Divine love was in him like a fire, and if he had been silent, he would ere long have had to cry with the prophet of old, "I am weary with restraining." He is the man who said, "Necessity is laid upon me; yea, woe is unto me, if I preach not the gospel." Paul, the extraordinary sinner, was saved that he might be full of extraordinary zeal and bring multitudes to eternal life. Well could he say—

> *The love of Christ doth me constrain*
> *To seek the wandering souls of men;*
> *With cries, entreaties, tears to save,*
> *To snatch them from the fiery wave.*
>
> *My life, my blood, I here present,*
> *If for thy truth they may be spent;*
> *Fulfill thy sovereign counsel, Lord!*
> *Thy will be done, thy name adored!*

Now, I will pause here a minute to put a question. You profess to be converted, my dear friend. What relation has your conversion already had to other people? It ought to have a very apparent one. Has it had such? Mr. Whitefield said that when his heart was renewed, his first desire was that his companions with whom he had previously wasted his time might be brought to Christ. It was natural and commendable that he should begin with them. Remember how one of the apostles, when he discovered the Savior, went immediately to tell his brother. It is most fitting that young people should spend their first religious enthusiasm upon their brothers and sisters. As to converted parents, their first responsibility is in reference to their sons and daughters. Upon each renewed man, his natural affinities, or the bonds of friendship, or the looser ties of neighborhood should begin to operate at once, and each one should feel, "No man liveth unto himself."

If divine grace has kindled a fire in you, it is that your fellowmen may burn with the same flame. If the eternal fount has filled you with living water, it is that out of the midst of you should flow rivers of living water. You are blessed that you may bless; whom have you blessed yet? Let the question go around. Do not avoid it. This is the best return that you can make to God, that when he saves you, you should seek to be the instruments in his hands of saving others. What have you done yet? Did you ever speak with the friend who shares your pew? He's been sitting there for a long time, and may, perhaps, be an unconverted person; have you pointed him to the Lamb of God? Have you ever spoken to your servants about their souls? Have you yet broken the ice sufficiently to speak to your own sister or your own brother? Do begin, dear friend.

You cannot tell what mysterious threads connect you with your fellowmen and their destiny. There was a cobbler once, as you know, in Northamptonshire. Who could see any connection between him and the millions of India? But the love of God was in his bosom, and Carey could not rest till, at Serampore, he had commenced to translate the Word of God and preach to his fellowmen. We must not confine our thoughts to the few whom Carey brought to Christ, though to save one soul is worthy of a life of sacrifice, but Carey became the forerunner and leader of a missionary band which will never cease to labor till India bows before Emmanuel. That man mysteriously drew, is drawing, and will draw India to the Lord Jesus Christ. Brother, you do not know what your power is. Awake and try it.

Did you never read this passage: "Thou hast given him power over all flesh, that he should give eternal life to as many as thou hast given him"? Now the Lord has given to his Son power over all flesh, and with a part of that power Jesus clothes his servants. Through you, he will give eternal life to certain of his chosen; by you, and by no other means, will they be brought to himself. Look about you, regenerate man. Your life may be made sublime. Rouse yourself! Begin to think of what God may do by you! Calculate the possibilities which be before you with the eternal God as your helper. Shake yourself from the dust and put on the beautiful garments of disinterested love to others, and it shall yet be seen how grandly gracious God has been to hundreds of men by having converted you. So far, then, Paul's salvation, because it had so clear a reference to others, was a pattern of all conversions.

II. Now, second, *Paul's foremost position as a sinner did not prevent his becoming foremost in grace, and herein again he is a pattern to us.*

Foremost in sin, he became also foremost in service. Saul of Tarsus was a *blasphemer,* and he is to be commended because he has not recorded any of those blasphemies. We can never object to converted burglars and chimney sweepers, of whom we hear so much, telling the story of their conversion; but when they go into dirty details, they had better hold their tongues. Paul tells us that he was a blasphemer, but he never repeats one of the blasphemies. We invent enough evil in our own hearts without being told of other men's stale profanities. If, however, any of you are so curious as to want to know what kind of blasphemies Paul could utter, you have only to converse with a converted Jew, and he will tell you what horrible words some of his nation will speak against our Lord. I have no doubt that Paul in his evil state thought as wickedly of Christ as he could—considered him to be an imposter, called him so, and added many an opprobrious epithet. He does not say of himself that he was an unbeliever and an objector, but he says that he was a blasphemer, which is a very strong word, but not too strong, for the apostle never went beyond the truth. He was a downright, thoroughgoing blasphemer, who also caused others to blaspheme. Will these lines meet the eye of a profane person who feels the greatness of his sin? May God grant that he may be encouraged to seek mercy as Saul of Tarsus did, for "all manner of sin and blasphemy" does he forgive unto men.

From blasphemy, which was the sin of the lips, Saul proceeded *to persecution,* which is a sin of the hands. Hating Christ, he hated his people too. He was delighted to give his vote for the death of Stephen, and he took care of the clothes of those who stoned that martyr. He hauled men and women to prison, and compelled them to blaspheme. When he had hunted all Judea as closely as he could, he obtained letters to go to Damascus, that he might do the same in that place. His prey had been compelled to quit Jerusalem and fly to more remote places, but "being exceeding mad against them, he persecuted them unto strange cities." He was foremost in blasphemy and persecution. Will a persecutor read or hear these words? If so, may he be led to see that even for him pardon is possible. Jesus, who said, "Father, forgive them; for they know not what they do," is still an Intercessor for the most violent of his enemies.

He adds, next, that he was *injurious,* which, I think, Bengel considers to mean that he was a despiser: that eminent critic says—blasphemy was his sin toward God, persecution was his sin toward the church, and despising was his sin in his own heart. He was injurious—that is, he did all he could to damage the cause of Christ, and he thereby injured himself. He kicked against the pricks and injured his own conscience. He was so determined against Christ that he counted no cost too great by which he might hinder the spread of the faith, and he did hinder it terribly; he was a ringleader in resisting the Spirit of God which was then working with the church of Christ. He was foremost in opposition to the cross of Christ.

Now notice that he was saved as a pattern, which is to show you that if you also have been foremost in sin, you also may obtain mercy, as Paul did: and to show you yet again that if you have not been foremost, the grace of God, which is able to save the chief of sinners, can assuredly save those who are of less degree. If the bridge of grace will carry the elephant, it will certainly carry the mouse. If the mercy of God could bear with the hugest sinners, it can have patience with you. If a gate is wide enough for a giant to pass through, any ordinary-sized mortal will find space enough. Despair's head is cut off and stuck on a pole by the salvation of "the chief of sinners." No man can now say that he is too great a sinner to be saved, because the chief of sinners was saved eighteen hundred years ago. If the ringleader, the chief of the gang, has been washed in the precious blood, and is now in heaven, why not I? Why not *you*?

After Paul was saved, he became a foremost saint. The Lord did not allot him a second-class place in the church. He had been the leading sinner, but his Lord did not, therefore, say, "I save you, but I shall always remember your wickedness to your disadvantage." Not so: he counted him faithful, putting him into the ministry and into the apostleship, so that he was not a whit behind the very chief of the apostles. Brother, there is no reason why, if you have gone very far in sin, you should not go equally far in usefulness. On the contrary, there is a reason why you should do so, for it is a rule of grace that to whom much is forgiven, the same loves much, and much love leads to much service.

What man was more clear in his knowledge of doctrine than Paul? What man more earnest in the defense of truth? What man more self-sacrificing? What man more heroic? The name of Paul in the Christian church stands in some respects the very next to the Lord Jesus. Turn to the New Testament and see how large a space is occupied by the Holy Spirit speaking through his servant Paul; and then look over Christendom and see how greatly the man's influence is still felt, and must be felt till his Master shall come. O great sinner, if you are even now ready to scoff at Christ, my prayer is that he may strike you down at this very moment, and turn you into one of his children, and make you to be just as ardent for the truth as you are now earnest against it, as desperately set on good as now you are on evil. None make such mighty Christians and such fervent preachers as those who are lifted up from the lowest depths of sin and washed and purified through the blood of Jesus Christ. May grace do this with you, my dear friend, whoever you may be.

Thus we gather from our text that the Lord showed mercy to Paul, that in him foremost it might be seen that prominence in sin is no barrier to eminence in grace, but the very reverse. Now I come to where the stress of the text lies.

III. Paul's case was a pattern of other conversions as an instance of longsuffering.

"That in me foremost Jesus Christ might show forth all longsuffering, for a cartoon or pattern to them which should hereafter believe." Thoughtfully observe the great longsuffering of God to Paul: he says, "He showed forth all longsuffering." Not only all the longsuffering of God that ever was shown to anybody else, but all that could be supposed to exist—all longsuffering.

> *All thy mercy's height I prove,*
> *All its depth is found in me,*

as if he had gone to the utmost stretch of his tether in sin, and the Lord also had strained his longsuffering to its utmost.

That longsuffering was seen first *in sparing his life* when he was rushing headlong in sin, breathing out threatenings, foaming at the mouth with denunciations of the Nazarene and his people. If the Lord had but lifted his finger, Saul would have been crushed like a moth, but almighty wrath forbore, and the rebel lived on. Nor was this all; after all his sin, the Lord allowed mercy to be possible to him. He blasphemed and persecuted, at a red-hot rate; and is it not a marvel that the Lord did not say, "Now, at last, you have gone beyond all bearing, and you shall die like Herod, eaten of worms"? It would not have been at all wonderful if God had so sentenced him; but he allowed him to live within the reach of mercy, and, better still, he in due time actually sent the gospel to him, and laid it home to his heart. In the very midst of his rebellion the Lord saved him. He had not prayed to be converted, far from it; no doubt he had that very day along the road to Damascus profaned the Savior's name, and yet mighty mercy burst in and saved him purely by its own spontaneous native energy. Oh, mighty grace, free grace, victorious grace! This was longsuffering indeed!

When divine mercy had called Paul, *it swept all his sin away,* every particle of it, his bloodshedding and his blasphemy, all at once, so that never man was more assured of his own perfect cleansing than was the apostle. "There is therefore now," says he, "no condemnation to them which are in Christ Jesus." "Therefore, being justified by faith, we have peace with God." "Who shall lay anything to the charge of God's elect?" You know how clear he was about that; and he spoke out of his own experience. Longsuffering had washed all his sins away. Then that longsuffering reaching from the depths of sin lifted him right up to the apostleship, so that he began to prove God's longsuffering in its heights of favor. What a privilege it must have been to him to be permitted to preach the gospel. I should think sometimes when he was preaching most earnestly, he would half stop himself and say, "Paul, is this you?" When he went down to Tarsus especially he must have been surprised at himself and at the mighty mercy of God. He preached the faith which once he had destroyed. He must have said many a time after a sermon, when he went home to his bedchamber, "Marvel of marvels! Wonder of wonders, that I who once could curse have now been made to preach—that I, who was full of threatening and even breathed out slaughter, should now be so inspired by the Spirit of God that I weep at the very sound of Jesus' name, and count all things but loss for the excellency of the knowledge of Christ Jesus my Lord."

O brothers and sisters, you do not measure longsuffering except you take it in all its length from one end to the other, and see God in mercy not remembering his servant's sin, but lifting him into eminent service in his church. Now this was for a pattern, to show you that he will show forth the same longsuffering to those who believe. If you have been a swearer, he will cleanse your blackened mouth, and put his praises into it. Have you had a black, cruel heart, full of enmity to Jesus? He will remove it and give you a new heart and a right spirit. Have you dived into all sorts of sins? Are they so shameful that you dare not think of them? Think of the precious blood which removes every stain. Are your sins so many that you could not count them? Do you feel as if you were almost damned already in the very memory of your life? I do not wonder at it, but he is able to save to the uttermost them that come unto God by him. You have not gone further than Saul had gone, and therefore all longsuffering can come to you, and there are great possibilities of future holiness and usefulness before you. Even though you may have been a streetwalker or a thief, yet if the grace of God cleanses you, it can make something wonderful out of you: full many a lustrous jewel of Emmanuel's crown has been taken from the dunghill. You are a rough block of stone, but Jesus can fashion and polish you, and set you as a pillar in his temple.

Brother, do not despair. See what Saul was and what Paul became, and learn what you may be. Though you deserve the depths of hell, yet up to the heights of heaven grace can lift you. Though now you feel as if the fiends of the pit would be fit companions for such a lost spirit as yourself, yet believe in the Lord Jesus, and you shall one day walk among the angels as pure and white as they. Paul's experience of longsuffering grace was meant to be a pattern of what God will do for you.

> *Scripture says, "Where sin abounded,*
> *There did grace much more abound";*
> *Thus has Satan been confounded,*
> *And his own discomfit found.*
> *Christ has triumphed!*
> *Spread the glorious news around.*

> *Sin is strong, but grace is stronger;*
> *Christ than Satan more supreme;*
> *Yield, oh, yield to sin no longer,*
> *Turn to Jesus, yield to him—*
> *He has triumphed!*
> *Sinners, henceforth him esteem.*

IV. *The mode of Paul's conversion was also meant to be a pattern,* and with this I shall finish.

I do not say that we may expect to receive the miraculous revelation which was given to Paul, but yet it is a sketch upon which any conversion can be painted. The filling up is not the same in any two cases, but the outline sketch. Paul's conversion would serve for an outline sketch of the conversion of any one of us. How was that conversion worked? Well, it is clear that there was nothing at all in Paul to contribute to his salvation. You might have sifted him in a sieve, without finding anything upon which you could rest a hope that he would be converted to the faith of Jesus. His natural bent, his early training, his whole surroundings, and his life's pursuits, all lettered him to Judaism, and made it most unlikely that he would ever become a Christian. The first elder of the church that ever talked to him about divine things could hardly believe in his conversion. "Lord," said he, "I have heard by many of this man, how much evil he hath done to thy saints at Jerusalem." He could hardly think it possible that the ravening wolf should have changed into a lamb. Nothing favorable to faith in Jesus could have been found in Saul; the soil of his heart was very rocky, the plowshare could not touch it, and the good seed found no roothold. Yet the Lord converted Saul, and he can do the like by other sinner, but it must be a work of pure grace and of divine power, for there is not in any man's fallen nature a holy spot of the size of a pin's point on which grace can light. Transforming grace can find no natural lodgment in our hearts, it must create its own soil; and, blessed be God, it can do it, for with God all things are possible. Nature contributes nothing to grace, and yet grace wins the day. Humbled soul, let this cheer you. Though there is nothing good in you, yet grace can work wonders, and save you by its own might.

Paul's conversion was an instance of divine power, and of that alone, and so is every true conversion. If your conversion is an instance of the preacher's power, you need to be converted again; if your salvation is the result of your own power, it is a miserable deception, from which may you be delivered. Every man who is saved must be operated upon by the might of God the Holy Spirit: every jot and tittle of true regeneration is the Spirit's work. As for our strength, it wars against salvation rather than for it. Blessed is that promise, "Thy people shall be willing in the day of thy power." Conversion is as much a work of God's omnipotence as the resurrection; and as the dead do not raise themselves, so neither do men convert themselves.

But Saul was changed immediately. His conversion was once done, and done at once. There was a little interval before he found peace, but even during those three days he was a changed man, though he was in sadness. He was under the power of Satan at one moment, and in the next he was under the reign of grace. This is also true in every conversion. However gradual the breaking of the day, there is a time when the sun is below the horizon, and a moment when he is no longer so. You may not know the exact time in which you passed from death to life, But there was such a time, if you are indeed a believer. A man may not know how old he is, but there was a moment in which he was born. In every conversion there is a distinct change from darkness to light, from death to life, just as certainly as there was in Paul's. And what a delightful hope does the rapidity of regeneration present to us! It is by no long and laborious process that we escape from sin. We are not compelled to remain in sin for a single moment.

Grace brings instantaneous liberty to those who sit in bondage. He who trusts Jesus is saved on the spot. Why, then, abide in death? Why not lift up your eyes to immediate life and light?

Paul proved his regeneration by his faith. He believed unto eternal life. He tells us over and over again in his epistles that he was saved by faith, and not by works. So is it with every man; if saved at all, it is by simply believing in the Lord Jesus. Paul esteemed his own works to be less than nothing, and called them dross and dung, that he might win Christ, and so every converted man renounces his own works that he may be saved by grace alone. Whether he has been moral or immoral, whether he has lived an amiable and excellent life, or whether he has raked in the kennels of sin, every regenerate man has one only hope, and that is centered and fixed in Jesus alone. Faith in Jesus Christ is the mark of salvation, even as the heaving of the lungs or the coming of breath from the nostrils is the test of life. Faith is the grace which saves the soul, and its absence is a fatal sign. How does this fact affect you, dear friend? Have you faith or no?

Paul was very positively and evidently saved. You did not need to ask the question, Is that man a Christian or not? For the transformation was most apparent. If Saul of Tarsus had appeared as he used to be, and Paul the apostle could also have come in, and you could have seen the one man as two men, you would have thought them no relation to one another. Paul the apostle would have said that he was dead to Saul of Tarsus, and Saul of Tarsus would have gnashed his teeth at Paul the apostle. The change was evident to all who knew him, whether they sympathized in it or not. They could not mistake the remarkable difference which grace had made, for it was as great as when midnight brightens into noon. So it is when a man is truly saved: there is a change which those around him must perceive. Do not tell me that you can be a child at home and become a Christian, and yet your father and mother will not perceive a difference in you. They will be sure to see it. Would a leopard in a menagerie lose his spots and no one notice it? Would an Ethiopian be turned white and no one hear of it? You, masters and mistresses, will not go in and out among your servants and children without their perceiving a change in you if you are born again. At least, dear brother or sister, strive with all your might to let the change be very apparent in your language, in your actions, and in your whole conduct. Let your conversation be such as becomes the gospel of Christ, that men may see that you, as well as the apostle, are decidedly changed by the renewal of your minds.

May all of us be the subjects of divine grace as Paul was: stopped in our mad career, blinded by the glory of the heavenly light, called by a mysterious voice, conscious of natural blindness, relieved of blinding scales, and made to see Jesus as one all in all. May we prove in our own persons how speedily conviction may melt into conversion, conversion into confession, and confession into consecration.

I have done when I have inquired how far we are conformed to the pattern which God has set before us. I know we are like Paul as to our sin, for if we have neither blasphemed nor persecuted, yet have we sinned as far as we have had opportunity. We are also conformed to Paul's pattern in the great longsuffering of God which we have experienced, and I am not sure that we cannot carry the parallel further: we have had much the same revelation that Paul received on the way to Damascus, for we, too, have learned that Jesus is the Christ. If any of us sin against Christ, it will not be because we do not know him to be the Son of God, for we all believe in his deity, because our Bibles tell us so. The pattern goes so far: I would that the grace of God would operate upon you, unconverted friend, and complete the picture, by giving you like faith with Paul. Then will you be saved, as Paul was. Then also you will love Christ above all things, as Paul did, and you will say, "But what things were gain to me, those I counted loss for Christ. Yea, doubtless, and I count all things but loss for the excellency of the knowledge of Christ Jesus my Lord." He rested upon what Christ had done in his death and resurrection, and he found pardon and eternal life at once, and became, therefore, a devoted Christian.

What say you, dear friend? Are you moved to follow Paul's example? Does the Spirit of God prompt you to trust Paul's Savior, and give up every other ground of trust and rely upon him? Then do so and live. Does there seem to be a hand holding you back, and do you hear an evil whisper saying, "You are too great a sinner"? Turn around and bid the fiend depart, for the text gives him the lie. "In me *foremost* hath Jesus Christ showed forth all longsuffering, for a pattern to them which should hereafter believe on his name." God has saved Paul. Back, then, O devil! The Lord can save any man, and he can save me. Jesus Christ of Nazareth is mighty to save, and I will rely on him. If any poor heart shall reason thus, its logic will be sound and unanswerable. Mercy to one is an argument for mercy to another, for there is no difference, but the same Lord over all is rich unto all that call upon him.

Now I have set the case before you, and I cannot do more; it remains with each individual to accept or refuse. One man can bring a horse to the trough, but a hundred cannot make him drink. There is the gospel; if you want it, take it, but if you will not have it, then I must discharge my soul by reminding you that even the gentle gospel—the gospel of love and mercy has nothing to say to you but this, "He that believeth not shall be damned."

> How they deserve the deepest hell,
> That slight the joys above;
> What chains of vengeance must they feel,
> Who break the bonds of love.

God grant that you may yield to mighty love, and find peace in Christ Jesus.

Onesimus: The Story of a Runaway Slave

Published in 1875; delivered at the Metropolitan Tabernacle, Newington. No. 1268.

Perhaps he therefore departed for a season, that thou shouldest receive him forever.—PHILEMON 15

Nature is selfish, but grace is loving. He who boasts that he cares for nobody, and nobody cares for him, is the reverse of a Christian, for Jesus Christ enlarges the heart when he cleanses it. None so tender and sympathetic as our Master, and if we be truly his disciples, the same mind will be in us which was also in Christ Jesus. The apostle Paul was eminently large-hearted and sympathetic. Surely he had enough to do at Rome to bear his own troubles and to preach the gospel. If, like the priest in the parable of the good Samaritan, he had "passed by on the other side," he might have been excused, for he was on the urgent business of that Master who once said to his seventy messengers, "Salute no man by the way." We might not have wondered if he had said, "I cannot find time to attend to the wants of a runaway slave." But Paul was not of that mind. He had been preaching, and Onesimus had been converted, and henceforth he regarded him as his own son. I do not know why Onesimus came to Paul. Perhaps he went to him as a great many scapegraces have come to me—because their fathers knew me; and so, as Onesimus' master had known Paul, the servant applied to his master's friend, perhaps to beg some little help in his extremity. Anyhow, Paul seized the opportunity and preached to him Jesus, and the runaway slave became a believer in the Lord Jesus Christ.

Paul watched him, admired the character of his convert, and was glad to be served by him, and when he thought it right that he should return to his master, Philemon, he took a deal of trouble to compose a letter of apology for him, a letter which shows long thinking, since every word is well selected: albeit that the Holy Spirit dictated it, inspiration does not prevent a man's exercising thought and care on what he writes. Every word is chosen for a purpose. If he had been pleading for himself, he could not have pleaded more earnestly or wisely. Paul, as you know, was not accustomed to write letters with his own hand, but dictated to an amanuensis. It is supposed that he had an affliction of the eyes, and therefore when he did write he used large capital letters, as he says in one of the epistles, "Ye see how large a letter I have written unto you with my own hand." The epistle was not a large one, but he probably alluded to the largeness of the characters which he was obliged to use whenever he himself wrote. This letter to Philemon, at least part of it, was not dictated, but was written by his own hand. See verse 19: "I Paul have written it with mine own hand. I will repay it." It is the only note of hand which I recollect in Scripture, but there it is—an IOU for whatever amount Onesimus may have stolen.

Let us cultivate a large-hearted spirit, and sympathize with the people of God, especially with new converts, if we find them in trouble through past wrongdoing. If anything needs setting right, do not let us condemn them offhand, and say, "You have been stealing from your master, have you? You profess to be converted, but we do not believe it." Such suspicious and severe treatment may be deserved, but it is not such as the love of Christ would suggest. Try and set the fallen ones right, and give them again, as we say, "a fair start in the world." If God has forgiven them, surely we may, and if Jesus Christ has received them, they cannot be too bad for us to receive. Let us do for them what Jesus would have done had he been here, so shall we truly be the disciples of Jesus.

Thus I introduce to you the text, and I notice concerning it, first that it contains *a singular instance of divine grace*. Second, it brings before us *a case of sin overruled*. And, third, it may be regarded as *an example of relationship improved by grace*, for now he that was a servant for a season will abide with Philemon all his lifetime, and be no more a servant but a brother beloved.

I. But, first, let us look at Onesimus as *an instance of divine grace*.

We see the grace of God in his *election*. He was a slave. In those days slaves were very ignorant, untaught, and degraded. Being barbarously used, they were for the most part themselves sunk in the lowest barbarism, neither did their masters attempt to raise them out of it; it is possible that Philemon's attempt to do good to Onesimus may have been irksome to the man, and he may therefore have fled from his house. His master's prayers, warnings, and Christian regulations may have been disagreeable to him, and therefore he ran away. He wronged his master, which he could scarcely have done if he had not been treated as a confidential servant to some extent. Possibly the unusual kindness of Philemon, and the trust reposed in him may have been too much for his untrained nature. We know not what he stole, but evidently he had taken something, for the apostle says, "If he hath wronged thee, or oweth thee ought, put that on mine account." He ran away from Colosse, therefore, and thinking that he would be less likely to be discovered by the ministers of justice, he sought the city of Rome, which was then as large as the city of London now is, and perhaps larger. There in those back slums, such as the Jews' quarter in Rome now is, Onesimus would go and hide; or among those gangs of thieves which infested the imperial city, he would not be known or heard of any more, so he thought; and he could live the free and easy life of a thief. Yet, mark you, the Lord looked out of heaven with an eye of love, and set that eye on Onesimus.

Were there no free men, that God must elect a slave? Were there no faithful servants, that he must choose one who had embezzled his master's money? Were there none of the educated and polite, that he must needs look upon a barbarian? Were there none among the moral and the excellent, that infinite love should fix itself upon this degraded being, who was now mixed up with the very scum of society? And what the scum of society was in old Rome I should not like to think, for the upper classes were about as brutalized in their general habits as we can very well conceive; and what the lowest scum of all must have been, none of us can tell. Onesimus was part and parcel of the dregs of a sink of sin. Read Paul's first chapter of the epistle to the Romans, if you can, and you will see in what a horrible state the heathen world was at that time, and Onesimus was among the worst of the worst; and yet eternal love, which passed by kings and princes, and left Pharisees and Sadducees, philosophers and magi, to stumble in the dark as they chose, fixed its eye upon this poor benighted creature that he might be made a vessel to honor, fit for the Master's use.

> *When the Eternal bows the skies*
> *To visit earthly things,*
> *With scorn divine he turns his eyes*
> *From towers of haughty kings.*
>
> *He bids his awful chariot roll*
> *Far downward from the skies,*
> *To visit every humble soul,*
> *With pleasure in his eyes.*
>
> *Why should the Lord that reigns above*
> *Disdain so lofty kings?*
> *Say, Lord, and why such looks of love*
> *Upon such worthless things?*

Mortals, be dumb; what creature dares
Dispute his awful will?
Ask no account of his affairs,
But tremble and be still.

Just like his nature is his grace,
All sovereign, and all free;
Great God, how searchless are thy ways,
How deep thy judgments be!

"I will have mercy on whom I will have mercy, and I will have compassion on whom I will have compassion" rolls like thunder alike from the cross of Calvary and from the mount of Sinai. The Lord is a sovereign, and does as he pleases. Let us admire that marvelous electing love which selected such a one as Onesimus!

Grace also is to be observed, in the next place, in the *conversion* of this runaway slave.

Look at him! How unlikely he appears to become a convert. He is an Asiatic slave of about the same class as an ordinary lascar, or heathen.. He was, however, worse than the ordinary lascar who is certainly free, and probably an honest man, if he is nothing else. This man had been dishonest, and he was daring withal, for after taking his master's property he was bold enough to make a long journey from Colosse to reach Rome. But everlasting love means to convert the man, and converted he shall be. He may have heard Paul preach at Colosse and Athens, but yet he had not been impressed. In Rome, Paul was not preaching in St. Peter's; it was in no such noble building. Paul was not preaching in a place like the tabernacle, where Onesimus could have a comfortable seat—no such place as that—but it was probably down there at the back of the Palatine hill, where the praetorian guard have their lodgings, and where there was a prison called the Praetorium. In a bare room in the barrack prison, Paul sat with a soldier chained to his hand, preaching to all who were admitted to hear him, and there it was that the grace of God reached the heart of this wild young man, and, oh, what a change it made in him immediately! Now you see him repenting of his sin, grieved to think he has wronged a good man, vexed to see the depravity of his heart as well as the error of his life. He weeps; Paul preaches to him Christ crucified, and the glance of joy is in his eye: and from that heavy heart a load is taken. New thoughts light up that dark mind; the very face is changed, and the entire man renewed, for the grace of God can turn the lion to a lamb, the raven to a dove.

Some of us, I have no doubt, are quite as wonderful instances of divine election and effectual calling as Onesimus was. Let us, therefore, record the lovingkindness of the Lord, and let us say to ourselves, "Christ shall have the glory of it. The Lord has done it; and unto the Lord be honor; world without end."

The grace of God was conspicuous in *the character which it worked in Onesimus* upon his conversion, for he appears to have been helpful, useful, and profitable. So Paul says. Paul was willing to have had him as an associate, and it is not every man that is converted that we should altogether choose as a companion. There are odd people to be met with who will go to heaven, we have no doubt, for they are pilgrims on the right way, but we would like to keep on the other side of the road, for they are cross-grained, and there is a something about them that one's nature can no more delight in than the palate can take pleasure in nauseous physic. They are a sort of spiritual hedgehogs; they are alive and useful, and no doubt they illustrate the wisdom and patience of God, but they are not good companions: one would not like to carry them in his bosom. But Onesimus was evidently of a kind, tender, loving spirit. Paul at once called him brother, and would have liked to retain him. When he sent him back, was it not a clear proof of change of heart in Onesimus that he would go back?

Away as he was in Rome, he might have passed on from one town to another and have remained perfectly free, but feeling that he was under some kind of bond to his master—especially since he had injured him—he takes Paul's advice to return to his old position. He will go back, and take a letter of apology or introduction to his master; for he tells that it is his duty to make reparation for the wrong that he has done. I always like to see a resolve to make restitution of former wrongs in people who profess to be converted. If they have taken any money wrongfully they ought to repay it; it were well if they returned sevenfold. If we have in any way robbed or wronged another, I think the first instincts of grace in the heart will suggest compensation in all ways within our power. Do not think it is to be got over by saying, "God has forgiven me, and therefore I may leave it." No, dear friend, but inasmuch as God has forgiven you, try to undo all the wrong, and prove the sincerity of your repentance by so doing. So Onesimus will go back to Philemon, and work out his term of years with him, or otherwise do Philemon's wishes, for though he might have preferred to wait upon Paul, his first duty was due to the man whom he had injured. That showed a gentle, humble, honest, upright spirit; and let Onesimus be commended for it; no, let the grace of God be extolled for it. Look at the difference between the man who robbed, and the man who now comes back to be profitable to his master.

What wonders the grace of God has done! Brethren, let me add: What wonders the grace of God can do! Many plans are employed in the world for the reformation of the wicked and the reclaiming of the fallen, and to every one of these, as far as they are rightly bottomed, we wish good success; for whatever things are lovely and pure, and of good report, we wish them God-speed. But mark this word: the true reforming of the drunkard lies in giving him a new heart; the true reclaiming of the harlot is to be found in a renewed nature. Purity will never come to fallen women by those hideous Contagious Diseases Acts, which, to my mind, wear, like Cain, a curse upon their forehead. Womanhood will but sink the lower under such laws. The harlot must be washed in the Savior's blood, or she will never be clean. The lowest strata of society will never be brought into the light of virtue, sobriety, and purity, except by Jesus Christ and his gospel; and we must stick to that. Let all others do what they like, but God forbid that I should glory save in the cross of our Lord Jesus Christ. I see certain of my brethren fiddling away at the branches of the tree of vice with their wooden saws, but, as for the gospel, it lays the ax at the roots of the whole forest of evil, and if it be fairly received into the heart it fells all the upas trees at once, and instead of them there spring up the fir tree, the pine tree, and the box tree together, to beautify the house of our Master's glory. Let us, when we see what the Spirit of God can do for men, publish the grace of God, and extol it with all our might.

II. And now, second, we have in our text, and its connections, a very interesting *instance of sin overruled.*

Onesimus had no right to rob his master and run away; but God was pleased to make use of that crime for his conversion. It brought him to Rome, and so brought him where Paul was preaching, and thus it brought him to Christ, and to his right mind. Now, when we speak of this, we must be cautious. When Paul says, "Perhaps he departed for a season, that thou shouldest receive him forever," he does not excuse his departure. He does not make it out that Onesimus did right—not for a moment. Sin is sin, and, whatever sin may be overruled to do, yet sin is still sin. The crucifixion of our Savior has brought the greatest conceivable blessings upon mankind, yet nonetheless it was "with wicked hands" that they took Jesus and crucified him. The selling of Joseph into Egypt was the means in the hand of God of the preservation of Jacob, and his sons, in the time of famine; but his brethren had nothing to do with that, and they were nonetheless guilty for having sold their brother for a slave.

Let it always be remembered that the faultiness or virtue of an act is not contingent upon the result of that act. If, for instance, a man who has been set on a railway to turn the switch forgets to do it, you call it a very great crime if the train comes to mischief and a dozen people are killed. Yes, but the crime is the same if nobody is killed. It is not the result of the carelessness, but the carelessness itself which deserves punishment. If it were the man's duty to turn the switch in such-and-such a way, and his not doing so should even by some strange accident turn to the saving of life, the man would be equally blameworthy. There would be no credit due to him, for if his duty lies in a certain line, his fault also lies in a certain line, namely, the neglecting of that duty. So if God overrules sin for good, as he sometimes does, it is nonetheless sin. It is sin just as much as ever, only there is so much the more glory to the wonderful wisdom and grace of God who, out of evil, brings forth good, and so does what only omnipotent wisdom can perform. Onesimus is not excused, then, for having embezzled his master's goods nor for having left him without right; he still is a transgressor, but God's grace is glorified.

Remember, too, that this must be noticed—that when Onesimus left his master he was performing an action the results of which, in all probability, would have been ruinous to him. He was living as a trusted dependent beneath the roof of a kind master, who had a church in his house. If I read the epistle rightly, he had a godly mistress and a godly master, and he had an opportunity of learning the gospel continually; but this reckless young blade, very likely, could not bear it, and could have lived more contentedly with a heathen master, who would have beaten him one day and made him drunk another. The Christian master he could not bear, so away he went. He threw away the opportunities of salvation, and he went to Rome, and he must have gone into the lowest part of the city, and associated, as I have already told you, with the very grossest company. Now, had it come to pass that he had joined in the insurrections of the slaves which took place frequently about that time, as he in all probability would have done had not grace prevented, he would have been put to death as others had been. He would have had short shrift in Rome: half suspect a man and off with his head was the rule toward slaves and vagabonds. Onesimus was just the very man that would have been likely to be hurried to death and to eternal destruction. He had put his head, as it were, between the lion's jaws by what he had done. When a young man suddenly leaves home and goes to London, we know what it means. When his friends do not know where he is, and he does not want them to know, we are aware, within a little, where he is and what he is at. What Onesimus was doing I do not know, but he was certainly doing his best to ruin himself. His course, therefore, is to be judged, as far as he is concerned, by what it was likely to bring him to; and though it did not bring him to it, that was no credit to him, but all the honor of it is due to the overruling power of God.

See, dear brethren, how God overruled all. Thus had the Lord purposed. Nobody shall be able to touch the heart of Onesimus but Paul. Onesimus is living at Colosse; Paul cannot come there, he is in prison. It is needful, then, that Onesimus should be got to Paul. Suppose the kindness of Philemon's heart had prompted him to say to Onesimus, "I want you to go to Rome, and find Paul out and hear him." This naughty servant would have said, "I am not going to risk my life to hear a sermon. If I go with the money you are sending to Paul, or with the letter, I shall deliver it, but I want none of his preaching." Sometimes, you know, when people are brought to hear a preacher with the view of their being converted, if they have any idea of it, it is about the very last thing likely to happen, because they go there resolved to be fireproof, and so the preaching does not come home to them: and it would probably have been just so with Onesimus. No, no, he was not to be won in that way, he must be got to Rome another way. How shall it be done? Well, the devil shall do it, not knowing that he will be losing a willing servant thereby. The devil tempts Onesimus to steal. Onesimus does it, and when he has stolen he is afraid of being discovered, and so he makes tracks for Rome as quickly as he can, and gets down among the back slums, and there he feels what the prodigal felt—a hungry belly, and that is one of the best preachers in the world to some people: their conscience is reached in that way. Being very hungry, not knowing what to do, and no man giving anything to him, he thinks whether there is anybody in Rome that would take pity on him. He does not know anybody in Rome at all, and is likely to starve. Perhaps one morning there was a Christian woman—I should not wonder—who was going to hear Paul, and she saw this poor man sitting crouched up on the steps of a temple, and she went to him and spoke about his soul. "Soul," said he, "I care nothing about that, but my body would thank you for something to eat. I am starving." She replied, "Come with me, then," and she gave him bread, and then she said, "I do this for Jesus Christ's sake." "Jesus Christ!" he said, "I have heard of him. I used to hear of him over at Colosse." "Whom did you hear speak about him?" the woman would ask. "Why, a short man with weak eyes, a great preacher, named Paul, who used to come to my master's house." "Why, I am going to hear him preach," the woman would say, "will you come and hear him with me?" "Well, I think I should like to hear him again. He always had a kind word to say to the poor." So he goes in and pushes his way among the soldiers, and Paul's Master incites Paul to speak the right word.

It may have been so, or it may have been the other way—that not knowing anybody else at all, he thought, "Well, there is Paul, I know. He is here a prisoner, and I will go down and see what prison he is in." He goes down to the Praetorium and finds him there, tells him of his extreme poverty, and Paul talks to him, and then he confesses the wrong he has done, and Paul, after teaching him a little while, says, "Now, you must go back and make amends to your master for the wrong you have done."

It may have been either of these ways; at any rate, the Lord must have Onesimus in Rome to hear Paul, and the sin of Onesimus, though perfectly voluntary on his part, so that God had no hand in it, is yet overruled by a mysterious providence to bring him where the gospel shall be blessed to his soul.

Now, I want to speak to some of you Christian people about this matter. Have you a son who has left home? Is he a willful, wayward young man, who has gone away because he could not bear the restraints of a Christian family? It is a sad thing it should be so—a very sad thing, but do not despond or even have a thought of despair about him. You do not know where he is, but God does; and you cannot follow him, but the Spirit of God can. He is going a voyage to Shanghai. Ah, there may be a Paul at Shanghai who is to be the means of his salvation, and as that Paul is not in England, your son must go there. Is it to Australia that he is going? There may be a word spoken there by the blessing of God to your son which is the only word which ever will reach him. I cannot speak it; nobody in London can speak it; but the man there will; and God, therefore, is letting him go away in all his willfulness and folly that he may be brought under the means of grace, which will prove effectual to his salvation. Many a sailor boy has been wild, reckless, godless, Christless, and at last has got into a foreign hospital. Ah, if his mother knew that he was down with the yellow fever, how sad her mind would be, for she would conclude that her dear son will die away at Havana or somewhere, and never come home again. But it is just in that hospital that God means to meet with him. A sailor writes to me something like that. He says, "My mother asked me to read a chapter every day, but I never did. I got into the hospital at Havana, and, when I lay there, there was a man near to me who was dying, and he died one night; but before he died he said to me, 'Mate, could you come here? I want to speak to you. I have got something that is very precious to me here. I was a wild fellow, but reading this packet of sermons has brought me to the Savior, and I am dying with a good hope through grace. Now, when I am dead and gone, will you take these sermons and read them, and may God bless them to you. And will you write a letter to the man that preached and printed those sermons, to tell him that God blessed them to my conversion, and that I hope he will bless them to yourself'?" It was a packet of my sermons, and God did bless them to that young man who, I have no doubt whatever, went to that hospital because there a man who had been brought to Christ would hand to him the words which God had blessed to himself and would bless to his friend.

You do not know, dear mother, you do not know. The worst thing that can happen to a young man is sometimes the best thing that can happen to him. I have sometimes thought when I have seen young men of position and wealth taking to racing and all sorts of dissipation, "Well, it is a dreadfully bad thing, but they may as well get through their money as quickly as ever they can, and then when they have got down to beggary they will be like the young gentleman in the parable who left his father." When he had spent all, there arose a mighty famine in that land, and he began to be in want, and he said, "I will arise and go to my father." Perhaps the disease that follows vice—perhaps the poverty that comes like an armed man after extravagance and debauch—is but love in another form, sent to compel the sinner to come to himself and consider his ways and seek an ever-merciful God. You Christian people often see the little gutter children—the poor little guttersnipes in the street—and you feel much pity for them, as well you may. There is a dear sister here, Miss Annie Macpherson, who lives only for them. God bless her and her work! When you see them you cannot be glad to see them as they are, but I have often thought that the poverty and hunger of one of these poor little children has a louder voice to most hearts than their vice and ignorance; and God knew that we were not ready and able to hear the cry of the child's sin, and so he added the child's hunger to that cry, that it might pierce our hearts. People could live in sin, and yet be happy, if they were well-to-do and rich; and if sin did not make parents poor and wretched, and their children miserable, we should not see it, and therefore we should not arouse ourselves to grapple with it. It is a blessing, you know, in some diseases when the patient can throw the complaint out upon the skin. It is a horrible thing to see it on the skin, but still it is better than its being hidden inside; and oftentimes the outward sin and the outward misery are a sort of throwing out of the disease, so that the eye of those who know where the healing medicine is to be had is thereby drawn to the disease, and so the soul's secret malady is dealt with. Onesimus might have stopped at home, and he might never have been a thief, but he might have been lost through self-righteousness. But now his sin is visible. The scapegrace has displayed the depravity of his heart, and now it is that he comes under Paul's eye and Paul's prayer and becomes converted.

Do not, I pray you, ever despair of man or woman or child because you see their sin upon the surface of their character. On the contrary, say to yourself, "This is placed where I can see it, that I may pray about it. It is thrown out under my eye that I may now concern myself to bring this poor soul to Jesus Christ, the mighty Savior, who can save the most forlorn sinner." Look at it in the light of earnest, active benevolence, and rouse yourselves to conquer it. Our duty is to hope on and to pray on. It may be, perhaps, that "he therefore departed for a season, that thou shouldest receive him forever." Perhaps the boy has been so wayward that his sin may come to a crisis, and a new heart may be given him. Perhaps your daughter's evil has been developed that now the Lord may convince her of sin and bring her to the Savior's feet. At any rate, if the case be ever so bad, hope in God, and pray on.

III. Once more: our text may be viewed as *an example of relations improved*, "He therefore departed for a season, that thou shouldest receive him forever; not now as a servant, but a brother beloved, specially to one, but how much more unto thee?"

You know we are a long while learning great truths. Perhaps Philemon had not quite found out that it was wrong for him to have a slave. Some men who were very good in their time did not know it. John Newton did not know that he was flying wrong in the slave trade, and George Whitefield, when he left slaves to the orphanage at Savannah, which had been willed to him, did not think for a moment that he was doing anything more than if he had been dealing with horses, or gold and silver. Public sentiment was not enlightened, although the gospel has always struck at the very root of slavery. The essence of the gospel is that we are to do to others as we would that others should do to us, and nobody would wish to be another man's slave, and therefore he has no right to have another man as his slave. Perhaps, when Onesimus ran away and came back again, this letter of Paul may have opened Philemon's eyes a little as to his own position. To doubt he may have been an excellent master, and have trusted his servant, and not treated him as a slave at all, but perhaps he had not regarded him as a brother; and now Onesimus has come back he will be a better servant, but Philemon will be a better master, and a slaveholder no longer. He will regard his former servant as a brother in Christ.

Now this is what the grace of God does when it comes into a family. It does not alter the relations; it does not give the child a right to be pert, and forget that he is to be obedient to his parents; it does not give the father a right to lord it over his children without wisdom and love, for it tells him that he is not to provoke his children to anger, lest they be discouraged; it does not give the servant the right to be a master, neither does it take away from the master his position, or allow him to exaggerate his authority, but all round it softens and sweetens. Rowland Hill used to say that he would not give a halfpenny for a man's piety if his dog and his cat were not better off after he was converted. There was much weight in that remark. Everything in the house goes better when grace oils the wheels. The mistress is, perhaps, rather sharp, quick, tart; well, she gets a little sugar into her constitution when she receives the grace of God. The servant may be apt to loiter, be late up of a morning, very slovenly, fond of a gossip at the door; but, if she is truly converted, all that kind of thing ends. She is conscientious and attends to her duty as she ought. The master, perhaps—well, he is the master, and you know it. But when he is a truly Christian man, he has a gentleness, a suavity, a considerateness about him. The husband is the head of the wife, but when renewed by grace he is not at all the head of the wife as some husbands are. The wife also keeps her place, and seeks, by all gentleness and wisdom to make the house as happy as she can. I do not believe in your religion, dear friend, if it belongs to the tabernacle, and the prayer meeting, and not to your home. The best religion in the world is that which smiles at the table, works at the sewing machine, and is amiable in the drawing room. Give me the religion which blacks boots, and does them well; cooks the food, and cooks it so that it can be eaten; measures out yards of calico, and does not make them half an inch short; sells a hundred yards of an article, and does not label ninety a hundred, as many tradespeople do. That is the true Christianity which affects the whole of life.

If we are truly Christians we shall be changed in all our relationships to our fellowmen, and hence we shall regard those whom we call our inferiors with quite a different eye. It is wrong in Christian people when they are so sharp upon little faults that they see in servants, especially if they are Christian servants. That is not the way to correct them. They see a little something wrong, and, oh, they are down upon the poor girls, as if they had murdered somebody. If your Master, and mine, were to treat you in that style I wonder how you would get on? How quick some are in discharging their maids for small [mistakes]. No excuse, no trying the persons again: they must go. Many a young man has been turned out of a situation for the veriest [slightest] trifle, by a Christian employer, when he must have known that he would be exposed to all sorts of risks: and many a servant has been sent adrift as if she were a dog, with no sort of thought whether another position could be found, and without anything being done to prevent her going astray. Do let us think of others, especially of those whom Christ loves even as he does us. Philemon might have said, "No, no, I don't take you back, Mr. Onesimus, not I. Once bitten, twice shy, sir. I never ride a broken-kneed horse. You stole my money; I am not going to have you back again." I have heard that style of talk, have not you? Did you ever feel like it? If you have, go home and pray to God to get such a feeling out of you, for it is bad stuff to have in your soul. You cannot take it to heaven. When the Lord Jesus Christ has forgiven you so freely, are you to take your servant by the throat and say, "Pay me what you owe"? God forbid that we should continue in such a temper. Be pitiful, easily entreated, ready to forgive. It is a deal better that you should suffer a wrong than do a wrong: much better that you should overlook a fault which you might have noticed, than notice a fault which you ought to have overlooked.

> Let love through all your actions run,
> And all your words be kind,

is said in the little hymn which we used to learn when we were children. We should practice it now, and—

> Live like the blessed virgin's Son
> That meek and lowly child.

God grant we may, of his infinite grace.

I want to say this, and then I have done. If the mysterious providence of God was to be seen in Onesimus getting to Rome, I wonder whether there is any providence of God in some of you being here tonight! It is possible. Such things do happen. People come here that never meant to come. The last thing in the world they would have believed if anybody had said it is that they would be here, yet here they are. With all manner of twists and turns they have gone about, but they have got here somehow. Did you miss a train, and so stepped in to wait? Does not your ship sail quite so soon as you expected, and so are you here tonight? Say, is that it? I do pray you, then, consider this question with your own heart. "Does not God mean to bless me? Has he not brought me here on purpose that this night I may yield my heart to Jesus as Onesimus did?" My dear friend, if you believe on the Lord Jesus Christ, you shall have immediate pardon for all sin, and shall be saved. The Lord has brought you here in his infinite wisdom to hear that, and I hope that he has also brought you here that you may accept it, and so go your way altogether changed.

Some three years ago I was talking with an aged minister, and he began fumbling about in his waistcoat pocket, but he was a long while before he found what he wanted. At last he brought out a letter that was well-nigh worn to pieces, and he said, "God almighty bless you! God almighty bless you!" And I said, "Friend, what is it?" He said, "I had a son. I thought he would be the stay of my old age, but he disgraced himself, and he went away from me, and I could not tell where he went, only he said he was going to America. He took a ticket to sail for America from the London Docks, but he did not go on the particular day that he expected." This aged minister bade me read the letter, and I read it, and it was like this: "Father, I am here in America. I have found a situation, and God has prospered me. I write to ask your forgiveness for the thousand wrongs that I have done you, and the grief I have caused you, for blessed be God, I have found the Savior. I have joined the church of God here, and hope to spend my life in God's service. It happened thus: I did not sail for America the day I expected. I went down to the tabernacle to see what it was like, and God met with me. Mr. Spurgeon said, 'Perhaps there is a runaway son here. The Lord call him by his grace.' And he did." "Now," said he, as he folded up the letter and put it in his pocket, "that son of mine is dead, and he is in heaven, and I love you, and I shall do so as long as I live, because you were the means of bringing him to Christ." Is there a similar character here tonight? I feel persuaded there is—somebody of the same sort; and in the name of God I charge him to take the warning that I give him from this pulpit. I dare you to go out of this place as you came in. O young man, the Lord in mercy gives you another opportunity of turning from the error of your ways, and I pray you now here—as you now are—lift your eye to heaven, and say, "God be merciful to me a sinner," and he will be so. Then go home to your father and tell him what the grace of God has done for you, and wonder at the love which brought you here to bring you to Christ.

Dear friend, if there is nothing mysterious about it, yet here we are. We are where the gospel is preached, and that brings responsibility upon us. If a man is lost, it is better for him to be lost without hearing the gospel than to be lost as some of you will be if you perish under the sound of a clear, earnest enunciation of the gospel of Jesus Christ. How long halt some of you between two opinions? "Have I been so long time with you," says Christ, "and yet hast thou not known me?" All this teaching and preaching and invitation, and yet do you not turn?

> O God, do thou the sinner turn,
> Convince him of his lost estate.

Let him linger no longer, lest he linger till he rue his fatal choice too late. God bless you, for Christ's sake. Amen.

Index to Key Scriptures